HOWARD
KAZANJIAN

A PRODUCER'S LIFE

J. W. Rinzler | FOREWORD BY *Marcia Lucas*

CONSULTING EDITOR *Brandon Alinger*

Cameron + Company
Petaluma, California

PAGE 2: *A letter from the Producer-DGA Joint Trainee Committee informed student Howard Kazanjian that they'd notify him when their assistant director trainee program was open for applications.*

ABOVE: *Circa 1964, film student Howard Kazanjian directs his "480" project at the University of Southern California, on the Cinema Department's small soundstage. The numerical 400s referred to senior year classes (300 denoted sophomore year, etc). The number 480 referred to a Senior Production Workshop, for which Kazanjian had to make two short films.*

"This book, my memoirs, was written not for the ego of it, but as a statement to young potential filmmakers and others about the challenges of our industry, both good and bad."

—*Howard Kazanjian*

Table of Contents

Foreword

My family didn't come from the music industry, the radio industry, the movie industry, or the TV industry. My uncle was a butcher. Another uncle was a chemist. A third uncle was a machinist. We were blue-collar families, and nobody knew anybody who had anything to do with the entertainment business. I'm sure my mother never earned what the other agents in her insurance office earned. She grew up under the glass ceiling.

My relatively short yet interesting career in the film industry was an accident—but, as Obi-Wan Kenobi says, "In my experience there's no such thing as luck." I grew up on the movies I saw on TV: Busby Berkeley musicals, World War II adventures, Errol Flynn swashbucklers, and the like. As an adult I worked as an assistant editor for years, on many commercials and later for directors Francis Ford Coppola, Haskell Wexler, and Michael Ritchie; I finally moved up to editor on movies directed by Martin Scorsese . . . and by my ex-husband, George Lucas.

I've added my voice to my good friend Howard's for his book because Howard is one of the most wonderful people I've ever met. He and his wife, Carol, are such amazingly pure, decent human beings. No affectations, no pretensions. Just wonderful, heartwarming, family-oriented people, and I love them both a lot. I'm also adding my voice to his book because, for more than forty years, I've stayed in the background, letting George do his thing and tell his stories. I

8

never wanted to come out. I never wanted to do an interview. I never wanted to write a book. I never wanted to do a documentary—because I thought, *what will the world think?* George Lucas is in the stratosphere, one of the greatest American filmmakers who ever lived, and his ex-wife is going to say she helped, she participated. She's going to sound like sour grapes. What could I say that people wouldn't interpret as the words of some bitter ex-wife?

So I stayed out of it. I was happy raising my daughters. Even when George and I were married, I never really went on the set that much. George used to like me to come to the set and I'd go sometimes. But being on a film set, it never really pushed my buttons.

See, I'm an editor, and I loved what I did. I was a post gal.

And in a way, this is a post book. So I'm happy to contribute to the story of my good friend, whose own career—from assistant director trainee, working with the likes of Hitchcock and Peckinpah, to his career that coincided with my own at Lucasfilm—is so interesting. It parallels the history of the movie industry that we both love so much.

I hope you enjoy it.

Marcia Lucas

Prologue

No one really wanted Harrison Ford to play Indiana Jones. Not Steven Spielberg, who had signed on to direct Raiders of the Lost Ark, *and not necessarily George Lucas, the film's creator and executive producer, who had mixed feelings. Spielberg and Lucas had decided on Tom Selleck.*

Only the film's producer, Howard Kazanjian, was lobbying for Ford.

And Kazanjian kept it up—Harrison Ford would be better. Even when Selleck proved unavailable, Kazanjian's suggestions, then his urgings went unheeded. Spielberg was getting tired of it. He told Lucas that if Kazanjian didn't lay off, he'd find another producer.

Spielberg finally consented to see Ford's latest films, Hanover Street, *a period romance, and* The Frisco Kid, *a comedy Western. After watching those, he said, in effect,* you've gotta be kidding me.

Spielberg couldn't see Ford in the role.

Day One of principal photography was only a few weeks away, but production didn't have their Indy.

Howard asked his wife, Carol, if she had any ideas on how to sway Spielberg, because he knew that she also felt that Harrison Ford was the real Indiana Jones.

She did have an idea—one last gambit . . .

George Lucas and Kazanjian on location in Tunisia filming Raiders of the Lost Ark, *1980.*

CHAPTER 1: *The Filmmaker's Apprentice*

P asadena is only a few miles away from Burbank, California—home to Warner Bros. Studio and the Walt Disney Studios. Another few miles away are the studios and soundstages of Universal, 20th Century Fox, Paramount, MGM, and Columbia. Howard Kazanjian recalls, "Growing up in Pasadena, you were very aware of Hollywood. In the 1940s, you knew about the real movie stars."

For his eleventh birthday, in 1953, Howard asked for a reel-to-reel tape recorder. His parents gave him instead their 8mm movie camera, which their son learned to use. He would wind up the fifty-foot loads (a few seconds of film time) and conduct youthful experiments: frame-by-frame clips of moving clouds or an apple quickly disappearing as if being eaten by an invisible man. He mostly shot hours of family vacations and family events. As a teenager he was a founding member of the Pasadena High School film club, acted in school plays, and recorded the dissection of a frog as an extra-credit project. "We even took the heart out—while it was beating," he says. "Movies got in my blood. My parents loved movies, too, and they would take me to the theater and, when I was little, I would sit on their laps. Later, I got my own seat."

They went to the local Pasadena movie houses: the Strand Theatre, State Theatre, United Artists Theatre, Crown Theatre, the Rialto Theatre, and the Academy (one of the few old movie houses that still exists). On special occasions the family would venture into Hollywood to see big-budget road-show films, such as *The Robe* (1953), at Grauman's Chinese Theatre; and *South Pacific* (1958), at the Egyptian Theatre; and *This Is Cinerama* (1952) at the old Warner Hollywood Theatre, long closed, once a grand movie palace.

The Kazanjians saw movies of all kinds, but Howard liked the costumed epics, such as *The Robe*, *Quo Vadis* (1951), and, above all, Charlton Heston in *The Ten Commandments* (1956). "They were spectacles, that's what intrigued me," he says. "Also re-creating the past, the sets, and putting a wardrobe on an actor. *The Ten Commandments* was a very vivid story. It was visual, it was wide-screen, it had visual effects. How often do you see the parting of the Red Sea? How often do you see ancient Egypt, the temples, and Moses and the chariots? It was one of the turning points where I said, 'I want to be in the movie business.' I loved the period pictures, and that's why I liked Westerns, too."

Shane (1953) was his favorite Western. Another was *Rio Grande*, which he saw in 1950 with his parents. "It left a lasting impression." A more obscure Western, *The Proud Rebel* (1958), starring Alan Ladd, directed by Michael Curtiz, left a mark, too, thanks to its vivid action, story, and music. "That spoke to me. A riveting movie." In addition to Ladd and John Wayne, actors such as Gary Cooper, Ken Curtis, Andy Devine, Dick Foran, Glenn Ford, Ken Maynard—and TV personalities Roy Rogers, Gene Autry, Hopalong Cassidy, the Cisco Kid, and Clayton Moore as the Lone Ranger—all left an indelible impression on Kazanjian.

After high school, he studied for two years at Pasadena City College. He applied to Yale and New York University. The former accepted him and he was about to go—when his sister, Janet, who was attending the University of Southern California (USC), located in Los Angeles, told him: "You're crazy. Go to USC." She reminded him that USC had the finest film program in the country and that it would make more sense to stay in California, study there, and meet people who worked in an industry that fascinated him.

CHARMED CLASSMATES

Howard Kazanjian applied, was accepted, and enrolled in USC's School of Cinema. He lived in an apartment off-campus. It was 1962 and he remembers that the cinema department's offices and rooms were located in what had once been a stable for horses. He and his fellow classmates were there to learn the basics of filmmaking, with an emphasis on writing and editing. The latter course was taught by Dave Johnson—one of the "Unholy Five," the faculty's backbone—and took place late afternoons. "That was a weird one," Kazanjian says. "A tiny room with about twelve wooden theater seats and a little screen, and, behind this, a little projection room for 16 millimeters."

Kazanjian's focus was directing, but all cinema majors were required to take courses on sound and sound editing, lighting, cameras and lenses, and requisites such as a foreign language course. In no particular order, undergrads took: Film Writing 315 (taught by Margaret Mehring); Audio Visual 477 (D. C. Daley); Cinema Directing 470; Senior Production Workshop 480a and 480b; Advanced Film Writing 415a (Irwin Blacker); Editing (Dave Johnson); Advanced Editing 435 (Mel Sloan); Production Planning 469; Technical Theater 300; Drama 300 (Bill White); Cinema 470 and 480b (John Cox); Camera (Richard Harber); Theatrical Film Symposium 460 (Arthur Knight); Stage Lighting 471b (Bill White); Recent Plays 425; Sound (Dan Wiegand).

More than one faculty member encouraged their cinema students to change majors, saying flatly that they'd never get a job in the industry. Another USC student, two years behind Kazanjian, Randal Kleiser recalls, "We were told that nobody was ever going to get into the film business. It was a closed shop. You needed to be related to somebody to get into the business; even to sweep a soundstage, you needed a contact. Being a film student was like studying basket weaving. Everybody on campus thought of us as idiots going after easy As, just watching movies and gliding through college. We lived next door to the Birnkrant girls' dorm, but the girls avoided the film students because we were thought of as geeks and lowlifes. They were all told to stay away from us because we were not good candidates for the future."

Film students were expected to make a series of short films of increasing complexity. They were given as one of their first assignments a previously filmed roll of 16mm black-and-white celluloid and told to edit it together. Kazanjian says, "It was raw footage of two guys walking out of the cinema building and having a fist fight, falling to the ground and rolling around. It's cutting back and forth between the two guys and a master shot of them on the ground. We had to decide how fast do you want that scene to go? Some students used nearly all the footage. Others used the two coming out—and *boom*! One guy gets knocked out, it's over."

Other undergrads either in the same class as Kazanjian or who enrolled a year or two later were future director John Milius, filmmaker Don Glut, writer-director Matthew Robbins, sound designer and editor Walter Murch, writer Willard Huyck, cinematographer Caleb Deschanel, producer Charles Lippincott, composer Basil Poledouris, director Randal Kleiser—and Kleiser's second-year roommate, George Lucas. (Producer Gary Kurtz attended a few years earlier; each year's class numbered about seventy-five.) "John Milius was the raconteur of the group," Kleiser says. "He held court in the courtyard and would tell stories, and we would all sit around and listen. Howard and Dennis [Galling] invited me to the Hollywood Bowl. Elizabeth Taylor and all these people showed up. I was wide-eyed. They were amused at how excited I was to see famous people. They were pretending to be sophisticated."

Kazanjian felt the instructors were of varying quality; he preferred teachers like Dick Harber, who taught camera and editing, and Dave Johnson, because they were ready to help and to answer questions. Other teachers were often retired from the industry and more lackadaisical. Mel Sloan reiterated to his students: "Here you are in Advanced Editing, but none of you will ever have the opportunity to use what you learn because you'll never get into the business."

Kazanjian's first directorial short was five or six minutes long and entitled, *This Picture Has No Title*, "mainly because I couldn't think of a title. Its subject matter more or less related to that."

"I got there in '64," says Kleiser. "Howard was the first person I met when I walked into the cinema department. I went up and introduced myself, and he was really, really nice to me. Took me on a tour of the department. Told me a little bit about where everything was and how it worked. Told me about the Delta Kappa Alpha cinema fraternity, which I immediately joined and was there for the whole time I was at USC. It was a group of film students that were not really living in a fraternity at all, it was just a social group for film students."

Students who chose to major in directing had to write and direct two short films for their senior year final assignment and were supplied with a limited amount of black-and-white film. "The equipment was not very good," Kazanjian recalls. "We went out to shoot on the university grounds, and the light meter didn't work because the glass was broken. But that's all we had." Finished shorts were projected in Room 108, their largest, which had 16- and 35-millimeter capability.

"The people who remained in the department," Kleiser says, "were the ones who really loved cinema and weren't there to make money or to become famous. We were there because we loved making movies, though we hoped we could get money and be successful, but were really told we wouldn't. We were all helping each other because we were downtrodden. John Milius, for example, ended up helping me with one of my senior thesis films called *Summer Days Don't Last*, about a surfer trying to adjust to the transition from the beach party days to the hippie days. John helped me with that script, because he was into surfing."

In turn, Kleiser was cast by George Lucas as the lead in the latter's short film called *Freiheit* (1966), about "someone who is running from authority," Kleiser recalls. "Basil Poledouris started out wanting to direct. I played a corpse in one of his movies. George shot one of mine." Kazanjian remembers playing Caesar in a film directed by Dennis Galling.

Despite reiterated threats of future unemployment, most of the cinema majors would speak of their time at USC as a golden era.

George Lucas had also transferred from a junior college, interested in illustration and photography, and didn't declare his major the first year. He visited the School of Cinema in 1964. "George and I were the only ones in the courtyard," recalls Kazanjian. "It must have been before class, and he said, 'Tell me about this place.' And I did. We met a couple of times. I suggested that he take Arthur Knight's class, because it was fabulous."

"I met George the first year," Kleiser says, "and then in the second year, my sophomore year, he needed a roommate. He had a little hideaway shack up in Benedict Canyon. The rent was maybe $150 a month. He knew that I liked art, and he did, too. He did paintings like Margaret Keane, the girls with big eyes, when we were rooming together and I thought, *Oh, he'll probably be a production designer, because he's good at art.* His personality was so shy, I never thought he would become a director."

Arthur Knight wrote for the two main industry papers, the *Hollywood Reporter* and *Variety*, and thanks to his connections, often brought in films that hadn't released yet with their producer, director, or star to speak with the students. In 1962, he screened *To Kill a Mockingbird*, followed by a Q&A with Gregory Peck; *Billy Budd* with producer Peter Ustinov; *Mutiny on the Bounty*, in the Cary Grant Theatre at the old MGM Studios; and *Lonely Are the Brave* with Kirk Douglas. Two years later, he showed *Dr. Strangelove or: How I Learned to Stop Worrying and Love the Bomb*, with Stanley Kubrick in attendance (according to at least one attendee).

Encouraged by Kazanjian, Lucas enrolled in Knight's Introduction to Film course, which was popular also because of Knight's self-effacing, wry humor. "Even a run-of-De-Mille production," Knight joked, was better than films produced by "former lawyers, accountants, agents, or TV executives who rarely go to the movies themselves, unless it be for a sneak preview of one of their releases."

"When I was in high school," Kleiser says, "my art teacher gave me the book *The Liveliest Art* by Arthur Knight. That book, I just loved it. So, when I got to USC and saw Arthur was teaching, I snuck into his class because I was a freshman and wasn't supposed to take film classes until I was a junior. It was 'Thursday *Knight* at the Movies,' that's what we called it. I would go every Thursday night to see the new films coming out, and the directors talking about it, and Arthur interviewing them. His class was our link to the industry. That link ended up helping a lot of people make the transition. For instance, the director Robert Wise was there one time. I went up to him and asked, 'Would you please look at my student film?' He said, 'Yeah, sure. Come to Universal, and I'll get a screening room and we'll look at it.' And he did. Then he took me to lunch and talked to me about it. That was so inspirational."

Lucas, Kleiser, and Kazanjian became friends, meeting now and again and taking one or two classes together. "I knew George the best of all those other people at that time—and he broke every rule," Kazanjian says. "He fought to get 'out of the box.' Rather than use five minutes of black-and-white 16mm film, George went out and bought 16mm color film and made his directorial film. You can say he was an innovator even then, maybe even a rebel."

At the time Howard was dating a young USC student named Carol, who would later become his wife; she was majoring in secondary education. "I had several occasions to meet and speak with George's parents and sisters at many social events," says Carol Kazanjian. "His parents would talk about him as a young man. His mother told me that he would take apart the toys she bought him to make other toys from them. He never liked the toys his mother bought him in their original form, so he made them something else. He was already out-of-the-box."

"George Lucas and I took Nina Foch's class," Kleiser says, "and we had to be on stage together, doing improv. George felt very uncomfortable." (Nina Foch had starred in *The Ten Commandments*, *An American in Paris* (1951), and *Executive Suite* (1954), among others, and taught acting in the drama department.)

| The Kazanjian Family

| Harry Kazanjian was, according to many experts, the finest precious-stone cutter in the world. He traveled the world in the service of a craft learned almost by chance, when his parents had to leave him with an uncle who worked in the jewelry business in Paris, France. It was not long before World War I, and Harry's parents were on their way from Armenia to America, but nine- or ten-year-old Harry had to stay in the French capital because of an eye infection. He went to work in his uncle's business, Paris Lapidary, where he learned his trade for about five years. In 1917, at the age of fourteen, he bought a first-class ticket to the United States and packed a pair of diamond earrings for his mother. He sailed across the sea—a dangerous journey due to prowling U-boats—to rejoin his parents and family in Springfield, Massachusetts. Proficient in jewelry cutting and polishing, he opened a shop in their attic. Business was

slow, so at seventeen years old, he opened a small shop in Springfield proper, where he also sold jewelry. His most successful stone was the aquamarine. Yet Springfield wasn't quite the right place either, so he moved to New York City and opened another store.

His brother, James, joined him a few years later. The two then moved to Southern California, where they established a jewelry business in downtown Los Angeles. They prospered. Harry became a renowned wholesale jeweler. He also discovered a number of precious stones. He met his future wife, Rose, at a church dance. Their firstborn was a girl, Janet. The second they named Howard, born in Pasadena on July 26, 1942. The third, Arthur, followed four years later.

Howard grew up in the jewelry business. "As a kid, I'd go down to the office. Just by living in the household and osmosis and reading journals and gem magazines, I learned," he says. "I know probably more about rubies, sapphires, and emeralds than many of the top salesmen in some of the finer jewelry stores today."

THE MAGNIFICENT TEN

Hoping to defy predictions, cinema majors and graduate students often scrounged for jobs in the industry during their time at the university. Kazanjian made the rounds at the studios and talent agencies on the prowl for any future position, from production assistant to mail-room clerk. "I met a great many people," he says. "I was ringing a lot of doorbells. But I'd definitely made up my mind that I wouldn't knock on doors for the next ten years out of school. I had given myself a limit. I would have gone into my dad's business."

Kazanjian's mother, Rose, recalled in 1983, "Howard couldn't get a job in the movies when he graduated from college."

Failing to find a job in the entertainment industry, he enrolled in the graduate program of the Business School (USC didn't have a PhD program in cinema) and lived at home to save money. He also continued his hunt, which led him to the vice president of Revue Studios, the television production arm of MCA. Executive and student talked in a bungalow and the former mentioned that the Director's Guild might be starting an assistant director training program.

"I truly didn't know what that job title meant," Kazanjian says. "But it sounded like you'd be working with a director and would be close to the film; it was a way to move up because you're right there. You're thinking and breathing with the director." He wrote to the guild on November 2, 1964. A typed response only a day later confirmed the program's potential existence, but explained that they were some time away from accepting applications.

From fall 1964 to late 1965 Kazanjian was president of USC's Delta Kappa Alpha National Honorary Cinema Fraternity (or "DKA," for short), whose membership numbered about ten students. Apart from fostering industry friendships and community work, the fraternity held prestigious black-tie banquets at the Town & Gown Banquet Hall on campus to fete luminaries such as Paul Newman, Groucho Marx, Roman Polanski, James Stewart, Mae West, George Cukor, and King Vidor. Arthur Knight would introduce the honorees on stage, show a few clips from their films, and conduct a one-on-one interview with them. *Variety*, the *Hollywood Reporter*, and news services covered each gala event.

Paul Newman arrived a bit late for his, and crossed the banquet room wearing a white tank shirt with a six-pack of beer hanging from his arm. "We were all stunned," says Kazanjian.

"Everybody in Hollywood would come to these things," Kleiser says, "because there was nothing like it. There was a cocktail reception ahead of time, black tie. There would be photographers shooting the students with the celebrities. I guess Howard arranged all that. Everybody was sitting at tables for the banquet. Somebody would get up and introduce every single person in the audience. They would stand up and get applauded, because they were all famous."

A star-studded dinner on February 7, 1965, honored actress Rosalind Russell, writer-director Norman Taurog, and director Robert

friday night films

DKA
Spring 1965

A program for one of the Delta Kappa Alpha National Honorary Cinema Fraternity's Friday film nights, this one featuring actor Paul Newman. The fraternity (DKA) held many events, including black-tie banquets at the Town & Gown Banquet Hall on campus to fete industry luminaries. From 1964 to 1965, Kazanjian was president of the fraternity. DKA alumni at that time included Gene Kelly, Harold Lloyd, and many other movie greats.

Wise. Wise wrote to Kazanjian afterward to thank him: "Sunday night was, I felt, a memorable few hours, not only because of the marvelous turnout, both in quality and quantity; nor because of the unusual and highly interesting program presentation; but because of the dinner itself which was, praise be, delicious."

Other honorees on other nights included Judy Garland, Jane Wyatt, Vera Miles, Mary Pickford, Jack Wrather, Ernest Lehman, Frances Marion, Ross Hunter, Gene Kelly, Irene Dunne, Delmer Daves, Harry Brand, Earl Bellamy, Daniel Taradash, and Dick Van Dyke. The DKA would also welcome Lucille Ball, Gregory Peck, and Hal Wallis. One night Kleiser was supposed to work Mae West's microphone, which was on a stand. "When she appeared, she was laying on a chaise lounge, the microphone at her level," he says. "At a certain point in the song, she stood up and continued singing, and I was assigned to raise the mic. I was so fascinated to be looking at Mae West from four feet away that I forgot to raise the mic. She glared down at me, and the sound went crazy."

"The moment I became president of the DKA," Kazanjian says, "and took the gavel, I stood up before the first meeting for new member nominations. Having met George Lucas and talking with him several times and liking George, I said, 'Let's vote for George.' Member Harvey Deneroff said, 'But George isn't a cinema student. He's just taking one or two classes.' I don't know why, but I said, 'If you don't vote George Lucas into DKA, I'm resigning.' As soon as I blurted that out, I said to myself, *Who am I to say this? They're going to throw me out!* But because of the emphatic manner in which I must have said it, every hand shot up and they agreed to bring George in as a member."

GREAT EXPECTATION

Kazanjian called his second film *So That Excellence and Enterprise May Flourish*. It took a look at USC's building and expansion program and the university's commitment to students and faculty. The film followed a female student in a small car who is simply trying to find a parking space and get to class, but is unable to do so. Contrasted against her frustration is the campus's five historic buildings—along with the university's future plans (to create, presumably, more parking spaces).

During the spring of 1965, the PGA/DGA wrote to inform him that applications for their training program were now being accepted ("PGA" for the Producers Guild of America). The letter noted that "personal history and character will be considered by the Committee in selection of candidates and each candidate will be required to take a written aptitude test before final consideration."

"I filled it out as I'd been filling out dozens of applications," Kazanjian says. "I got a letter back saying that they wanted to give me a test at USC. I had nothing to lose because I was already at USC. One Saturday I went over to the School of Business and took this eight-hour-long test and then forgot about it."

The exam consisted of a lot of math. Similar to a college prep test but oriented toward the motion picture industry, it tested personality traits, intelligence, reading skills, and more math.

Weeks later, Kazanjian received a letter informing him that he had received a high score on the exam and that he should appear for an interview at the Directors Guild of America at 7:30 PM. On the appointed evening outside the appointed office, he found several other students also waiting to be interviewed; one of them was the son of a well-known director. This didn't bode well for the unconnected Kazanjian. They were accepting only ten into the program. Each interview was scheduled for twenty to thirty minutes. "I walked in and mine lasted about seven minutes; I walked out with my shoe in my mouth, thinking, *Boy, you've really blown it, Howard!*"

He attended the first few days of his second year of grad school with little hope of being accepted into the program. His mother picked up a ringing telephone while he was at home after class, asked who it was, and handed the telephone to her son. It was Joe Youngerman, national executive director of the Directors Guild of America. He suggested that Howard attend a meeting that same evening with studio human resources personnel and other trainees. The problem was the meeting was about to start. Kazanjian raced over, not exactly sure what his status was, and found himself in a large boardroom with people sitting around a large table, two deep,

23

staring at him. "One of the suited gentlemen shouted out, 'Great start—already late!' I believe it was William Schaefer, Jack Warner's right-hand man. Youngerman hadn't told the group he'd failed to notify me. I was mortified."

The good news was that he'd been accepted as one of the new trainees in the inaugural class of the PGA/DGA program. Kazanjian was the youngest, at age twenty-three, and was introduced to the group (later the program would be renamed "DGA/PGA" to emphasize that trainees were to be assistant directors, not assistant producers). The 10 had been chosen from 640 applications; starting compensation was $100 a week, "escalating to $165 per week, for the third year of such training." There was no guarantee of continuous employment during the training period.

George Sidney, Directors Guild of America president, and Charles Boren, executive vice president of the Association of Motion Picture and Television Producers, announced the selections, made by a committee of Alliance of Motion Picture and Television Producers (AMPTP) and DGA reps. The other nine trainees were: Kenward Cosper, Robert Doudell, Lee Erickson, Malcolm Harding, Arthur Levinson, Wolfgang Marum, Philip Parslow, James Westman—and Walter Hill Jr. (who would go on to direct many films, such as *The Warriors*, *The Driver*, and *48 Hours*, and produce and cowrite the first *Alien* movie). The industry newspaper *Variety* wrote that the "idea of training program had been kicked around several years by both management and the guild, according to Sidney. Feeling was such a program was necessary to set up some standards for applicants qualifying as assistants." (At that time, the DGA had 2,600 members, 664 of them assistant directors, with 503 on the West Coast and 161 on the East Coast.)

"For a while I thought I must have been a last-minute pick," Kazanjian says. "Later I found out from Walter Hill that I had been top of the class. It was just that at first the new trainee program was a bit unorganized."

EARLY, LONG DAYS

On Friday, September 3, 1965, *Variety* reported: "Training program for assistant directors for the film industry goes into operation today as ten trainees start three-year apprenticeships in feature and TV production." Kleiser says, "When Howard's name was in the *Hollywood Reporter* for the DGA, that was very impressive to all of us. It was great for somebody from our school to get accepted, because they didn't accept a lot of people. Howard was one of the first people who broke into the industry. This was a big event for us—because we had been told nobody would ever get in."

Kazanjian, however, had no idea where his designated studio was located. "I really never got out into the Valley. I barely knew where Universal Studios was, let alone Four Star, where I was being assigned!" With the help of a map, he reported for work on the following Monday at Four Star Television, a triangular plot of land at 4024 Radford Avenue in Studio City. (Now CBS Studios. Long before, it had been home to Mack Sennett's studio. Then Mascot Pictures had merged with Monogram Pictures and Consolidated Film Corporation to form Republic Studios.) The studios' four founding stars were actors Dick Powell, Joel McCrea, David Niven, and Charles Boyer. The first executive Kazanjian met was Norman Powell, Dick's son, who ran the place. He was cordial and welcoming.

The DGA program planned for two hundred days of training; then, if one qualified, he (no women had been admitted) would be able to pay his dues to the DGA and become a professional second assistant director (or "2nd AD"). On Wednesday evenings, the ten trainees were required to attend seminars for a period of two years on various topics at the Association of Motion Pictures offices on San Vicente Boulevard. Kazanjian took advantage of the four-week course on the Screen Actors Guild, taught by Lindsay Parsons Jr., to learn everything he could. It would prove invaluable. "I was now a 2nd AD trainee," he says. "The first day at Four Star, after meeting Norman Powell, I met some of the people, looked at the paperwork, but didn't go on set. My job the first week was to make sure the actors were in makeup for their early morning call, offer them breakfast, and so on, being with the 2nd AD and learning

25

Assistant 2nd director trainee Kazanjian leans on a horse-hitching rail during the production of the TV pilot High Noon *(1965) at Four Star Television (now the CBS Studio Center, or CBS Radford, lot). On far left is Peter Fonda, who starred as Will Kane Jr. (Fun fact: The comedy TV show* Seinfeld *was also filmed at CBS.)*

everything from paperwork to hiring or dismissing extras, and being at the beck and call of the 1ˢᵗ AD."

Kazanjian spent those early days on *Burke's Law* (later *Amos Burke, Secret Agent*, to capitalize on the James Bond craze), starring Gene Barry, directed by John Peyser. Bill Derwin was 1ˢᵗ AD; Ricci Rondell was 2ⁿᵈ AD and he explained to Kazanjian in more detail his responsibilities in television production. (The character Amos Burke was chief of detectives in LA, a millionaire with a chauffeur-driven Rolls-Royce and a highfalutin lifestyle. In the show's intro, he hops into his luxury car, and a sexy female voice whispers the show's title.) Kazanjian arrived on time for his second day at 6 AM. He met Rondell, who blurted out, "Oh my God! I forgot to give a call to . . ." He gave the name to Kazanjian and said, "Here's the phone number. Call and apologize. Say, 'We forgot to give you a call. Can you please get here as quickly as possible?'"

The 2ⁿᵈ AD didn't mention that the actress they'd forgotten to notify was with the show's powerful producer, Aaron Spelling. At the time Spelling had three shows in production at Four Star. "So, I dial the number and a man answers the phone," Kazanjian says. "I don't know to whom I'm talking. I'm calling the number given and I deliver the message. Not long afterward, Norman Powell gives me a call—he's laughing, because he knew it wasn't me who forgot to give her the call the day before. But he tells me that Aaron Spelling had just called—and he wanted to know who *had* forgotten."

Kazanjian was talking with Spelling himself a few days later on the set of *Honey West*, which starred Anne Francis. "His paper coffee cup was on the step of a ladder hidden from my view—and I knocked it into Aaron's pants. I nearly died. He walked away. A stand-in came over to me, who was very close to Aaron, and said, 'Don't worry. Aaron's not going to fire you. This happens all the time.'"

Upon completion of the episode, "Prisoners of Mr. Sin" (broadcast on October 27, 1965), Kazanjian worked under director Jim Goldstone and the ADs on the next *Burke's Law*: "Watch the Man Die" (broadcast as "Peace, It's a Gasser" on November 3). Second assistant director Rondell again supervised Kazanjian. The 1ˢᵗ AD on that show was Jim Brown, because the previous 1ˢᵗ AD had rotated out. Each 1ˢᵗ AD had to prepare *and* shoot their assigned episode, and would therefore alternate; the 2nd ADs worked only on the actual shoot, which took a week per show, but weren't needed for prep.

Kazanjian was then moved onto *The Big Valley* for three episodes, under 2nd AD Ed Teets. The show starred an actress who was already a legend, Barbara Stanwyck (*Meet John Doe* and *The Lady Eve* from 1941; *Double Indemnity*, 1944; etc.). Stanwyck played the widow of a wealthy nineteenth-century Californian rancher who participates in the adventures of her family and sons. One of the episodic directors was Paul Henreid, who had costarred in *Casablanca* (1942); *Now, Voyager* (1942); and other classics. Kazanjian was immersed among professionals who had venerable cinematic histories and loads of experience. He worked long hours to get up to speed. "It's not nine to five; it's five to nine," he says. "It could be tough on me, but I've got that smile on my face. And I don't walk, I run. You had to show that you were there, and smart. I did the show's paperwork and whatever else I had to do. I loved it. Every second of it. The magic of making something out of nothing. Seeing the sets, even walking the back lot was fun and inspiring. And Barbara Stanwyck was a great lady. She was the boss. When she walked on the stage, dead quiet. Respect. For her good work and her character."

"I've always loved the Western," Stanwyck told a reporter from the *San Francisco Chronicle* on set. "It's pure drama, tried and honest. Many actresses look down on them, but I never have. I wanted to do *Big Valley* in '61 but it took four years to make it jell. We had to add the daughter and the illegitimate son, which gave us more characterization to work with. Listen, honey, I try to make Victoria Barkley as human as possible. She doesn't come waltzing down the staircase in calico to inquire as to the progress of the cattle. She's an old broad who combines elegance and guts."

Kazanjian again made sure the actors knew where the production wanted them to be each hour of the day, from makeup to the set. Each afternoon he delivered the all-important call sheets, which told actors and crew about the following day's shoot: location(s), times, scenes, etc. Early mornings, he'd check the extras to make sure they were wearing the right clothing or send them to wardrobe. An extra might come to work with a hat or an extra coat; they could then walk across a set or street, remove their coat or add a hat and cross back looking different. He also had to make sure extras didn't disappear for whatever reason. On a Western set on the back lot, he dealt with wagons, buggies, horses, and so on. "On the stages, everyone was smoking all the time," he says. "God, it was terrible. I'd wear a sweater on a soundstage because it was freezing, but when I'd come home, I'd leave the sweater outside to air."

He was next assigned to the studio's *The Smothers Brothers Show*, a sitcom starring comedians Tom and Dick Smothers, for another three shows. He couldn't know then how big and influential the Smothers Brothers would be in just a few years. "The one that wore a hairpiece I remember," Kazanjian says. "The one that didn't, looked like he did. That's all I remember about those guys. They were nice, they were cordial, but as a new trainee, I didn't see that much." Following that sitcom, he worked on more episodic TV and a few pilots, including one based on the film *High Noon* (1952). "I'd seen *High Noon* a couple of dozen times, and it was fun to see and compare the actors to the original actors. I was able to see how they built a Western town, how they brought in trees, and added snow. I loved that. The whole process."

Kazanjian interned on two other pilots: *The Sea Wolves*, a few days of location work in San Diego; and *Ace of the Mounties*, starring Ron Husmann and Joan Blondell. He recalls: "Then, after three months, the DGA said, 'Your next assignment is Warner Bros.' But Four Star didn't want me to leave. And I didn't want to leave, because it had already become a home. I knew the people. But all of us, all ten trainees, had to move to their next assignment." The DGA wanted their apprentices to be exposed to different studios and production centers, to work on both TV shows and theatrical movies in order to acquire a complete toolbox for any situation. The program was designed to provide trainees with the widest view of all aspects of the industry, the real world of Hollywood, which was quite different from the schooling at USC. It meant not only working with extras and actors, but with directors and producers, while learning about cameras, filming, editing, sound, wardrobe, makeup, and the art department.

AD trainee Kazanjian stands in the conning tower of a World War II submarine set during production of the TV pilot The Sea Wolves *(1965), another Four Star production. This was filmed in San Diego, with Don Taylor directing.*

The great Japanese director Akira Kurosawa had also tested into an assistant director training program at a studio called Photo Chemical Laboratories (PCL), or Toho, in the late 1930s. Kurosawa wrote in *Something Like an Autobiography*: "Management theory at PCL regarded the assistant directors as cadets who would later become managers and directors. They were therefore required to gain a thorough mastery of every field necessary to the production of a film. We had to help in the developing laboratory; carry a bag of nails, a hammer, and a level from our belts; and help with scriptwriting and editing as well. We even had to appear as extras in place of actors and do the accounts for location shooting."

VETERANS OF THE GOLDEN AGE

Kazanjian arrived at renowned Warner Bros. Studios in Burbank on January 17, 1966. This was the studio that had made such wonderful films as *Casablanca; Now, Voyager; The Adventures of Robin Hood*; and many others. It had a fully equipped lot with two dozen large soundstages and dependent workshops and departments, such as grip and electric houses, as well as a large mill. Kazanjian explored everything and walked the legendary back lot, taking in Spanish Street, Western Street, New York Street, and Brownstone Street; traversed a huge jungle; skirted a lake; and he toured the still-standing sets of recent films, such as London's Covent Garden for *My Fair Lady* (1964). (Years later, when Columbia Pictures moved in, the back lot was replaced with new office buildings and parking areas.)

He also observed productions in action. Against a stage wall on rollers was the miniature house where Professor Fate from *The Great Race* (1965) blew up. Hoisted above stage doors were vintage wagons and buggies. On one soundstage was the house from *Who's Afraid of Virginia Woolf* (1966). Hidden behind the walls of the New York buildings were dozens of classic cars from the 1920s and '30s.

As an assistant director, he could drive his own car up to the stage door and park. On his first active set, what struck the young trainee was that everyone else seemed very old. They looked to be between the age of sixty-five and seventy. "I don't recall any young people," Kazanjian says. "During the war, each department had guaranteed employment for five prop men, five special effects men, and five electricians and grips, most likely as part of a union negotiation. Many of these talented crew were life members. They were left over from the studio system, which was still functioning." One of the old-timers was Robey Cooper, "one of the best prop guys I've ever worked with"; Lee Wilson was a veteran gaffer. Kazanjian learned from these "masters of their art. Old had nothing to do with their talent. They were seasoned professionals."

From January to February, he would go from a few days on one production to a week or only a day on another, from the episodic *The F.B.I.*, *F Troop*, and *Mister Roberts* to two days on a remake of *Hotel* (1967), directed by Richard Quine and starring Rod Taylor, Karl Malden, Melvyn Douglas, and Merle Oberon. "I was called in to work with a hundred extras and actors in the main lobby and corridor set with Malden," Kazanjian says. "I was more of a fill-in. The studio wanted me to get exposed to what was going on throughout the lot and with the handling of large crowds." Central Casting issued the call for extras; the supplier was the studio's extras casting department, headed by Jim Martel.

Sometime around 1966, Kazanjian had the opportunity to work on a one-day job for a minute-long Oscars commercial starring Bob Hope. "For years I had seen him as host of the Oscar telecast," he says. "My job was to see that he was notified when the crew was ready and the small set was lit. After one or two takes, he was finished for the day and his entourage escorted him off the stage. I moved on to my next assignment. To this day, I believe he was the very best host the Oscar telecast ever had."

Another early assignment was a month on the TV pilot for *House of Wax*, directed by Hy Averback (who was also executive producer of *F Troop)*. Kazanjian, energetic as always, was observed by director of photography (DP) Richard "Dick" Kline, who remarked on the young man's enthusiasm and abilities. He once spotted the trainee on two phones at once while still being attentive to what was happening on set. (Kline had assisted and operated on more than two hundred motion pictures before becoming

33

a DP in 1963; his most famous assignment was perhaps as an assistant cameraman on Orson Welles's *The Lady from Shanghai*, 1947.) Kazanjian would run errands to and from the set all day long. Because he was efficient, gradually the 2nd ADs shifted much of their work to the trainee. "I could handle it," he says. "Many of the shows kept both myself and the 2nd busy." (The pilot for *Wax* was turned down by the TV network, but the studio later released it as a 1966 feature film, *Chamber of Horrors*.)

A slightly lengthier assignment for Kazanjian, about six weeks, was *Not with My Wife, You Don't!* (1966). Helmed by Norman Panama, a veteran comedy director, the production had a seasoned staff that included production designer Edward Carrere, a standard at Warner Bros. since 1932. Carrere had collaborated with directors Raoul Walsh, Michael Curtiz, and Alfred Hitchcock on films such as *White Heat* (1949), *Adventures of Don Juan* (1948), and *Dial M for Murder* (1954). The film also had an all-star cast—Tony Curtis, George C. Scott, and Carroll O'Connor—and told the story of an Italian nurse (Virna Lisi) who falls in love with two American fliers during the Korean War.

Kazanjian worked under 1st AD Jack Aldworth and 2nd AD Mike Daves (son of Delmer Daves, a veteran writer-director of such films as 1957's *3:10 to Yuma*). "I was told to never speak with Tony Curtis," Kazanjian says. "Tony was a million-dollar actor, literally; he had his own makeup person, his own wardrobe person, stand-in, and driver. I hadn't seen that kind of staffing before. Whenever I would go to Tony's dressing room on stage or on location to tell him we were ready for him, usually his wardrobe man answered the door. He told me on two occasions not to fear Tony and that I could give him the call sheet directly, answer any of his questions, or tell him we were ready on the set for him."

Kazanjian crossed paths with the film's composer, John "Johnny" Williams, and was introduced to Joel Freeman, the film's associate producer. During World War II, Freeman had been drafted into the air force, where he spent his time in the First Motion Picture Unit as a script supervisor and assistant director on training films. After the war, he joined David O. Selznick's International Pictures as a production clerk on *Duel in the Sun* (1946) and slowly moved up on Alfred Hitchcock's *The Paradine Case* (1947); two consecutive Cary Grant vehicles, *The Bachelor and the Bobby-Soxer* (1947) and *Mr. Blandings Builds His Dream House* (1948); and many other features. "I worked for eight years without taking a vacation day off," Freeman says.

"Joel was a legend," Kazanjian recalls. "As for the actors, George C. Scott played chess often with O'Connor. They certainly were second fiddle to Tony when it came to dressing rooms and staff. Tony had a nine-to-six work day. He showed up on time and left on time. He would do his close-ups first when his face and makeup were the freshest and then he would leave the other actors' close-ups for after he'd gone home. If Scott was doing his close-ups, and Tony had left for the day, someone else would read Tony's lines off-screen."

While shooting exteriors on a military air field, it began to rain. Director Panama asked Curtis to look skyward and invent some dialogue about the rain. "However, the way the picture was photographed and later cut together, we never could see the rain," Kazanjian says. "Tony's line seemed to make no sense at all."

In the spring of 1966 Kazanjian moved onto *An American Dream* (1966), a William Conrad production directed by Robert Gist. Its story was about a TV talk show host who may have killed his wife and who is therefore pursued by both the police and a gang of hoodlums. Conrad would be most remembered for his distinctive voice as an overweight investigator in the TV series *Cannon* (1971–1976) and *Jake and the Fat Man* (1987–1992). The movie starred Janet Leigh, Stuart Whitman, Barry Sullivan, Murray Hamilton, and George Takei (just before he became Sulu on *Star Trek*). The script was based on popular writer Norman Mailer's novel and had a modest budget of a million dollars. "Most of television is crap," Conrad said in a 1976 *Los Angeles Times* interview, and their film's story exemplified his words.

Kazanjian had already come across Conrad as a director. While shooting a TV show, after watching a couple of takes, Conrad would ask for another take, then turn his back to the actors. He'd listen to their performed dialogue and, if he liked what he heard, would tell them, "Cut! Print!" This technique came from his early days doing radio (Conrad had been the original Marshal Matt Dillon on the *Gunsmoke* radio drama in the 1950s).

The director of *An American Dream*, Gist, was a difficult personality, gruff and somewhat egotistical. He'd debuted as an actor in *Miracle on 34th Street* (1947) and may have been awarded his job thanks to his role as one of the soldiers in the film version of Mailer's *The Naked and the Dead* (1958), which the influential writer had liked. Gist was making the switch to director under the aegis of director-producer Blake Edwards, who was running the TV series *Peter Gunn*. Not only was Kazanjian learning the technical side of moviemaking, he was becoming fluent in its personal politics.

For a scene in which the talk show host's wife falls to her death from a thirtieth-floor penthouse, production moved to a downtown Los Angeles skyscraper to film Janet Leigh's walk into the building. Kazanjian recalls, "While we were shooting, a fire broke out on the twentieth floor. An exterior window burst from the heat and crashed down to the street only feet from where we were shooting."

A New Generation

Kazanjian was laid off in April 1966. Without full-time contracts, many on the production crews lived an itinerant lifestyle. Usually the studio would give them a week's severance. Fortunately, Kazanjian was back at work on another Conrad production by July. The film was *The Cool Ones* (1967) and starred Roddy McDowall, among others. The story—about a young millionaire rock-and-roll promoter (McDowall) who decides to create a new boy-girl duo for his teen TV show—was written by Joyce Geller, a classmate of Kazanjian's from USC. Geller had won the first Samuel L. Warner Memorial Opportunity Award. Her original screenplay had been titled "The Wiggy Plan of Tony Krum," but Warner Bros. changed it in order to cash in on the new music craze of hip or "cool" young people.

To that end, Conrad and the studio hired Gene Nelson, who had most recently directed two Elvis Presley films (*Kissin' Cousins*, 1964; and *Harum Scarum*, 1965). Nelson came from a dance background and had played the part of Will Parker in the film version of *Oklahoma!* (1955). The film's DP, Floyd Crosby, had worked on beach party movies

FOUR STAR TELEVISION
CALL SHEET

ST ~~UNIT~~

11TH DAY OF SHOOTING

7:30 SHOOTING ~~OR LEAVING CALL~~

PICT. DEADLY MUSIC NO. 6543 DIRECTOR MURRAY GOLDEN

SERIES AMOS BURKE
PRODUCER AARON SPELLIN
DATE TUES 11-30-65

		SCS.		LOC.
SET INT. ANNA'S STUDIO	D	X38 (CONTINUED) 17/8		STAGE 6
SET INT. ANNA'S STUDIO	D	107-108 33-57-38-59-40 3 1/8 5 7/8		↓
SET EXT SORREL LODGE	D	42 TO 53-55-56-57 109-1014		N.Y. SQUAR
SET INT. MAN'S PLANE	D	103-104-X27 X84 X89-90 5 7/8		STAGE 1
SET INT. COFFEE SHOP	D	3 THRU 12 4 1/8		↓
SET				LOC.
SET				LOC.

CAST AND DAY PLAYERS	PART OF	MAKEUP	SET CALL	REMARKS
GENE BARRY	AMOS	10:00	10:30	M.U. ON SET
LYNN LORING	ANNA	7:00	8:30	M.U. IN DEPT
KEVIN MC CARTHY	BILL	8:00	8:30	
WILL WHITE	MOTORCOP		WILL NOTIFY	M.U. ON SET
HARRY BASCH	O'BRIEN		WILL NOTIFY	
TROY MELTON	TAYLOR		WILL NOTIFY	
	DR. O'BRIEN		WILL NOTIFY	
CARL BENTON REID	MAN		WILL NOTIFY	
JAMES EDWARDS	NORTON	9:30	10:00	
DON HAGGERTY	1st/POLICE	9:30	10:00	↓

ATMOSPHERE AND STANDINS		THRU GATE	
3 STANDINS		8:00 A	
10 ATMOS		10:00 A	

ADVANCE SCHEDULE OR CHANGES

WED, 12-1-65

~~HONEY WEST~~ #6438 "KING OF THE MOUNTAIN"

ASST. DIR. JOE CRAMER / H. KING   PROD. MGR. Larry Crane

Assistant director trainee Howard Kazanjian's handwritten call sheet for "Deadly Music," an episode of the Amos Burke *TV series for Four Star Television, dated November 30, 1965. Call sheets were typically generated by assistant directors to let production know what was happening the next day on their movie: cast needed, location, makeup calls, extras and special crew needed, set names, scene numbers, and any other important information.*

37

and several of Roger Corman's low-budget horror productions (and was the father of David Crosby, at the time a member of the Byrds). Choreographer Toni Basil brought along her friend, actress and fellow dancer Teri Garr (who appeared in the background of some shots and would go on to star in many hits of the 1970s, such as *Young Frankenstein* and *Close Encounters of the Third Kind*). A small speaking/singing part was given to a young guitarist named Glen Campbell, who would become a huge TV and recording star. Composer Lee Hazlewood was busy helping Nancy Sinatra to the top of the charts with such hits as "These Boots Were Made for Walking." Hazlewood brought in Billy Strange for the arrangements. Strange was a guitarist and member of the Wrecking Crew, legendary studio musicians utilized by dozens of performers and rock groups in recording sessions, from Frank Sinatra to the Beach Boys. (Even the film's carpet had a pedigree: veteran lighting gaffer Lee Wilson told Kazanjian that it was the same carpet used for the Ascot race scene in *My Fair Lady*.)

One day Campbell got lost off-set. "We were ready for him and he had disappeared," Kazanjian says. "While everyone was waiting, I had to shout, 'Where are you? Get out here!' Then I had to go out and find and reprimand him. I really didn't pay any attention to him, which is unusual for me, because I pay attention to all actors and extras and handle them with respect. The lesson here is one never knows who the next Glen Campbell is going to be." (Campbell became a member of the Country Music Hall of Fame and the Musicians Hall of Fame, and Kazanjian had the "pleasure" to meet him again, years later, at one of his concerts.)

Kazanjian reported to 1ˢᵗ AD Gil Kissel, another old-timer, who had begun as a set decorator on director John Huston's *The Maltese Falcon* (1941). "Gil was a little slow and envious of the younger people coming up," Kazanjian recalls. "He looked askance at them, not viewing them so much as assistants but rather as replacements."

And Kazanjian was about to move up the ladder.

CHAPTER 2: *Movie Reality*

I had proved myself on some of these other Warner Bros. shows, so the head of production, Dutch Meyer, said, 'Your next assignment is *Cool Hand Luke.*'"

On September 19, 1966, Kazanjian joined the film, which starred Paul Newman as the eponymous hero, during its preproduction. Director Stuart Rosenberg had a budget of around $4 million, double anything Kazanjian had worked on before. This one had potential. Hank Moonjean, 1st AD and the film's associate producer, may have recommended the trainee and would mentor him throughout. Kazanjian met key crew and was given a script to break down. He and the assistant directors went over the scenes with Rosenberg, deciding where to shoot and how to schedule it as efficiently as possible. In doing so, Kazanjian learned that screenwriter Donn Pearce had based the story on his experiences working on a chain gang in a Southern prison. Pearce had been a safecracker in the late 1940s and was arrested. Luke and his inmates were amalgams of what Pearce had seen and heard. Luke is arrested for lopping the tops off parking meters; in prison he refuses to be broken, doesn't fit in at first, but eventually wins the respect of the other prisoners—before dying tragically, shot by a sadistic guard. Some analysts would say that Luke, a war veteran, was suffering from post-traumatic stress disorder before it was a diagnosed condition. He couldn't be broken because his psyche had already been destroyed by the horrors of combat and killing.

Stuart Rosenberg had discovered Donn Pearce's original novel *Cool Hand Luke* in a Hollywood Boulevard bookstore and taken it to actor Jack Lemmon's production company, Jalem, to get the ball rolling.

39

Jalem had bought the film rights and hired Pearce to write a screenplay draft. "It was the first time I had come across an existentialist hero—not an antihero—in American literature," Rosenberg told the *New York Times* in 1968.

"It's one of the few roles I've committed myself to on the basis of the original book, without seeing a script," Newman said. "It would have worked no matter how many mistakes were made." Newman was doing his own research for his part as Luke, spending time in West Virginia, talking to locals, recording their accents, and asking their opinions on a range of subjects.

In his copy of the screenplay, dated September 29, 1966, Kazanjian read eight pages that described in detail the cast of characters, from Dragline (George Kennedy, a veteran of many John Ford films) to Dog Boy (Anthony Zerbe), something he'd never seen before in a script. Other supporting actors were Dennis Hopper as Babalugats, Strother Martin as Captain, and Oscar winner Jo Van Fleet as Arletta, Luke's mother. Kazanjian recalls: "In reading the script, and the sequence where Luke has to eat dozens of eggs, I felt there was Christian symbolism. But I never heard it discussed. What it gave me was an introduction to each character before actually meeting the actor cast for that part. Luke's character was described as 'not believing in God, or fate, nor implied morality.' Any reference to 'Christ-like' would have come from Paul Newman, producer Gordon Carroll, or director Rosenberg. But in the church scene at the end of the picture, Luke does call out to God as his 'Old Man.' That could connote a Christ-like figure."

In another scene, a teenager, The Girl (Joy Harmon), originally named Lucille, gets off of a school bus, goes into her house, and changes into a bikini: "a blonde-haired schoolgirl, a vision of American high school sensuality," per the script. She then performs a drum-majorette routine executing erotic moves with her baton. "That wasn't going to pass the censor," Kazanjian says.

Cast and crew were a mixture of veterans and first-timers. Newman was an established star (*Cat on a Hot Tin Roof*, 1958; *Exodus*, 1960; etc.) and DP Conrad Hall was the equivalent in his craft (1966's *The Professionals* and *Harper*, the latter of which also starred Newman).

40

But most of the cast were New York stage actors relatively new to movies. It was Gordon Carroll and Stuart Rosenberg's first film; backing them up, however, were top-notch technicians, such as Moonjean. In post, film editor Sam O'Steen and sound mixer Larry Jost would work their magic. Producer Carroll (who would go on to coproduce *Alien*, 1979) was often around during preproduction. Kazanjian met him and had lunch several times with Newman's brother, Arthur, who managed the star's production company and was the film's titular unit manager. Paul had once told Arthur, upon deciding to attend the Yale School of Drama: "I don't care if I have to live out of an orange crate, I'm gonna learn my craft."

"It wasn't just luck," Arthur would say. "Paul worked hard. He was always punching ahead."

SECOND ON THE ROAD

Associate producer Carter de Haven Jr., who functioned as the actual unit manager, locked in various sites in Stockton, California. Following the pattern of most productions, they would shoot on location first before doing studio work. If the weather was bad, they always had a "cover set" nearby to shoot alternative scenes. To authenticate the prison atmosphere, Rosenberg reportedly banned all women from the set, even the wives of the actors. Actress Joy Harmon was segregated from the rest of the cast and stayed in a different hotel.

Although Kazanjian was a "trainee" in name, his duties were now actually those of a second assistant director. He was usually the first to arrive on location. Once "action" was called, he stayed within ten feet of the camera in case the director or ADs needed something. His job was also to know exactly what work was scheduled next and for the following days, and to anticipate what 1st AD Moonjean was about to say. He had to keep his ears and eyes open and keep track of everyone's whereabouts; he verified that cast members were dressed and in appropriate makeup at all times and nearby. "I learned many things from Hank Moonjean that seemed so simple in nature," Kazanjian recalls. "One: An assistant director never sits, even if given a chair with his name on it, unless in a meeting. Two: An assistant never puts his hands in his jean pockets,

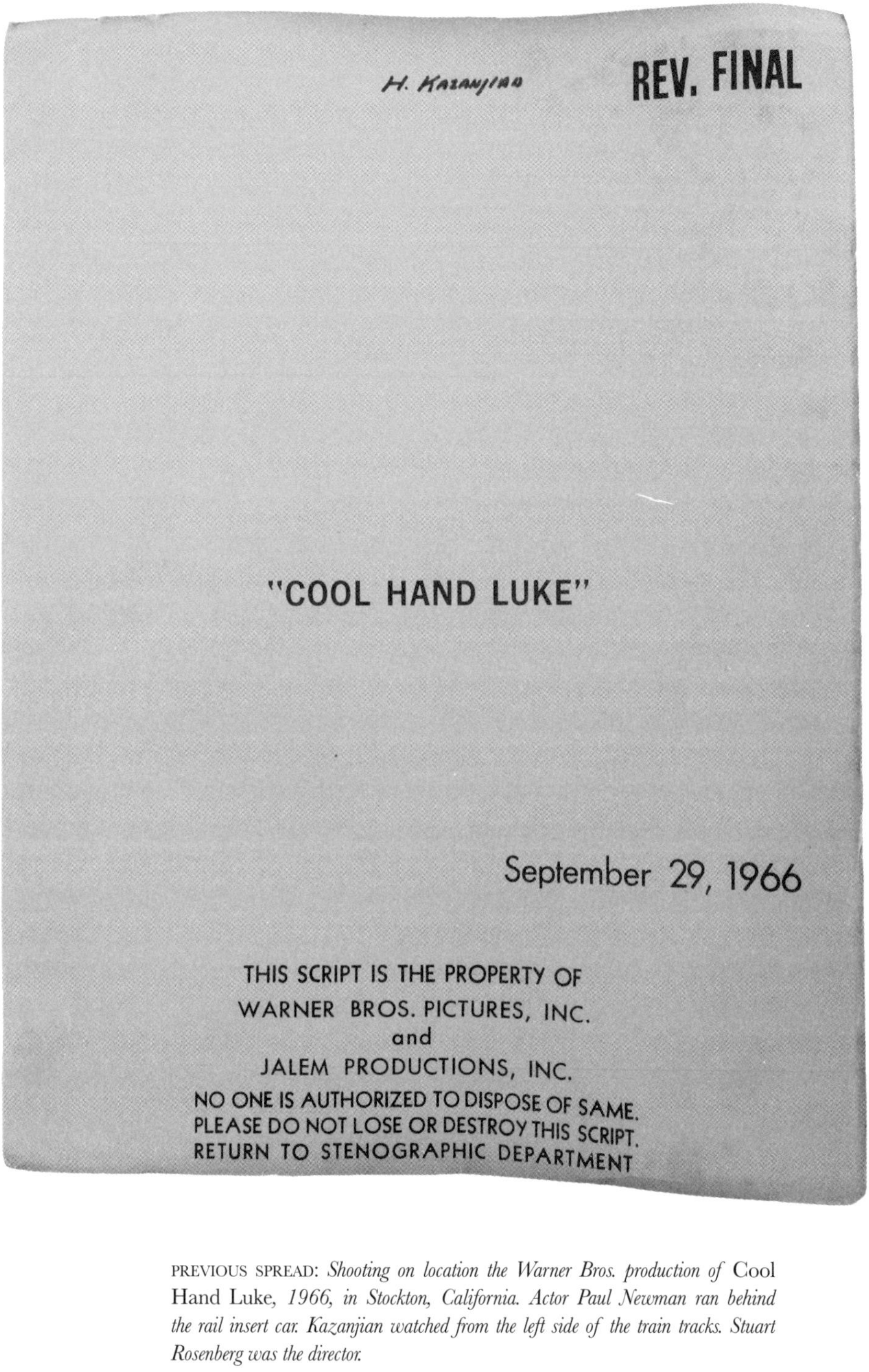

H. Kazanjian

REV. FINAL

"COOL HAND LUKE"

September 29, 1966

PREVIOUS SPREAD: *Shooting on location the Warner Bros. production of* Cool Hand Luke, *1966, in Stockton, California. Actor Paul Newman ran behind the rail insert car. Kazanjian watched from the left side of the train tracks. Stuart Rosenberg was the director.*

ABOVE: *Kazanjian's copy of the* Cool Hand Luke *revised final draft screenplay.*

no matter how cold the weather may be. I studied what Hank said and watched others on the set, then and forevermore. Hank was right. Body language plays an important part in how one takes control of the set. I studied body language in any conversation or meeting. Head movements to how one stands, sits, shifts, or uses his hands and arms tells me many things, including what they may be thinking. The color of one's shirt or clothes is also an indicator."

Kazanjian made sure Paul Newman's car was at his hotel door and that the actor left for the set on time, that he had advance notice of when needed, and had everything he required throughout the day. Actors J. D. Cannon (who played the character Society Red) and George Kennedy rode together in a car. A bus transported the rest of the chain gang. Kazanjian sat up front to make sure the large cast was accounted for before the vehicle left for the location. He recalls, "Each day Strother Martin boarded the bus, usually last and often late. He'd insinuate it was my fault and say, 'What we've got here is a failure to communicate!'"— repeating what would become the film's famous line.

Kazanjian's duties also included making sure the caterer was on time and had the correct food count; he coordinated dressing rooms, transportation, makeup, props, and wardrobe. He verified that the call sheets were ready for the next day's work and sent in by 9:30 AM to the production office to be typed up and distributed by end of day, or earlier if a cast member had to leave the set. "You *run* all day long, not walk, on your feet for ten to twelve hours." At day's end, he filled out production reports and time cards for the cast, turned them in to the production office, drove home, and went to bed, often without having had time to eat dinner. Craft service in those days was "the guy who would move a red bucket around for the cigarette butts and make a cup of coffee and maybe, *maybe* donuts, which cost ten cents. Coffee was usually free. A producer might say, 'I'll pay for the donuts.'"

Their first location was Lodi, California, where Rosenberg filmed Newman snapping the heads off the parking meters. "I had a great time with that part," Newman said in an interview. "I liked that character." Kazanjian recalls, "That night we had a smaller crew. Stuart Rosenberg was well prepared and seemed to know exactly what he wanted. He worked well with cast and crew. His concentration was on Paul, followed by the other leading actors." (Kazanjian notes that the meter scene may have been reshot later as a pick-up at Warner Bros., on "Midwestern Street.")

In one scene with the chain gang digging a ditch, Luke picks up a live rattlesnake, which is then shot in the head by the sadistic prison guard. A snake handler sewed the mouth of the snake shut for its scene with Newman; then an expert marksman was brought in to shoot its head off, with a stand-in or stuntman holding the snake. When Luke is sentenced to three nights in "The Box," a scene shot with a small crew, the female script supervisor broke into tears of embarrassment when she happened to see Newman stripping to put on his nightshirt; Hank Moonjean apologized and comforted her. The boxing duel between Luke and Dragline took a day to film, and one or both actors reportedly may have fainted due to exhaustion in the severe heat. Kazanjian was about thirty feet away and remembers Newman lying on the ground for a while, perhaps to catch his breath. Between setups, cast and crew played poker and gambled on sporting events. Kazanjian placed a bet on when the baby of Buck Kartalian (Dynamite) and his wife would be born (and won).

Production imported tons of Spanish moss straight from Louisiana in order to make the prison set more convincing on location in Stockton, California. A construction crew erected a dozen buildings, including barracks, mess hall, warden's quarters, guard shack, and dog kennels. (While passing by the "prison complex," a San Joaquin County building inspector mistook it for a migrant workers' shanty and posted condemned notices on the structures for not being up to code.) DP Conrad Hall and his crew would set up their lighting for the chosen angles. According to *American Cinematographer* magazine, Hall was experimenting with realism. "In the pioneering days of cinematography," Hall said, "the idea was to strive for a kind of visual perfection, a beauty that came from an almost surreal perfection—skin that glowed, focus that enhanced the romantic senses, lighting that was always beauteous. Then things began to change."

Hall and other cinematographers such as Haskell Wexler were after a grittier, more naturalistic look. Hall used techniques previously considered no-no's—a certain movement, a lens flare—throughout *Cool Hand Luke*, particularly when shooting the chain gang under the blazing sun. "With Connie's photography you always thought you were there right in the scene," Kazanjian says, "right in the barracks or out in the field with a sickle and shovel. His contribution to the film was immense, and Stuart depended on Connie 100 percent. Usually Stuart would set the cast and Connie would stand with him and then move in the camera(s), often with little or no discussion with Stuart. Stuart directed the actors, Connie directed the camera and usually the placement of the camera, what lens to use, and often how the camera moved, panned, tilted, and so on. This isn't to say Stuart didn't speak with Connie on what he wanted, or on a specific move or shot, but it was a very smooth operation between director and DP."

They filmed Luke's death out of continuity, night for (cold) night, in a church. As usual, Hall lit the scene with special care. "Certain kinds of violence viscerally affect me," Hall said in 2007. "I don't mind doing a picture that is psychologically violent . . . I just try to stay away from pictures that seem to be gratuitously violent." Kazanjian recalls: "Whenever I see that church, or one similar, I recall Hank Moonjean asking me to find twenty-four black farmworkers for another scene. We weren't prepared for that. The answer was, 'Go to an all-black church and ask for help.'"

As the shoot moved from location work to studio photography, Kazanjian remarked that actor Dennis Hopper, who had a reputation as a hell-raiser, was instead behaving between scenes more like his movie character: "quiet." Morgan Woodward, the de facto prison-guard executioner, "the man with no eyes," was "scary, as was his character, but really a nice person." Kazanjian was in the swing of things, enjoying his job on the film.

Then, while shooting in the barracks set on the Warner Bros. lot, just before they wrapped production, he was whisked away to *Camelot*.

CHAPTER 3: *Kingdoms Gone*

T he production team of *Camelot* had just returned from a location shoot in Spain, where its small Hollywood crew had been supplemented with a European crew. Because it had rained more than anticipated, they'd captured only a few of the needed shots against backdrops of real-life castles and landscapes, such as the scene in which Lancelot (Franco Nero) sings his way down to the sea to take a boat bound for England. (A castle in Coca, Spain, had been chosen as a stand-in for Camelot, and the Alcázar palace in Segovia as Lancelot's fortress, "Joyous Gard," from Arthurian legend.)

Cast and crew were now staffing up on the Warner Bros. lot. Producer Jack Warner had been watching Dick Kline, son of cinematographer Benjamin H. Kline (who'd worked in the industry since the silent film days), and had liked what he'd seen during Kline's turn as DP on the *House of Wax* pilot. Kline was given the same job on *Camelot*. Kline, in turn, championed Kazanjian. Impressed by his get-up-and-go attitude on *House of Wax*, Kline had gone to the powers that be and requested the young man. The studio and the DGA had complied, and Kazanjian was pulled from the training program six months early and promoted to second assistant director status. He'd proved himself to Warner Bros. and to all concerned, and became the youngest member of the DGA.

The Lerner-Loewe *Camelot* musical had been a mega-success on Broadway. Its cinematic adaptation promised to be a huge affair, one of the biggest movies of the year, and was Jack Warner's baby. Its director was Joshua Logan, its stars, Richard Harris and Vanessa Redgrave. Kazanjian's mentor, Joel Freeman, was also on the film as

Director of the Warner Bros. production Camelot, *Joshua Logan presents newly promoted 2ⁿᵈ assistant director Howard Kazanjian with his own chair on the set. DP Dick Kline gave Kazanjian the nickname "Bambi" because of his brown eyes and long eyelashes! Kazanjian doesn't recall ever using the on-set chair other than while doing paperwork after wrapping for the day.*

an uncredited associate producer. Kazanjian read the script in catch-up mode that December 1966, having missed the first round of prep. The film was already over budget. He recalls, "I was given a great deal of responsibility, some control, and a certain amount of creative and artistic leadership. It was true Hollywood filmmaking, what I had always dreamed about as a kid."

He broke down the script by underlining in color the speaking cast. In another color he underlined set descriptions, such as "EXT. MERLYN'S WOODS & POND" and "DAY" or "NIGHT"; in yet another color he indicated special props, animals, or effects. He made summaries on single pages of each set and/or scene, then transferred them to abbreviated strips, a half-inch wide by one and a half feet long, with a coding system ("1," Richard Harris; "2," Vanessa Redgrave, etc.), and pinned them to a long board on a production office wall. A black strip between white strips defined single days of shooting. Exteriors would, as usual, be filmed first, but other key components were each star's availability and the number of days for which they'd contracted. Kazanjian and the other assistant directors studied the board, the contracts, and moved the strips around. When the board was complete, they created "Day-out-of-Days," totals of days worked, days off, paydays, and travel days for the actors, which helped the studio's casting and legal departments to negotiate salaries and logistics. (Supplemental lists included animals, costumes, prerecording of songs, extras, and so on. These lists were not trivial and were overseen by Freeman. When megastar John Wayne was contracted for a single-day cameo on a different film, things had gone wrong. Because they were supposed to complete his scenes in one day, when Wayne went into overtime, that production ended up paying him substantially more than if they'd contracted Wayne for two or three days.)

Kazanjian then condensed much of the assembled information into the all-important shooting schedule. If a revised script was delivered from the front office, oftentimes, the new script would have to be broken down again and a new shooting schedule generated. Meanwhile, carpenters in the soundstage-size Mill, an all-purpose construction site, were building sets based on production designer John Truscott's vision of Camelot. Truscott had designed the London and Sydney productions of *Camelot* and

50

had the facility bustling. They were also fabricating props, large and small, including metal or rubber armor and swords. The property department aged the props as needed. About 1,500 suits of armor were needed in all. (A few genuine chain mail shirts and leather boots had been brought back from London. Actors would always wear lightweight rubber armor on horses; actual metal was reserved for close-ups.)

"Nobody knows when Camelot existed, if it did exist," Logan explained to film critic Roger Ebert, "but I was damned if I was going to set it in one of those clammy old stone castles furnished with a flickering torch, suits of armor, and moss-covered stairs. Our castle is a place King Arthur could call home." He noted that Truscott's aesthetic had attracted Warner Bros. to the project for it was "neither Gothic nor Romanesque but an in-between period, suggesting a legendary time."

Kazanjian was happy to work again with art director Edward Carrere. "Many of the costumes and props were being manufactured while they were in Europe," he says, "and schedules changed as new actors were cast and sets were built. During lunch I would go to the Mill and watch armor being made, sets constructed, and so on. Visiting wardrobe on occasion, once I walked into a large room where fifteen seamstresses were behind their sewing machines. This was old Hollywood at its best." Kazanjian had seen Merlyn's costume in tests and thought it a marvel. Basing his concept of the character on the description by author T. H. White in *The Once and Future King* (published in 1958 and used as source material for the musical), Truscott, who doubled as costume designer, told the seamstress to weave into Merlyn's robe images of strange beasts, slugs, and bugs. Actor Laurence Naismith was also fitted with mirrored contact lenses to enhance his otherworldly appearance, but these made it impossible for him to see. Kazanjian had to lead the actor to his position near the set's tree for one of his first scenes; an animal wrangler would place a live owl on his shoulder. Other trained animals—fox, rabbit, and so on—were then placed in the forest.

"In all my years as a filmmaker," Kazanjian recalls, "I've never seen such beautiful clothing as those Vanessa wore in *Camelot*. Harris, as King Arthur, also had a great wardrobe—all designed with fine fabrics and materials by John Truscott."

Star Richard Harris (King Arthur) of Camelot *(1967) signed a photo to Kazanjian, writing in praise of his diligent work on the set, "I suppose one day you will own the studio."*

Kazanjian also worked with a storyboard artist on the big joust scene. On other days, he might be needed during costume and hair tests. The more he knew, the better the 2nd AD could assure each department's smooth functionality and facilitate inter-departmental action. Kazanjian arranged auditions for scenes requiring dozens of extras. It seemed to him that Logan interviewed every male extra in Hollywood. The 2nd AD would line them up outside of Logan's office, on the street across from several dressing rooms, and organize them into groups for review: potential knights, street musicians, townspeople. One group was ordered to return in their underwear, for they'd have to be fit enough to wear a knight's skin-tight clothing, rubber armor, or tights.

Alfred Newman, a longtime fixture and legend at Fox, was employed to put the Broadway musical's famous songs onto tracks in prerecording sessions. These would be used for lip-synching on set. Unusually, Logan planned to record several songs live; that is, at least one of the stars was going to sing her own songs instead of being dubbed by a professional singer. "It really will be Vanessa's own voice," Logan told Ebert. "Ever since *West Side Story* [1961], people have gotten very bothered about dubbing in the voices of other singers. I can't imagine why. When I did *South Pacific* [1958], Ezio Pinza was the only actor who sang his own songs, and nobody seemed to care. But Vanessa herself will sing, all the same. She has a marvelous voice, but nobody over here has heard it because she's known only as an actress."

MISADVENTURES

Production days started at 6 AM. Kazanjian would first look in on the film's stars, Richard Harris and Vanessa Redgrave (King Arthur and Guenevere, respectively), in makeup. Redgrave's wash and hairdo alone took almost an hour; Bob Schieffer was her makeup artist and, early mornings, when Redgrave was in her chair, Kazanjian would ask if she wanted breakfast. "Bob was always generous with small talk, or offering suggestions both to me and cast" (Schieffer's long list of credits included 1935's *Top Hat* with Fred Astaire; he was later head of the makeup department at Disney Studios). Harris was made up either in his bungalow suite facing the tennis courts or in a ten-by-ten-foot dressing room on wheels (to be closer to the soundstages). The 2nd AD would bounce between the two actors, as well as other cast members, fetching anything needed and solving problems or clearing up misunderstandings. He kept studio vehicles on hand for both stars at all times.

"Harris had a slightly bent or broken nose," Kazanjian recalls, "but Frank Prehoda was his makeup man, a brilliant guy, and he knew how to use shadowing to make it look straight. Those are things I learned, the tricks, not just in makeup, but in many departments. One day Harris wore a certain wig, another day a different one, because Arthur aged, as did his armor, as did lots of things in the movie. You're shooting out of continuity; his mustache changed, too."

Actors had to be ready and on set, generally, by 8:00 AM. Kazanjian had been given an office on the lot, but as the days passed, he spent very little time there; instead he orbited the set while in his "standing office." He updated reports and was on hand in case the director or DP needed him.

A winter's day was the setting for Guenevere's arrival in Camelot. Stagehands and special effects created a blanket of snow (salt) in front of a painted miniature of the castle, fabricated in the Mill, and shot in forced perspective. Logan was under pressure to cut costs, so he gave a good deal of latitude to Kline in setting up the camera, which allowed him the time to concentrate on the actors' performances. Kazanjian noted that Kline toned down the overall light, but would throw extra light on smaller areas. For a dolly shot that followed Guenevere's horse litter, Kline focused a handheld PAR light (parabolic anodized reflector) on Redgrave. "Oftentimes, Dick and I would discuss what lens he had on or why a dolly shot," Kazanjian says. "Dick took me under his wing and explained many things. Several years later I realized how valuable those lessons were."

One early morning in makeup, Redgrave's "wonderful longtime hair person," Lenore Weaver, told Kazanjian that a special guest was going to visit that day. Only Logan and Kazanjian would be introduced to her. Later that morning, while shooting the snow scene with Redgrave and Harris, Weaver appeared—accompanied by Princess Grace Kelly of Monaco. "Grace Kelly was first introduced to Joshua, who spoke with her for a minute, then myself," Kazanjian recalls. "Previously I had asked Lenore if I should bow, take her hand, what? Lenore said I would know what to do. The crew just stared at Grace." Kazanjian was honored to meet the star he'd seen in Alfred Hitchcock's *Rear Window* (1954), *Dial M for Murder* (1954), and *To Catch a Thief* (1955), as well as Fred Zinnemann's *High Noon* (1952); Kelly had abandoned her career upon marrying Rainier III, Prince of Monaco.

Ebert was on hand perhaps a week later while Logan filmed Redgrave singing a verse of "Take Me to the Fair." It was slow going thanks to a prop man who had stepped backward into a spray of mustard grass that the director had intended to shoot through. "Part of the trouble was the clearing, hardly big enough to build a campfire in," according to Ebert, was overcrowded with a hammock slung between two saplings; Redgrave; Anthony Rogers (Sir Dinadan); an "epic-sized" film crew; and at least a dozen visitors, "fiancées, reporters, and out-of-work knights . . . trees, carpeted with thick green grass, and lit with romantic yellow beams from the sun and the rich hues of Logan's vocabulary."

"I'm going to sing softer this time," Redgrave said. "I don't want to be making opera faces."

Richard Harris was also eager to sing live and not to a prerecorded track because he'd heard that fellow Englishman and actor Rex Harrison was singing live as the eponymous Doctor Doolittle on the nearby Fox lot. Harris was not as accomplished a singer as Harrison, however, so director and music associate Ken Darby had tried to dissuade him. The compromise was that when both Redgrave and Harris sang together, they would lip-synch to a prerecorded track. When Harris sang his solos, he'd sing live. As insurance, he'd prerecorded his songs, as had Redgrave and Nero, months earlier under Newman's supervision, as mentioned; it would be up to the director to choose what to go with in the editing room later. Darby was always on the set watching the performers whether it was live or prerecorded.

Redgrave recalled that for her "Lusty Month of May" showstopper, "there were hundreds of daffodils and dozens of apple trees in blossom all planted and watered and timed to blossom at the beginning of January.

Joshua Logan's excitement and enthusiasm, and the skills of hundreds of Warner's craftsmen and women . . . had transformed the back lot and the soundstages into an extraordinary series of tableaux vivants. Guenevere's dress was made of finely crocheted cream wool cobwebs, hung with bleached melon seeds, each cobweb with a seashell at the center."

On set, it was "Mr. Logan." Logan was a respected director, writer, and producer for film and stage, but approachable. He spoke to Kazanjian about the difficulties of his life and how, when he was three years old, his father had committed suicide. Although happily married and with children, he hinted of challenges and struggles that dogged his steps. (Logan's credits include *Picnic*, 1955; *Mister Roberts*, 1955; *Bus Stop*, 1956; *South Pacific*, 1958; *Fanny*, 1961; and others.)

Richard Harris, his male lead, had his own challenges, most of which revolved around excessive carousing and drinking. Kazanjian describes the actor as "a true gentleman and a professional," but Harris often arrived late after a night out. "The studio driver would kiss his ass, so Richard would ask for the same driver. A couple of times, he would say to the driver after being driven home, 'Wait a minute, I'm changing my clothes; I want you to drive me to so-and-so.' Then he would go out all night and the driver would sit there, eventually going into 'gold' or 'double gold' overtime. If he was late, I couldn't call the driver. The driver would have to find a pay phone down the street and hope that Richard didn't walk out.

"Richard sometimes had to be woken up at home," adds the 2nd AD. "There were one or two times he was in the makeup chair, and I would have to hold his head so he wouldn't move it. A few times when he was late, I'd have to go on set and up to Dick Kline and say, 'We have a problem, can we start with something else?' Kline would always know what I was referring to. And Richard became a friend. He joked with me because I was saving him so many times. I thought, *Why not try to help him?*"

One day Harris was already late when he slipped and fell in the shower, cracking his head. It happened to be the morning Logan was to shoot King Arthur's soliloquy at the Round Table. "Frank Prehoda and

I are waiting in his room because he's late. Richard finally arrives and Frank's trying to put a Band-Aid on his wound and then put makeup over the bandage, so I said, 'Why don't you just tilt his crown down?' Frank tilted it down to cover the mark and nobody knew the difference."

At the end of a long day, Harris would sometimes indulge in a bottle of Johnnie Walker Red Label Scotch whiskey. Although Kazanjian was unaware of their activities, it would later be reported that Harris and costar David Hemmings (Mordred, the villain) were drinking buddies. Hemmings apparently saved Harris's life when the latter, at a low point during filming, was going to jump from a second-story house into a dry pool. At least once the two actors smuggled alcohol onto the lot in a prop van, drank with abandon, then filled up a porta-loo with their empties. Jack Warner, who rarely came on set, happened to discover their shenanigans during an impromptu visit and, after ordering crew to clean it all up, told Harris and Hemmings, "This bar is now closed."

THE STUDIO BELL TOLLS

Kazanjian generated the call sheets' several pages each morning based on the shooting schedule. Page one went out to everyone on set; page two, from the production office, listed what other productions were doing and went out only to management and executives (for example, on April 28, 1967, *Sweet November*, directed by Robert Ellis Miller, was on Stage 12; and director Richard Lester was on location in San Francisco, shooting *Petulia*); pages three and four usually listed on-set times and equipment, and were distributed to the crew.

On Tuesday, April 25, Kazanjian drove his new 1966 GTO onto the lot and hurried over to the makeup department. Lionel Jeffries (King Pellinore) had a 5:45 AM makeup call, followed by Harris and Redgrave. Other key actors were to follow at 6:30 and 7. He then drove to Devil's Gulch on the back lot where the "Exterior Jousting Field" had been created (south of the Camelot Castle courtyard in front of the large Camelot Castle set). A tent had been set up for the extras to be costumed and made-up, where they started arriving at 6:30 AM. Upon entering the men's tent, Howard found twenty-two wardrobe assistants preparing the knights, noblemen, and peasants (the day before he'd ordered from Central Casting a variety of extras, from four doubles and one "fire-eater" to a "sword-balancer" and juggler—in addition to "atmosphere" extras: forty noblewomen, twenty-five peasant men, twenty-five peasant women, twenty-five noblemen, one "queen of love & beauty," six street singers, twenty knights, two street ladies, five Eastern peddlers, ten children [minors], and so on).

To keep everyone awake, associate producer Joel Freeman had ordered forty gallons of coffee in addition to fifteen dozen Danish pastries; thirty more gallons of coffee would arrive that afternoon. The stuntmen, including Joe Canutt and his brother Tap, had come on early in production to work with the coordinator and the art department. To simulate being hit by a lance and knocked off their horses, riders were yanked by a strong wire, invisible onscreen, by off-camera stagehands. When anyone hit the dirt, Kazanjian had to check them out quickly to make sure they weren't hurt (in one shot, a stuntman had to fall and hit a rail that separated the charging knights, a section of which was balsa wood).

A large *Camelot* sequence was shot at night with twenty-five mounted stuntmen clad as knights and thirty dressed as guards holding burning torches for a battle of "knights vs. knights." Kazanjian's challenge was keeping track of what each stuntman was doing for each stunt, for each was paid accordingly. Extras who held torches received an additional "bump" in pay (those holding the reins of a horse were also paid more). All this had to be logged onto time cards at the end of the evening. It was the right of assistant directors to select extras they'd worked with before or those they knew. Kazanjian thus hired his old USC classmate Randal Kleiser, who at that time was directing commercials, modeling, and moonlighting as an extra. "It was on the back lot, where they had the big castle built," Kleiser recalls. "There were all these other peasants, so I was a peasant. As an extra, if you held a torch, you got $10 extra, if you held a horse, you got $10. Howard tried to be nice to me, gave me three torches and a horse, but the horse was terrified of the torches. So I spent the whole night with my arms pulled apart by the horse and the torches for $40 extra."

58

Kazanjian didn't leave the set until about 2:30 the next morning. "As an AD, you had to have your fingers on the pulse of all situations," he explains, "so as to not fall afoul of any SAG or other union regulations and incur monetary penalties. Chief among these regulations were those governing work hours and mealtimes."

Overtime didn't actually kick in until after ten hours worked, which meant the studio could use people nine hours before incurring multiples of the normal rates. If the production did go into overtime, the AD had leeway to send certain crewmembers home—greensmen, electricians, unneeded extras—to keep costs down. Mealtimes had to be respected; if the actors ate breakfast at 6 AM, lunch had to be offered within the next five and a half hours. Dinner, if served, had to be within the next six hours. "As AD, you had to keep all these things in mind and watch your clock, for there were penalties when these time frames were exceeded."

One day, after a long morning on the throne room set, Kazanjian called for lunch, "one hour." Toward the end of the hour break he went to the dressing rooms to check on the artists. "All the cast get touched up with makeup, hair, and have their wardrobe checked," he says. "I went to David Hemmings's dressing room, a little portable box, and I said, 'David, we're ready for you.' David responded, 'When are we going to lunch?' 'David, we called lunch, you were on the stage. Everyone heard the call.' He says, 'No, you have to come to me and say, 'David, one-hour lunch.' I said, 'We'll get you a sandwich. What would you like?' 'No, I want to break for lunch.'"

Up until recently David Hemmings had been an unknown, a struggling actor, but he'd become "one of the hottest screen properties in the world," according to Ebert, on the basis of his first starring role in Michelangelo Antonioni's *Blow-Up* (1966).

"So, I went to the stage telephone, because David's in this first shot after lunch and I have a hundred and fifty dressed extras waiting on this huge stage, and I call Joel Freeman. I explain the situation. Now Joel is a very experienced old-timer who has been in situations like this before. Joel knew the business inside and out. He hangs up. A little while later the phone rings onstage. We had a studio policeman there answering the phone. He says it's for David Hemmings. David takes the phone and it's

59

his agent, who says—I'm paraphrasing because I wasn't on the phone—'What did you do?! Jack Warner just fired you and is replacing you.' Joel had gone to Jack. This all happens within five minutes. Jack Warner stood up for me. David came flying back on set so fast. That's how it was taken care of. You learned to work things out and find solutions."

The studio still had its original boss, Jack Warner, but his crew was working for the last time on permanent contract. During preproduction of *Camelot*, Warner had announced that he was selling his stock to the Canadian film and distribution company Seven Arts Productions. The news sounded the death knell for the original Warner Bros. studio. "I recall when the new Seven Arts administration moved in," Kazanjian says. "One of their first moves was to have a crew from the back lot break up and haul away the Warner Bros.' 'WB' logo, which was made of concrete. I used to walk by the logo, located on the lawn of the circle drive outside the administration building, and I felt sad about seeing the 'WB' fade away. I also didn't like the new 'W7' logo that began appearing on stationery and films."

BEHIND-THE-SCENES DRAMA

Logan was relying more and more on Kazanjian to run the set. His 1st AD was about sixty-six years old and, for his own reasons, preferred to remain sitting in his chair during production. Kazanjian, on the other hand, had memorized the shooting schedule and associated logistics; he had a visual mind and could instantly see the implications of any change on various aspects of production. He would also notice things in dailies that occasionally escaped others ("dailies" refers to the review of the previous day's shoot, usually attended by the director, studio execs, and a chosen few). "We're watching dailies on the big screen," Kazanjian recalls, "and to the right, I see the wheels of the sound boom crawling up on the salt/snow with its black wheels on white. The lights come up, and Logan and Jay Lerner, the talented man who wrote the music and the script, are there, and I mention it. Logan asks the projectionist to thread up the shot again and we watch it. The second time through they again see nothing of the black wheels on white snow." A similar incident occurred in dailies when

Kazanjian noticed a round bandage on the back of Richard Harris's neck during a forest scene. Again, he pointed it out, this time to editor Folmar Blangsted and Logan; again, they couldn't see it.

At the end of each day, Howard took the time cards, made the calculations, and handed them to payroll. He earned the respect and approval of the studio for his attention to detail. They began grooming him for a bigger job, even though the future ownership of the studio was in question. Kazanjian was also liked by the actors and the extras, because he usually had answers to their questions; if he didn't have an answer, he would get one, especially for the extras (a rule he would keep throughout his career for any actor or crewmember). He was sympathetic to their situation; he knew that if an extra was not working, they'd need to be looking for their next job. On the other hand, they didn't want to move on if there were any chance the film could still employ them. Extras often asked if they could step outside and use a pay phone to call Central Casting to look for work. Unlike many ADs worried about logistics, Kazanjian would keep track of who was needed when and let them make their important calls. "I've always made it a practice to answer questions from cast, crew, or corporate. If I don't have an answer, I explain that I'll find out and get back to them."

Kazanjian would confer often with Mr. Logan, fifty-eight at that time, who was always impeccably dressed in a dark suit and tie and highly polished shoes. In gritty dirt and salt/snow, his shoes would lose their shine by late afternoon, yet the next day they'd be restored to their former glory. When Logan once invited Kazanjian to his rented home in Beverly Hills, the mystery of their rejuvenation appeared—in the form of a butler, towel over his arm, who answered the door.

Logan had an office on the lot, where a secretary typed up his correspondence and production materials. Mornings, he would drive over to inspect the sets with Kazanjian and Kline, tell them what he wanted, then return to his office until preparations were completed for shooting. Once when Kazanjian called the secretary to relay the ten-minute warning, she informed him that Logan wasn't in and hadn't been seen for a while. Kazanjian called Freeman, who called the motor gate, where the guard confirmed that Logan had driven off the lot. They were bewildered. Logan had apparently gone home without explanation. After their director was located and returned, Freeman left a standing order with gate guards that if it were only midday, they weren't to let Logan off the lot. Kazanjian wondered if Logan's meanderings had anything to do with the director's hints about a troubled childhood.

The scope of the movie could be overwhelming at times. The immense winter forest set, built on Stage 8, required more than four hundred 10K lights. For the wedding between Arthur and Guenevere, Kline used more than one thousand real candles, lit all at once by a team of thirty prop men (the union allowed only property men to move or light candles). Kline doubled the candlelight by placing mirrors in strategic positions; to add a glow, he placed an eight-by-eight-foot pane of glass in front of the camera at a thirty-degree angle; behind the camera, he had a light beamed onto a twenty-by-twenty-foot white flat, which was reflected by the glass into the lens. Shot through glass, the mythical couple onscreen would seem to pass through a mystical haze. Kline controlled his colors and contrast by pre-flashing his negative, a technique Kazanjian had heard about but never seen used. Because the process opened up the shadows slightly, Kline used far less fill-light than usual. Pre-flashing also muted the colors, lending the realm of Camelot a storybook glow.

The DP always kept his AD informed. He would let him know when his cameras were in place and the set was lit. He warned him about delays. Kline also offered advice on the business and people, and explained his methods. "You have to pick a style," the cameraman told him, "you move or you don't." Kline moved the camera only when he had to, but liked to use a camera crane when possible. For an establishing shot of the Round Table set (built at one end of the throne room set, though separate from it, to save time and money), the camera operator was told to pan up from the knights at the Round Table to the stained glass windows above. During the take, Kazanjian saw that the operator hadn't done it right and brought his concern to Kline. The operator denied it. When dailies came back, Kazanjian was proved right, but the set had already been broken down and was too expensive to set up again.

Kazanjian continued to learn from associate producer Joel Freeman, who would constantly ask for numbers: How many extras? How many hours worked? When did they start? What time did they go to lunch? The 2nd AD learned to count everything, right down to the number of lunches consumed. He recorded what time the company moved from one stage and arrived at another in the daily production reports. "But there was another side to Joel," Kazanjian says. "He continued to be a master teacher to me and a long-lasting friend."

When a big press junket was announced for the day, Freeman took Kazanjian aside and told him he was invited. When Kazanjian pointed out that he wasn't dressed for it, Freeman ordered him to the wardrobe department. There, they fitted him on the spot, selected a suit, marked and pinned it up, and told him to come back later. When he did, the costume department had already altered the suit and were pressing it. They supplied him with socks and shoes, and sent him off to the junket properly attired. (A name tag from a previous film indicated that the suit had originally been fabricated for actor Christopher Plummer in *Inside Daisy Clover*, 1965.)

SECRETS

As production came to a close, soundtrack composer Alfred Newman spent more time outside his office door at his piano, which he kept in the hallway across from Kazanjian's office. Newman supplied music for the film's new scenes to complement Frederick Loewe's Broadway score. Newman, who would be given a black-and-white work dupe of the assembled film after wrap, would tell Freeman that his cue arrangements for Camelot were the most difficult of his career.

Logan showed up on set one day—and was told that Jack Warner was pulling the plug on the film due to overruns. The director had only one more day to shoot everything they needed. "I began to pile up in my mind all the various things that we still had to do," Logan said. "Arthur's speech at the Round Table, bits and pieces of Lancelot's miracle at the jousting match—so we kept on shooting until three or four in the morning."

"For the very last scene of the picture," Kazanjian recalls, "King Arthur is preparing for battle, and Ken Darby wanted a few words picked up. We brought in Richard Harris to sing just those one or two words to a music playback onstage. One of the words was 'Camelot' and Darby had him sing it six or seven times with different accents on the word."

Logan recalled: "Finally, I called a halt, deciding that if we missed anything we'd just have to come back. But we never shot another foot. Jack wouldn't allow it. And we squeezed by."

Kazanjian was put to work in post. The master shot for the last scene had been filmed on location in Spain, but Logan needed a few pick-ups, close-ups of Harris as Arthur and Gary Marsh as the boy, Tom. With a little set dressing, makeup, and armor to match, Logan shot these pick-ups on a soundstage with some new dialogue. In editorial, Logan then compared the close-ups shot on stage to what had been filmed months earlier on location. The pick-ups needed a little "magic," or what they referred to as "color timing" (done in a lab), so the colors would match. Other scenes might need more green or less blue, as the director and producer saw fit.

Next up was "looping." Actors would be called into a sound studio on the lot, placed at a microphone stand, and given headphones. On a screen they'd see projected in a continual "loop" a scene that needed dialogue to be rerecorded for one reason or another. In some cases, the words might be "wild," meaning that the dialogue wasn't synched to anyone's lips; in most cases, their words would have to be synched to what was shot. Occasionally, dialogue had been rewritten but was close enough to what was said to match. (This process was referred to as "looping" well into the 1970s, due to the edited, repeating loop. In the 1980s, thanks to more sophisticated equipment, the process became known as ADR, or Automated Dialogue Replacement.)

Kazanjian attended all the major cast looping sessions for two reasons: Warner Bros. wanted him to learn more about overall production, and to make sure Richard Harris and the actors found the correct recording studio, arrived on time, had lunch on time, and so on (as usual, time cards and production reports had to be completed each day). Franco Nero was perhaps the first to be called in. Nero had to tame his heavy Italian accent, an exercise that took about three weeks. "Each week his English improved so we would rerecord his voice over and over again," Kazanjian says. "One day Logan and Jay Lerner come in and they're looking at that scene in the snow, and it's repeated in a loop, over and over. And the wheels of the sound boom roll up, visible at last, and Lerner screams out, 'Oh my God! There are wheels in the picture.' Dead quiet. Nobody says anything to me. Like they had never been told. I was learning that the assistant director is either wrong or invisible." (To solve the problem of the wheels in the picture, they either did an optical blow up, pushing in to crop out the wheels, or they manually blurred them out.)

Finally, the negative was sent off so theatrical prints could be made.

The reviewer for *Variety* wrote that *Camelot* was "a musical with wit . . . A musical with wisdom, which says and demonstrates so much about human belligerency and the slow nature of 'progress' . . . It must generate a great deal of discussion of its substance and not its means. The means are magnificent. The heart is beneath the trappings of knighthood. This is especially a great picture for Harris whose performance is rich in nuance and heartbreak, abounding in the kind of nobility which has temporarily gone out of fashion in fiction."

"The end result was a pretty nice film that I was very proud of," Kazanjian says. However, he did notice that the release print had a scene where the bandage on the back of Harris's neck was plainly visible in a quick cut (for the film's DVD release, the bandage was optically removed). Logan said, "Since it did turn out to be the most beautiful picture I ever made, perhaps Jack was right" about pulling the plug. A couple of years later Logan made public his bipolar disorder and the relief that lithium was bringing him. The disclosure made Kazanjian more conscious than ever that those who worked so diligently on films, who were fitted into the cogs of the studio production machines, were nothing more than frail humans.

But there was little time for reflection that May of 1967. Kazanjian was told to follow Freeman across the Warner Bros. lot to take up another position as 2nd AD, this time for *Finian's Rainbow*—under the direction of Francis Ford Coppola.

CHAPTER 4: *Once Upon a Lullaby*

O ne might assume that because Kazanjian had recently worked on one musical, he was being put on another, *Finian's Rainbow*. The truth was that nothing much else was happening on the Warner Bros. lot that summer. The sale of Jack Warner's stock to Seven Arts Productions had slowed production. The founding movie moguls were retiring or dying off. There were still a few second-generation titans, such as Lew Wasserman at MCA-Universal, but Jack Warner was on his way out. New management had new ideas, but often knew little to nothing about the motion picture industry. Sensing that the studios were weakening, younger, more independent filmmakers were determined to work in less restrained environments; they wanted more creative control. One such director was Francis Ford Coppola, an improbable choice for *Finian's Rainbow*, a musical starring arguably the world's greatest dancer and singer Fred Astaire as Finian McLonergan. Coppola had been a staff writer at Seven Arts; his hiring was a case of "right place at the right time." "It was quite a coincidence related to my directing *Finian*," he said.

In fact, the new Warner Bros.-Seven Arts studio had been looking for an energetic, younger director to helm the big-screen adaptation of the Broadway musical. Coppola's second feature, *You're a Big Boy Now* (1966), had been released theatrically even though it was his postgraduate thesis project at UCLA film school. His first theatrical movie, *Dementia 13* (1963), a low-budget horror flick, had been produced by Roger Corman. More importantly, Coppola had written several scripts to some acclaim, including *This Property Is Condemned* (1966) and *Is Paris Burning?* (1966). Production execs had therefore narrowed the choice to

Coppola or William Friedkin, whose Sonny and Cher film, *Good Times* (1967), had gone over well. They chose Coppola.

"My first thought," Coppola said, recalling his decision to accept, "was what I should have said is no." He said yes because he knew it would make his father, Carmine, a professional musician and composer, happy. He also recognized that it "was an extraordinary opportunity for a young director. I had done a lot of stage musicals, so I had experience with the genre." Upon reading the script and seeing the musical, Coppola thought it best to film the whole movie on location, somewhere like Tennessee. He felt its "book," which touched upon Civil Rights issues in a "dumb" way, would work only if the story were told in real environments. The studio, however, wasn't about to let a relatively untried, iconoclastic bearded twenty-something run amok with their money where they couldn't control him.

For Kazanjian, the *Finian* production marked the end of his trial period with the DGA. He'd taken, on his own time, the PGA/DGA courses that covered the rules and regulations of SAG, the Teamsters, IA (IATSE, all three the large labor unions of trade professionals), and so on. Consequently, not only was he a bona fide second assistant director, Kazanjian was more familiar than most with the more arcane rules and regulations of several unions. As such, he redeemed himself in William Schaefer's eyes, the executive assistant to Jack Warner who had been at the studio since 1933 and who had once been critical of Kazanjian. When a question arose about a SAG regulation, Kazanjian explained to Schaefer how the rule could benefit production. Schaefer called SAG to confirm what the upstart was telling him. They confirmed, and Kazanjian's stock rose at the studio.

CHE COPPOLA

On May 15, Kazanjian was sent to San Francisco to join Coppola, whom he'd never met. The studio had consented to a couple of weeks of location filming before the rest of the movie was shot on soundstages and the back lot. "I think Francis didn't want an old-timer 2nd AD," says Kazanjian, who arrived at the Holiday Inn and took an elevator up to his room from the underground parking. "An older man and a younger bearded man got in at the lobby. At about the fourth floor the younger man, who turned out to be Francis, asked the older man, who turned out to be his temporary unit manager, when the assistant director was arriving. I said, 'I'm here!' That's how I met Francis."

Coppola wanted to keep the crew small for location work: an electrician, a grip, a special effects man, DP Philip Lathrop, and his operator. Lathrop, a Warner Bros. regular, usually wore a suit and tie, and worked with veteran gaffer Lee Wilson. The crew traveled in one station wagon and one truck, while their unit manager traveled ahead of them in another car to make preparations for each location. Their first task was the title sequence for the film. Many musicals of the period began with lavish location shots, of cities (*West Side Story*, 1961) or the countryside (*The Sound of Music*, 1965), to establish a sense of place. Fred Astaire (Finian McLonergan) was also on hand in San Francisco, as was his young costar, Petula Clark (Sharon McLonergan). Coppola wanted to film the actors crossing the picturesque Golden Gate Bridge, but the city was not granting permits. Undeterred, the director resorted to guerilla filmmaking tactics, in imitation of the European filmmakers he admired so much. It was Kazanjian's first exposure to the technique. They rented a second station wagon and some equipment, picked up Astaire and Clark, and headed for the bridge.

Coppola dropped Kazanjian and the actors at the south/city end. With Kazanjian off-camera directing pedestrian traffic, the two actors pretended to be tourists on a sightseeing excursion, while Coppola, with camera, had the station wagon crawl along ahead of them, tailgate down, so he could shoot their promenade. The unit manager trailed in his car. Because annoyed drivers had to swerve around the convoy, their actions didn't go unnoticed. By the time they arrived at the north/ Marin County end of the bridge, a police car was following them with red lights flashing. They pulled over onto a scenic lookout; fortunately, the manager happened to know the officer. (This shot won't be found in any iteration of the film, but the original "roadshow" version used some of the footage, which included even the flashing red lights of the police car in the background.) "While the police were being pacified,"

Kazanjian says, "Coppola continued driving up the coast for an unknown destination. We didn't see the unit manager for two days because Coppola changed travel directions. We never arrived at two hotels where we had reservations."

For a shot on location south of San Francisco, they used the station wagon and the truck; Astaire and Clark rode with Kazanjian and Coppola in the car. Kazanjian sat on the middle hump in the back seat between the actors. Beyond the city limits, the director spotted sheep grazing on a hill and shouted to the driver to stop. In pursuit of a bucolic moment, Coppola told Kazanjian to get out and herd the fleecy critters past his camera and the stars. "As Francis positioned the cast in the field, the sheep ran off," Kazanjian recalls. "Now Francis is yelling for me to keep the sheep behind Fred and Petula. I tried, but it didn't happen because I'm not a sheepdog—not to mention I was in some farmer's fenced-off field, chasing his sheep."

By the time they reloaded the station wagon, Kazanjian was worried about a possible meal-infraction penalty. It was already late afternoon. Half-joking, he gestured to the empty countryside and asked if they wanted to eat "here" or wait for the hotel in Sonora, as scheduled. "Let's wait for the hotel," said Astaire, who understood their predicament. Clark agreed. According to the arcane rules of SAG, the assistant director having made the proper legal offer to his cast and production was spared the meal penalty.

Despite a rocky start, Coppola impressed his stars and Kazanjian over the next few days on location in Tuolumne and Napa Counties. He was always on the lookout for a more interesting backdrop, whatever their schedule or destination. He spotted a riverboat when they were driving through Stockton and quickly set up a shot of Astaire and Clark traveling upriver on its deck because the whole locale could pass for the Deep South. "Francis was closer to my age and treated me as a companion rather than someone working for the studio," Kazanjian says.

In Sonora, director, cast, and crew did several setups on a train, for a sequence in which the film's romantic lead Woody Mahoney (Don Francks, who had been flown in) is returning home to Rainbow Valley. They shot on top of the train—though only exteriors had been

69

planned—and then Coppola added one more element. He had seen an effect in a short directed by Charles and Ray Eames called *Toccata for Toy Trains* (1957), which he wanted to emulate. In this shot, a toy train drove right "through" an exterior camera. "No one on the crew could figure out how it had been done," Kazanjian says. "Phil, the DP, made some calls and discovered it had been done with a mirror."

The truck driver was sent out to find the biggest mirror available, and came back with one measuring about six by six feet. They didn't have the exact tools or materials needed, but the crew jerry-rigged the mirror at a forty-five-degree angle across the tracks. From its side, the operator zoomed into the mirror, which was reflecting an image of the train. As the heavy train rolled toward the mirror, it began vibrating. "As the train came down the track and passed the camera, it hit the mirror. That ended the shot," Kazanjian continues. "Then Francis called for the camera to be inside a passenger car with Woody." It was another ad hoc shot, and the DP and one electrician had only the one battery and a six-light lamp. They were using ASA 200 film, so gaffer Lee Wilson stood in the corner of the passenger car holding the six-light in the air, while the camera was walked through, handheld.

Coppola made it clear to his AD and others throughout the location shoot that he found the film's "book" clunky and out of touch. He added a new subplot to give the film a more contemporary feel: mentholated tobacco hybridization vs. bigoted land rights, a dispute— complete with activism, sit-down strikes, and protest songs—that threatens to destroy the story's picturesque, unspoiled Rainbow Valley. The final script told that story in the context of an Irish immigrant and his daughter who move to the American South with a magical pot of gold that could change people's lives, including those of struggling farmers and African-Americans threatened by a racist politician.

In the coastal town of Bodega Bay, farther northwest, Coppola created another impromptu moment. He filmed Astaire and Clark walking along a fence with small village houses beyond, one of which was the recognizable schoolhouse from Hitchcock's *The Birds* (1963). A more ambitious location shot was from a helicopter of Astaire and Clark. The pilot had to hit the filming switch as soon as the pair was visible below, a difficult maneuver that added up to about thirty "takes." To maximize their chances of getting it right, Coppola had every take printed because he couldn't be sure which had succeeded, if any.

SHALL WE DANCE?

On Monday, May 22, 1967, *Variety* reported that one of the film's producers, Joseph Landon, was reactivating an old studio technique: "a live performance of a film play before principal photography begins. Film musical, which today starts six weeks of rehearsals, sans camera or lights, rolls July 5 at Warner Bros. Francis Ford Coppola will direct cast headed by Petula Clark and Tommy Steele." The article also noted that because Fred Astaire would be shot out of continuity, production felt that a live run-through would shorten shooting time. Coppola began his rehearsal period by having his principals do a table read of the script. Kazanjian sat in. The director wanted to get a feel for the story and the songs, how it all fit together, particularly for Astaire. The "live performance" followed, which Kazanjian describes as a "full-blown Broadway Musical," without sets, but with a few props. Coppola even brought in his father to provide the musical accompaniment. Kazanjian was cast as stage manager. He would cue everyone and everything from his place in one of the six theater seats.

The day of the show, the audience consisted only of the AD, a few guests, and Carol (whom Kazanjian was still dating). Gaffer Wilson operated the dimmers. Kazanjian recalls: "We put on a whole spectacle for Francis, like a theatrical performance, no stops, just keep going, going, going. We saw and heard a complete private live-action showing of *Finian's Rainbow*—with Fred Astaire—something I shall never forget. I was the stage manager, but had little to do but enjoy the show. A lot of the dance numbers were in there, but some hadn't been finished or rehearsed as yet. Even so, it's possible that Francis saw that it wasn't going right, and started thinking about Hermes Pan."

Hermes Pan had co-choreographed Astaire's dances since the 1930s, but nothing was sacred to the young director. "One thing that impressed me so very much was the rehearsal time Fred spent on his dance numbers,"

71

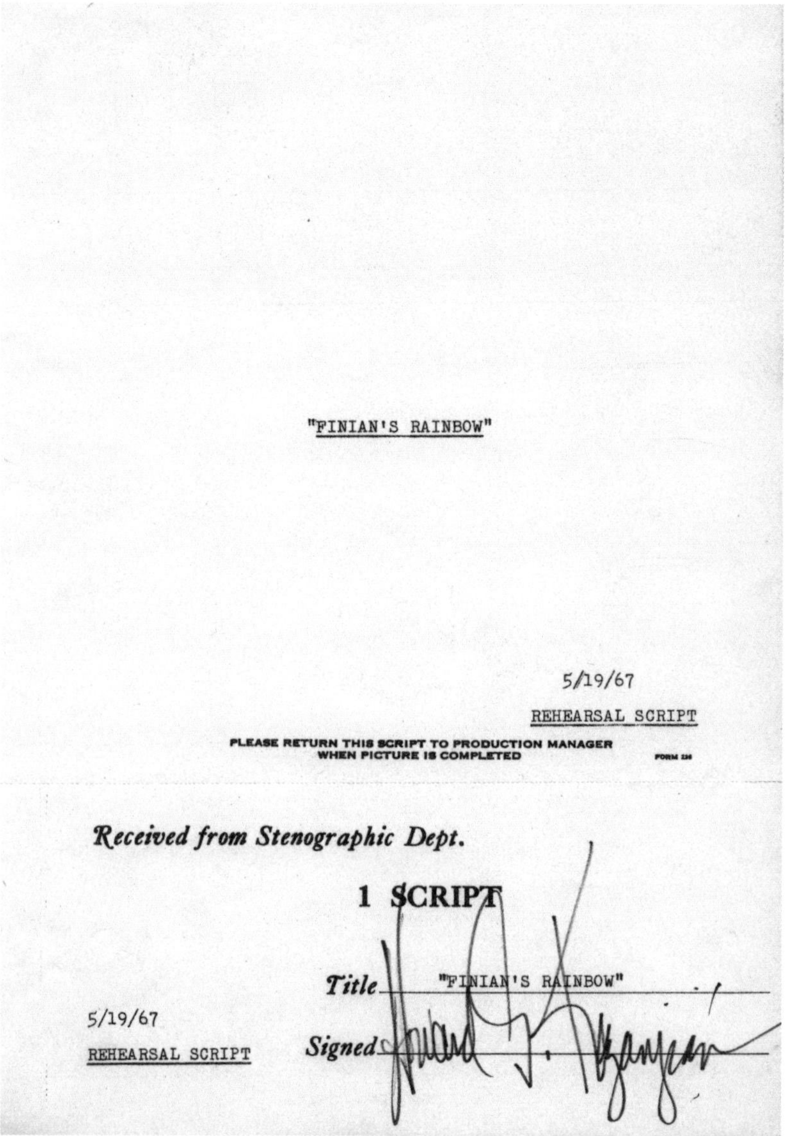

"FINIAN'S RAINBOW"

5/19/67

REHEARSAL SCRIPT

PLEASE RETURN THIS SCRIPT TO PRODUCTION MANAGER
WHEN PICTURE IS COMPLETED   FORM 136

Received from Stenographic Dept.

1 SCRIPT

Title _____ "FINIAN'S RAINBOW" _____

5/19/67

REHEARSAL SCRIPT

Signed _____

ABOVE: *Kazanjian's copy of the "rehearsal script" for* Finian's Rainbow *(1968).*

OPPOSITE, CLOCKWISE FROM TOP LEFT: *Fred Astaire signed his photo portrait to Kazanjian, "To Howard—I'll be there!!" a testament to the 2nd assistant director's efforts to keep all the actors punctual. • Tommy Steele (Og), director Francis Ford Coppola (in shorts), and Petula Clark (Sharon McLonergan) in conversation on location in Griffith Park, not far from the studio, for* Finian's Rainbow. *• On stage at Warner Bros. studio, Coppola directs Astaire on the "green set," an interior build complete with trees, lawn, and a real running stream.*

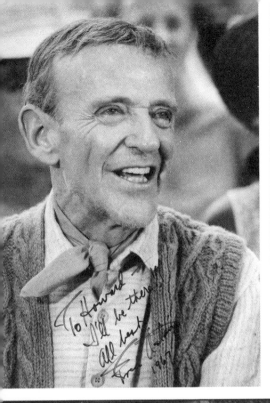

Kazanjian says. "Fred would spend the entire day in the rehearsal hall working with Pan practicing one dance, day after day after day. He'd begun rehearsing long before even the reading and performance."

"During the making of any show," Astaire told Johnny Carson in 1979, "it's worrisome because you're always wondering if you're going to put it all together."

A FOGGY DAY

When Coppola found time to sit down and watch dailies of the location shoot, he watched the helicopter shots one by one, nervously. He recalled: "I'd heard a story that one thing Jack Warner, the old man, hated was when a director printed more than two takes. He thought it was a waste." As take after take unfurled, the director saw that the helicopter camera had filmed nothing but empty corn fields—and then discovered when the lights came up, to his horror, that Jack Warner was sitting a few seats from him. "He never said anything. He just got up and left, but my God, my heart was in my mouth."

Finian's Rainbow occupied two soundstages and its crew revamped and resod the forest green sets on the back lot still standing from *Camelot*, adding fake trees and bushes, and so on. They used the stage with the tank for a set that had a running brook bound by sheer rock walls. Another set consisted of a bridge for the film's ending. As 2nd AD, Kazanjian was once again making sure that the production machine hummed: actors on time and in makeup, meals satisfactory, etc. He quickly realized that Don Francks was going to be difficult. "He had that 'star' mentality that sometimes infects performers," Kazanjian says. "It goes like this: On a first film, an actor will talk to you; on the second, you have to knock on his door; by the third, it's 'Who are you?' Francks had jumped to stage three in his first major film" (similar to Hemmings on *Camelot*).

One morning, out of the blue, Kazanjian got a call from George Lucas, his former USC classmate and fraternity brother. Lucas had won Warner Bros.' six-month scholarship on the strength of his postgraduate film *THX 1138.4EB* (1967). Kleiser says, "We were all blown away by *THX*, especially the sound design, the different types of voices and sounds and squeaks. It just felt very futuristic. The soundtrack was quite amazing. George had been very clever about working the system. The government was giving all this 16mm color film to the air force, whose students were at USC to learn how to work cameras so they could film planes. George corralled them together and therefore got all their film, the raw footage, and was able to make *THX* for his big graduate film" (he also used the air force students as crew and extras).

Unlike the previous winner of the studio award, Joyce Geller, Lucas didn't want to write; he wanted to study animation, but had found that studio department shut down, another sign of Warner Bros.' decay. With nothing to do, he'd called Kazanjian, who remembers, "George was sitting there in an office, bored out of his skull. He saw my name on a call sheet and decided to reach out."

Kazanjian invited Lucas down to the set to watch them shoot. They happened to be on a scene that revolved around the largest (fake) tree of Rainbow Valley (where Finian's gold is hidden). The film's three stars participated in a midsize song-and-dance number that culminated with Astaire dancing down a country road followed by the village's children. While Coppola filmed "Look to the Rainbow," Lucas arrived. Between setups, Coppola noticed the young man in a sweater with a similar-looking beard to his own standing next to Kazanjian. When the director asked what he was looking at, Lucas replied, "Nothing much."

Kazanjian introduced them, and Lucas asked if he could hang around. Coppola agreed, but required his visitor to let him know if he had any suggestions or ideas about how to shoot the picture. "He was very open about it," Kazanjian says. "You have to keep in mind that most of the crew was much older than Francis, George, and myself. We three somewhat stuck together in thinking and relationship." Their meeting may have occurred on the day Seven Arts officially concluded their purchase of Warner Bros.—July 15—for Lucas would maintain that the morning he arrived, Jack Warner exited the studio for the last time. (Actually, Jack Warner left the grounds toward the end of October, accompanied by his loyal assistant William Schaefer, who would continue to work for Warner until the latter's death in 1978.)

"One day I was working on the show," Coppola said in 1968, "and

I kept seeing this skinny kid with a beard and he was always looking at me. So I went up [to my AD, Kazanjian] and I said, 'Who's that?" and he said, 'Well, he's observing you.'"

Gary Young, while making his documentary *The New Cinema* (1968), would ask Lucas about the transition from student to professional filmmaker. "I think they're slowly beginning to realize that the students know what they're doing," Lucas replied. "They're not just silly kids out there playing around. They're serious and they're dedicated and they're trained in all the aspects of film, not just one area. A student out of film school can not only run a camera, run a sound unit, produce and direct and write, but he can also act, in many cases."

The three young film school graduates quickly formed a bond. And if Coppola needed a film clip from editorial for a retake or a matching shot, or if he wanted something from his office, Lucas was dispatched. Eventually Coppola allowed his "observer" to join him in dailies.

| They All Laughed

| At the time he met Coppola, Lucas was dating Marcia Griffin. "When George got the Warner Bros. scholarship, my apartment was closer to Warner Bros. studio," says Marcia. "So George started living with me more or less full-time. Francis was a party animal and he would have big social events at his house, dinner parties, and George would take me along, so I met Francis and Ellie, his wife, and their kids."

Lucas had met Marcia when they both happened to be working for editor Verna Fields. Marcia Griffin had been working as an assistant editor on television commercials, but had hit the glass ceiling when she tried to find a job on a TV series or a film. She recalls, "Time after time, they said, 'We just can't have a lady in the editing room. Our editors are very foul-mouthed and they get angry and blah, blah, blah.' So then this friend of mine told me he knew a lady who lived out in the valley in Van Nuys who liked to hire women, and

76

she was working on a project and needed assistance. So I called her. Her name was Verna Fields."

Fields hired Griffin. Fields was cutting a documentary on President Lyndon Johnson's trip to Southeast Asia while also teaching part-time at USC. The trip had been shot in 16mm for the United States Information Agency, but the camera teams hadn't been "slating" them—so the sound was out of sync. Fields therefore also hired several USC students to log the film. One of them was George Lucas. "George was very quiet," Marcia says, "but Verna had seen some of his student films and thought he was really talented and she was under a deadline to get the film cut, so she asked George to cut some scenes for her. He was probably the least experienced editor she had and I was the best assistant she had. So she made me George's assistant while he cut. And I'm a motormouth, of course. Later on, he told me he thought I was full of beans, but I thought he was a cold fish, and so that's how I met George."

Despite their wariness, they were both interested in films and often went together to see screenings of student shorts; Lucas would drive them. On one trip they discovered that they'd both been born in Modesto, which created a "Modesto bond." "But we were always oil and water," she says. "We'd go to films, go to a French movie, black-and-white, and I'd be sitting there asking, 'Where's the story? Where's the characters?' We'd leave the theater and George would say, 'That was such a good film' and I would say, 'I was bored out of my skull.'" One of the films they saw together was Stanley Kubrick's *2001: A Space Odyssey*. "I remember George saying, 'Now it's possible to make a movie in outer space and have it be real,'" she says, "because of the miniatures, and the starfields, and so on."

Never Gonna Dance

Clark divulged in 2012: "There was a lot of Flower Power going on." When she was asked if she and her costars were "smoking certain substances," she replied, "Yes, all that stuff. It [making the movie] was a wonderful experience. A lot of good things were going on there. It was California in the late '60s and it was kind of great." Trouble was afoot, however. Coppola wasn't happy with Hermes Pan. The songs had been prerecorded, but the rehearsals and performances (often to the rhythms of a live piano) weren't going right. "Fred Astaire was grand," Kazanjian says. "He was a gentleman, a pro. He and Hermes would arrive early at the studio and spend the whole day rehearsing, rehearsing, and more rehearsing. But it was a little old-fashioned and it wasn't working for Francis. There was an assistant working with the other thirty-three dancers, taking his orders from Hermes. Maybe they complained—I don't know where it started—but I know Francis was concerned."

Coppola went to Astaire, who told him it was okay to fire Pan. "Fred approved," Kazanjian says. "That was the first question I asked Francis, if Fred had approved." Hermes Pan departed about halfway through production.

Francks also continued to disappoint. There was little chemistry between him and Clark. Coppola and the producer called for closed-door meetings to discuss the situation. "There was one day when Francis cleared the theater," Kazanjian says. "I found out later that day or evening that he didn't like Don Francks. None of us did. But he couldn't fire him. We had shot too much." Clark and her husband/manager were also proving difficult. The latter informed Kazanjian that Clark's schedule had to be rearranged to suit British tax laws; she needed more time out of the United States.

Production carried on and Astaire kept at it. "Fred would do a dance and Francis would say, 'Cut and print.' But Fred would ask to do it again, even though it looked perfect to us," Kazanjian says. "What a perfectionist. Normally, the crew close to the camera knows if there will be another take. We sense this. With Fred, one never knew.

"However, his big dance number in the barn was nothing special. It wasn't designed to show Fred's true talent at that time. Fred could have done better. I watched him dance his heart out all day long in those rehearsals. He was much more agile than that. He could have done much more and better than what was filmed."

Not only had Astaire's longtime choreographer been axed, his choice of dance partners, the experienced Barrie Chase, for the role of Susan the Silent, was passed over in favor of Coppola's preference: a younger unknown dancer named Barbara Hancock. "She turned out to be a real trouper," Kazanjian says. "In the dance number in the rain, Barbara persevered despite suffering from the flu."

But Coppola's choice may have thrown Astaire off his rhythm.

As for Francks, Coppola felt the actor had a chip on his shoulder. Later he would realize that the actor was "giving me, for real, the character" and admitted that he hadn't known enough at the time to recognize Francks' method acting style.

NICE WORK IF YOU CAN GET IT

Evenings, Kazanjian and Lucas would sit around Coppola's office. The 2nd AD had learned that his director was not a great communicator and would often change his mind about what he was going to shoot the following day, regardless of what the call sheet said. He might also neglect to tell anyone about key details related to his change of heart: a Titan crane or a late call, a dance number with more or fewer dancers. Kazanjian would have to scramble and spend hours making dozens of calls to cover for Coppola or have to explain to the director that they hadn't yet rehearsed the number he suddenly wanted to film.

In addition to the next day's work, the three men would discuss movies, their plans, and the future. Coppola didn't like Hollywood and its rigid systems; neither did Lucas. Coppola wanted to move up north and establish his own production house in San Francisco. He suggested his two friends go with him. Lucas was ready to sign up, but Kazanjian was on a director's path within what was left of the studio system. "George hated Hollywood so much," Kleiser says. "When they got George and a bunch of film students to go and shoot a behind-the-scenes of *Mackenna's Gold*, George did a movie about the desert where they were with only one shot of them filming; a long, long, long shot. He was saying "fuck you" to Hollywood. It's strange, because I was so enthusiastic about Hollywood, and he saw that in me. For some reason, it didn't cross over to him. He thought it was all fake, and the people were fake, and he thought that they were just after money. That it wasn't art. He didn't like the surface-y quality of the people."

"George was always anti-Hollywood," says Marcia. "Definitely anti-Hollywood. You have to remember all the French filmmakers were the rage because they wrote and they directed and they edited and they produced their own movies; it was a 'film by' credit, it was never 'directed by.' And so George, Francis, I think Scorsese, I think Brian De Palma, a lot of these young people wanted to make their own films and they didn't want to have the studio telling them who they could cast, who could produce their film. They wanted to make more independent films."

Lucas wanted to turn *THX 1138.4EB* into a feature. He'd written the short film with fellow USC student Matthew Robbins, but Coppola suggested he write the feature script alone. "George was articulate and smart and was a rebel," Kazanjian says.

To conclude the *Finian* story, cast and crew took a short trip to another location, Griffith Park. There, they filmed the outdoor wash-line scene, followed by a location shoot on the rolling hills, oak trees, and green lawns of Disney Ranch. "Joe Landon was a fun producer," Kazanjian says. "He was usually on the set, on local locations, or on the back lot. The dancing ensemble loved Joe, so while we were shooting at Disney Ranch, they 'stole' his '65 Mustang convertible and washed it themselves. It was the first time in months it had been washed."

They returned to the studio for Barbara Hancock's ballet on the running brook and meadow soundstage set. The stage effects department had rigged sprinklers above; a flashing arc light simulated lightning, as the dancer performed in the rain. "The master shot was done in one take," Kazanjian remembers, "with several pick-up shots and close-ups captured next."

During post, Coppola sent another fellow ex-film student, Carroll

Ballard, to shoot more scenic locations using doubles for the stars. The director was at work on his edit. Before Jack Warner departed, Coppola had argued for editor Melvin Shapiro, and won. However, Coppola was more interested in the preproduction of his own independent road film, *The Rain People*, than working with Shapiro in editorial. He invited Lucas to join him on the road as a production assistant and documentarian (which would result in *Filmmaker*). Coppola wanted only a small crew with a single assistant director. "I was a second assistant director and needed two more months to become a first assistant director," Kazanjian explains. "Francis asked the DGA for a waiver so I could become a first, but they rejected his request." (Coincidentally, in Lucas's documentary, one can see Coppola on the telephone arguing with Joe Youngerman, head of the DGA, and threatening to quit the guild if Youngerman doesn't grant the waiver to Kazanjian. Unsuccessful, Coppola hangs up.)

"He fought hard on my behalf but lost," Kazanjian continues. "Francis suggested I quit the DGA and come along. But I loved what I was doing and if I quit, there was no way I could get back into the guild as an assistant director. A director can quit and then rejoin by paying his initiation fees again, but not assistant directors. In the end, Francis couldn't wait two months, so I got left behind."

Coppola drove off with Lucas and his crew, leaving *Finian's Rainbow* to be completed by associate producer Joel Freeman. Coppola would say, "I left it to the producer and others to finish it after I had done a preliminary edit and went off to make *The Rain People*." Because Kazanjian had excelled in his work, producer Joseph Landon fought for and succeeded in obtaining a screen credit for the 2nd AD (second assistant directors were rarely given screen credit; years later the DGA would negotiate credits for that position into standard contracts).

Associate music supervisor Ken Darby would write to Kazanjian: "*Finian's Rainbow* is in the can. Sealed and delivered. We were two weeks at Todd-AO dubbing the 6-track 70mm version—and it turned out better than anything I've worked on since *The King and I*. We finished the album today! It's at least ten times better than *Camelot*. EVERYBODY

81

could be nominated for the film except the one guy who SHOULD BE NOMINATED AND WIN—a certain H. G. Kazanjian who had to see to it that everybody was where they were supposed to be at the time they were supposed to shoot. In my book, you're the best!'"

The film was released in October 1968 to mixed reviews. Ebert, however, loved it: "*Finian's Rainbow* . . . gives you that same wonderful sense you got from *Swing Time* or *Singin' in the Rain*, or any of the great musicals: that it knows exactly where it's going and is getting there as quickly and with as much fun as possible. Remarkably, because it is only Francis Ford Coppola's second film, it is the best-directed musical since *West Side Story*. It is also enchanting, and that's a word I don't get to use much. . . . A lot of the fine things in the film come from Fred Astaire, who possibly danced better thirty years ago, but has never achieved a better characterization. In most of the Astaire musicals we remember, he was really playing himself, and the plot didn't make much of an effort to conceal that. This time he plays arthritic, wizened, wise Finian McLonergan (with some songs and dances the original stage *Finian* didn't have). And it is a remarkable performance."

It would be Astaire's last dance film, for, he told Johnny Carson, "Who wants to be the oldest dancer in captivity?" Astaire signed a photo to his 2nd AD, saying, in recognition of Kazanjian's doggedness about punctuality: "I'll be there!!"

"Now when I look at *Finian's Rainbow*," Coppola said decades later, "I think my only dissatisfaction is that I feel I could have greatly improved it if I had done the final postproduction. I might do that someday just for the fun of it—not to ever show it, but just to amuse myself, to see how good I can make it."

While the director was disappointed in his own effort, the Coen brothers—directors-writers of *Fargo* (1996) and many critical and box-office hits—enjoyed the movie: "When we worked with Nicolas Cage on *Raising Arizona* [1987], we talked about his uncle, Francis Ford Coppola, and told him that *Finian's Rainbow*, which hardly anyone has ever seen, was one of our favorite films. He told his uncle, who I think has considered us deranged ever since."

THE ASSISTANT DIRECTOR IS STILL WRONG

A couple of weeks after finishing his duties on *Finian's Rainbow*, Kazanjian was assigned to another Warner Bros.-Seven Arts production, *I Love You, Alice B. Toklas!*, which started shooting on November 14, 1967. Its script told the story of an attorney named Harold Fine, who forsakes his conservative lifestyle for the hippie lifestyle, only to find that both are unfulfilling. The title referred to Alice Toklas, writer Gertrude Stein's life partner, whose 1954 *The Alice B. Toklas Cook Book* had a recipe for cannabis brownies.

By this time, Kazanjian was developing his assistant-director skills to a fine point: He could anticipate what was going to happen an hour, two hours, or even five days ahead of time. However, his abilities were to be tested by a contentious production without clear leaders. The film's director was Hy Averback, who'd had a long career acting in radio, TV, and film, with whom Kazanjian had worked before. Its cowriters were Larry Tucker and Paul Mazursky. The film's megastar, Peter Sellers, wanted Mazursky to direct. Sellers had made a number of successful films, including Kubrick's *Dr. Strangelove* (1964) and Blake Edwards's *Pink Panther* films, and had forced producers to replace a director before. He was notorious in the business for being difficult. His secretary carried a suitcase with a portable phone in it for emergency calls. No one doubted Sellers's brilliance, but, by all accounts, he had inner demons. Some of them resulted in shuffling writers, producers, and directors. Some of his anxieties expressed themselves in "superstitions." The bed in his bedroom, for example, had to face due north. The bed couldn't simply be rotated; the room had to have been originally laid out that way. Nor could the bed have a window above it.

Kazanjian tried to mollify his star, but without success. To make matters worse, Sellers had recently divorced from his wife, Britt Ekland; his mother had passed away; and he'd suffered a series of heart attacks. As usual, the 2nd AD handed out call sheets toward day's end to crew and cast or to their assistants. "Often we would say goodnight and we'll see you at 6 AM tomorrow, etcetera," Kazanjian says. "But telling them the time the next morning was not protocol."

One morning Sellers didn't show up. Producer, director, production managers, and 1ˢᵗ AD Jack Cunningham all asked Kazanjian if he'd given Sellers his call sheet. "'Yes' was my answer, 'and we'll see you in the morning at six o'clock,'" he says. "After we found out why he was not coming to work—Peter's assistant said the stars had not aligned and he would not be coming in—they asked me if I'd asked him if he would be at the studio tomorrow? 'No,' I responded. 'No one asks that question! You don't ask someone if they're coming to work tomorrow.'

"That was my mistake. Now my instruction was to ask him every night, when I gave him the call sheet, 'Will you be here tomorrow?' Well, at the end of the next day when I gave him the call sheet and asked him—you should have seen his expression and heard what he said to me. He was swearing at me. After that, he'd just take the call sheet and wouldn't answer."

The day before a Friday the thirteenth, Sellers informed Kazanjian that he would not be coming to work the following morning. The AD let everybody know. The next day, Timothy Leary, Harvard psychologist and advocate of LSD—whom Nixon once described as "the most dangerous man in America"—was brought in by production as an impromptu substitute "dressed like a guru," Kazanjian says. "He sat in the bakery set onstage, with the camera facing him filming, and they asked him questions. I'm floating around in the background listening. I had no interest in standing next to the camera watching Leary, nor did most of the crew. It was a one camera setup all day long. The crew relaxed way behind the camera. One of the things he said was that everybody should smoke marijuana every day, and have LSD once a week." (Leary's monologue would be cut from the final film by the studio, as would poet Allen Ginsberg's scene.)

Sellers would spend some nights partying. One morning before dawn he told his driver to take him directly to the location, which was near Sunset Boulevard. At 4:00 AM, he was the first and only person there. There was no honey wagon (dressing and/or washroom). "Boy, did I get it," Kazanjian says. "My new orders were that whenever we were on location to be sure that his dressing room was out there at 4:00 in the morning no matter what time his call time might be. You see, Jack Warner is no longer running the studio. There's no one to stand up to Sellers."

84

In a publicity photo for I Love You, Alice B. Toklas! *(1968)
are actor Peter Sellers, writer-executive producer Larry Tucker, and
director Hy Averback.*

When a wardrobe assistant mentioned to Sellers that he'd missed a belt loop in the back of his pants, the actor screamed that he'd dressed that way on purpose. On another occasion he shouted at the script supervisor, who burst into tears. Her offense was that she was wearing purple, which Sellers said gave him "bad vibes." The next day, *Variety* ran an article about Sellers's awful behavior on set. After reading it, Sellers went on another rampage, telling the "dumb Americans" they weren't "any good; you're not good filmmakers. Your crews are lousy."

"Well, guess what?" Kazanjian says. "The next day, *Variety* ran another article. For three days they did. Nobody knew who was talking to *Variety*. I later found out it was a stand-in by the name of Mike Lally, an old-timer, the ex-union guy for the extras. Basically, it was hell working with Sellers. He's the one person out of the hundreds who I've said I'd never work with again."

As filming wound down, toward Christmas, Sellers gave every crewmember a gift, except to the two assistant directors. "Both Jack Cunningham and myself were pleased we were not included in his gift-giving," Kazanjian says.

I Love You, Alice B. Toklas! was released fall of 1968 and received generally good reviews: "Film blasts off into orbit via top-notch acting and direction," *Variety*, ironically, decided. "Sellers's performance—both in scenes which spotlight his character as well as ensemble sequences in which everyone is balanced nicely—is an outstanding blend of warmth, sensitivity, disillusion, and optimism."

In another counterculture filmmaking experience, Kazanjian spent a day working on what would become one of the seminal films of the decade, *Easy Rider* (1969).

Director Dennis Hopper needed to film a few pick-ups and retakes, and, legally, had to have a DGA assistant director on location. "It was about an hour away, so I drove over to the cold night location," Kazanjian recalls. "I was there about an hour, and they said, 'Look, you don't need to hang around. Just don't say anything and go home.' Which I did. That was the pot-smoking scene around the fire with Peter Fonda and Jack Nicholson, and Dennis Hopper. They obviously didn't want me there. I really only worked about two hours on that film."

In those turbulent times, when every rule was being questioned and old traditions tossed out, Kazanjian was about to meet another rebellious director—Sam Peckinpah, who was in preproduction on *The Wild Bunch* (1969).

W ord was out at the studio that director Sam Peckinpah was hunting for two assistant directors for his next feature. Warner Bros. executives pushed for their up-and-comer Kazanjian. The clock was ticking, for Peckinpah wanted to shoot his script and get it onto theaters before Fox's production of *Butch Cassidy and the Sundance Kid* (1969). The Fox film was to star Robert Redford and Paul Newman in a somewhat romantic, clean-cut Western, written by William Goldman— compared to what Peckinpah had in mind: a gritty, realistic Western called *The Wild Bunch*, starring a collection of older, beat-up leading men. Consequently, Peckinpah's choice for 1ˢᵗ AD Phil Rawlins was already in Mexico preparing locations.

"I was never interviewed regarding the script by Peckinpah," Kazanjian says, "although all the other key crew had been. His team had overlooked me in the interview process, or perhaps thought I had been interviewed. *The Wild Bunch* screenplay was by Walon Green and Sam Peckinpah from a story by Roy N. Sickner. I only saw Walon Green once while in Mexico. Sickner, I never saw." With only weeks to go before day one of principal photography, instead of going through Peckinpah's normal grilling procedure, Kazanjian was called into the director's outer office only to find it empty. The director was on business elsewhere. Instead a female voice called out from behind a closed door to the inner room, "Be right with you."

Kazanjian waited until the woman revealed herself to be a nurse and asked him to come into the inner room, where she told him to drop his pants. Out came a hypodermic, and Kazanjian received a shot in his derriere—a painful surprise that formed a knot for a month. "On the positive side," he says, "I knew I'd gotten the job and would soon be going south of the border, down Mexico way." Kazanjian, having grown up on classic Western TV shows and movies, was excited to be working on a big-budget film in that genre, one with potential.

He'd be joining a director, however, whose reputation was in need of resuscitation. Peckinpah's *Major Dundee* (1965) had gone over budget and hadn't made enough money. The mercurial Peckinpah had been fired from his next project, *The Cincinnati Kid* (1965). To some extent, Kazanjian was a fail-safe for the studio, someone in addition to the producers who, executives hoped, might be able to keep the volatile director on schedule, on target, and on budget. Peckinpah had been allotted seventy days and about $3 million dollars to film in Mexico. The director wrote to his friend and star of *Major Dundee*, Charlton Heston, to say that *The Wild Bunch* might turn out to be "reasonably good."

BURSTING BLOOD

Kazanjian traveled to Mexico to join *The Wild Bunch* officially on March 7, 1968. He checked in to the Hotel Río Nazas in Torreón, a town convenient for production due to its small airport. He'd been warned by his friend, script supervisor trainee Crayton Smith, during *Camelot*, about Peckinpah; Smith would also be on *Wild Bunch* as script supervisor. Sure enough, when Kazanjian met the director, the latter had just been asked to vacate the hotel for having peed in one of the lobby's potted plants during a drunken binge. "Sam was always a bit cold and aloof," Kazanjian says of their first encounter.

The entire crew left a few days later for Parras de la Fuente, six hundred miles north of Mexico City, where they fulfilled the last chores of preproduction. Here the 2ⁿᵈ AD met the film's all-star veteran cast: William Holden (Pike Bishop), Ernest Borgnine (Dutch Engstrom), Robert Ryan (Deke Thornton), Edmond O'Brien (Freddie Sykes), Warren Oates (Lyle Gorch), Ben Johnson (Tector Gorch), Strother Martin (Coffer), and Bo Hopkins (Clarence "Crazy" Lee). Together they'd act out the story of a band of older bandits and gangsters (led by Bishop/Holden) as they rob a railroad station, are pursued by a posse (headed by Thornton/ Ryan), before one last orgy of violence in a relatively noble attempt to rescue one of their own from a despotic Mexican general. The action would take place against a backdrop of changing times, the end of the wild frontier and the advent of the industrial age. "In my eyes, Bill Holden was an icon," Kazanjian says, "a very talented and successful actor in our business, always on time, he knew his lines, was social with me, but was there to make a picture."

In Parras, Peckinpah brought the cast in for a script read-through at the Hotel Rincón del Montero, at a rather long table. The read-through would last five days. Kazanjian was the only nonactor allowed in the room. They would break only when wardrobe or prop crew had questions for Peckinpah, such as the proper selection of hats, guns, holsters, and horses for the five leads. "There was a little bit of, 'Read it this way,' or, 'Change that,'" Kazanjian recalls. "One day the special effects crew came in and said, 'We're ready,' and I said, 'Ready for what?' They wanted to show us something.

"We went out the door to a nearby corral. Up against the fences they had a cutout of a human being with a uniform on it in order to show us squibs that would simulate gunshot wounds. I didn't know what was going on. They said, 'Ready—watch.' They pushed a button and a squib went off. I had never seen that before. They went off blowing holes in the clothing. Sam said, 'That's not what I want! That's not what I want!' He got a gun. 'This is what I want.' BANG! BANG! *BANG*! With a real gun and real bullets. 'That's the effect I want.'

"So the next day, same thing. We stopped the reading, went out, and it was bigger, with blood this time. Sam said, pointing to the target, 'The bullet would come in here and go out over there, so we need to set up the squibs like that, front and back.' From there they began testing with even bigger squibs loaded with blood and pieces of meat."

The Hotel Rincón del Montero was not fancy (though it is today): six bungalows in a half circle housed most of the American crew. Each bungalow was built of adobe bricks and had thatched wood ceilings; the interiors had stone floors, a big room, and a bathroom. Kazanjian and Crayton Smith, promoted to script supervisor, were about the same age, and assigned to share one bungalow. With limited lodging available, most of the cast and crew had to double up. On the whole, the Parras community cooperated with production, but a few businesses were out to gouge the Hollywood transients. Taxi fares doubled or tripled. The town's one sizeable restaurant, a country club on the outskirts of town, increased prices. Due to the housing shortage, rentals quickly became exorbitant. Charges for laundry skyrocketed.

"I'd send my jeans and clothes out to the hotel laundry, and they always returned clean and pressed," Kazanjian says "My Wrangler jeans could almost stand up on their own. Crayton, who was newly married, would wash his jeans in the sink. One night both Crayton and I woke up at the same time in the middle of the hot night. As we stepped out of bed—our feet touched water. Crayton had pushed so hard on the sink washing his clothes it had broken away from the adobe walls and water was flooding our room. The challenge was to find someone at the hotel to stop the water and fix the sink. This was the first of two incidents of the sink coming off the wall."

The Sunday before they were to begin principal photography, 1st AD Rawlins and Kazanjian were walking from one of the adobe bungalows to the dining room, when production manager Bill Faralla crossed paths with them and said, "Your replacement will be here tomorrow." "Phil turned to me and said 'What was that he said? Did he say *your* replacement is coming—who was he saying that to?'" Kazanjian remembers. "I got a bit worried because the replacement could have been for me, though I had just arrived in Parras and certainly hadn't done anything to be fired for. Shortly thereafter, I found out Phil was being removed from the picture for no good reason. That certainly scared me and put a great deal of pressure on me—I was going to be the only assistant director for the start of principal photography."

Kazanjian was told that Rawlins's replacement would arrive in the morning, but on the first day of shooting, Monday, March 25, he was the only crewmember tasked with harnessing the hundreds of disparate elements necessary for cameras to roll. "I had only the Mexican assistant directors, who were also our translators and who were used to working mostly with the fifty Mexican army members who often worked as extras."

The town's look had been modified by art director Eddie Carrere, with whom Kazanjian was working a third time. Carrere was an ideal choice for the film, having been born in Mexico City and educated at Polytechnic High School in Los Angeles. He knew how to juxtapose the script's socioeconomically linked townships on either side of the border, each caught up in the violence of the film's Mexican Revolution. "I felt at times the great pressure put upon him," Kazanjian recalls. "The entire long street for the opening sequence had new store facades built on the fronts of the existing buildings by Carrere and his crew."

Usually directors schedule something relatively easy to shoot for the first couple of days, in order to shake out cast and crew. Not Peckinpah. He had his people take on the film's opening—an ultraviolent, ultracomplex choreographed holdup and shoot-out, during which Holden, Borgnine, and the rest of the gang trade bullets with Ryan's posse, catching civilians in their crossfire amidst a marching band, rampaging horses, buggies, and an assortment of dangerous stunts.

The temperance union band had to play their instruments, sing, and march down the main street, followed by a sizable crowd. One of Kazanjian's jobs had been to teach the Mexican locals how to sing in English. It was also his duty to wrangle chickens or dogs as needed, recording everything used in detailed daily production reports that were sent back to the studio.

While filming the opening, they discovered that it was difficult to choreograph the shooter, a squib going off, and the actor's reaction with the proper timing. Often the actor couldn't feel the squib going off. "He'd only maybe hear a faint pop," Kazanjian says. "So Sam had them add a little bit of black powder, so when the squib went off, it would hit the skin. Some of the actors got burned that way, but it worked to cement the three actions together." Rawlins's replacement, Cliff Coleman, arrived late in the day with a folded script in his back pocket. His first words to Kazanjian were: "I haven't even read it yet." But Coleman turned out to be an excellent extras talent herder. He excelled in setting the background extras and the 2nd AD learned from him.

After filming the opening shoot-out in Parras, cast and crew moved to locations nearby for various scenes. Peckinpah traveled to the set each morning with his DP, Lucien Ballard. Ballard was a "good-looking man," sixty-four years old, a veteran and accomplished DP who had shot nearly a dozen Westerns, several with Peckinpah. Legend has it that during a three-day party at actress Clara Bow's house in 1929, she convinced then-camera assistant Ballard to make movies his life's work. Director Josef von Sternberg, and his star Marlene Dietrich, later promoted him to director of photography. But Ballard had a mean streak. The people who knew him, his camera crew, attributed it to an injury sustained by one of his sons, who was blinded during a Fourth of July fireworks display. He carried a stick that hung on a strap from his wrist and would use it to prod his crew or adjust their "barn-door" lights.

Kazanjian recalls: "After the director said, 'Cut,' and explained the next shot, Ballard wouldn't allow the assistant directors to do anything. He wanted everyone behind the camera. When it was lit, he'd say, 'Ready, bring 'em in'—but we wouldn't be ready because we hadn't had the time to prepare the background, the horses, or anything. Yet Sam was always down on the assistant directors, and not Lucien." Kazanjian tried reasoning with the DP several times to no avail. "We were shooting one scene and Lucien was really being mean and nasty, and he was blaming me for not having the background ready, so I grabbed his stick and broke it. The crew watching was stunned. One of the camera assistants appeared with another stick. Evidently, Lucien had a backup stick in the truck."

For the next week, DP and 2nd AD didn't exchange a word or look each other in the eye. "Both of us would turn away. That was silly. Did we kiss and make up? Yeah. But he didn't change. He just didn't want people in front of the camera or even in the way background while he was lighting."

At the end of each long shoot day, in addition to putting together call sheets and delivering them to dozens of people, Kazanjian was up late keeping personnel records, scheduling, writing those production reports, and making sure that the entire show was on track.

DEPUTY DIRECTOR

"How-ward!"

This was Peckinpah's preferred, exaggerated two-syllable shout for Kazanjian. He never seemed to call his first assistant if there was a problem. Only *How-ward*.

Cast and crew became accustomed to the director's frequent, elongated calls, which would bring work on set to a halt. Everyone would go silent and turn toward the 2nd AD, who would brace himself for the director's gale-force onslaught. Even if a day went by and Peckinpah didn't single him out, there was always the threat.

A third 1st AD arrived from Hollywood, but he didn't last long either.

Three down.

"Sam, as everyone knows, was extremely difficult," Kazanjian recalls. "But I think deep down, when not behind the camera, he was a gentle man. I do think Sam wanted to have a good time and be comradely with the crew. He just didn't know how. I looked for that in him, and when Sam would yell for me, I would appear next to him and say, 'Yes, Sam.' He would then ask for the impossible, but I quickly learned my response must be, 'Coming in, Sam.'"

For a scene in which Pike/Holden and the Wild Bunch discover that their stolen money from the railroad is in fact only metal washers, the director asked his 2nd AD to place, deep in the background, a dead man lying in front of a window with a candle lit by him. Kazanjian made it happen. He recalls another instance: "One day we were standing on a high bluff preparing a shot overlooking virtually nothing but desert, where the posse was going to be riding. Sam says, '*How-ward*,' and he kinda talks with this deep voice. Everything gets quiet again. 'When we were here scouting, I told you I wanted this valley greened in.' First of all, I had never been to this location or on any scout; second, it was basically an impossible request, but I'd already learned, so: 'Coming in, Sam,' and stepped back."

Kazanjian ordered a standby water truck, already loaded with various colors of dye (to be used later in the "wine barrel scene"), to spray down the immediate area below the bluff with a green color. "The slightly greened-in patch compared to a thousand-acre vista made little difference," he says. "But it gave Sam time to set up the shot."

At a similar location a few days later, Peckinpah told Kazanjian he wanted four pack horses with the bounty hunters, not the usual five. They reshot the scene, which took the better part of the morning. "I asked Tony the wrangler how many horses were always in the pack. He told me always five. So I asked him to always keep five horses around even though Sam said there were only four."

For a scene in which Holden was on his stomach looking through binoculars at the posse a mile away, Peckinpah wanted to place Holden and Borgnine in a patch of very small, but sharp cacti. "While the green crew dug out and planted cacti, Sam had time to plan the shot." Many of the director's requests were stalling tactics so he could plan.

Typically, when filming was wrapped for the day, cast and crew knocked off to a bar or parts unknown. Kazanjian then had to deliver call sheets to recipients scattered all over town. Borgnine recalled that the cast would go out regularly and "get drunk all night long." Sometimes Kazanjian would find Peckinpah smoking a different-looking cigarette; crew informed the somewhat naive 2nd AD that his director was smoking a marijuana joint.

Stuntmen were housed farthest out, in a hacienda, so were the last ones served their call sheets (if they had not been on set to receive them). One evening Kazanjian arrived during dinner and was impressed to find a dozen stuntmen at a dining room table being waited on by help they'd hired. (These stuntmen had been hired on as units: a man and a specially trained horse responsive and able to tolerate noisy gunshots, capable of performing falls, and so on.)

After making his rounds, Kazanjian would do paperwork. The days and nights were so long, often without time to eat, that he was losing weight. He eventually shed 20 pounds during the shoot, down to 163.

One day the director lashed out and called Kazanjian a terrible name.

"He called me a word I'd never heard before, but it hurt me to the extent that I went to producer Phil Feldman," he says. "I told him it was unnecessary for Peckinpah to treat me like he did. I was there working for him. I enjoyed working for him and he shouldn't mistreat me or the others. This message was not just for me, but for the entire crew. It did make a difference thereafter."

The name-calling ended.

Another long telephoto shot took forever to set up with Deke (Robert Ryan) and the posse riding from left of screen through the desert, right. "After Sam said cut, he asked me to bring the posse back into camera," Kazanjian recalls. "That took about twenty minutes because they were so far away. But during this time Sam is not talking or giving us the next setup. We wait and wait. As the actors on horseback arrive back to camera, Sam goes up to bounty hunter Paul Harper. In the actor's costume vest the strings of a tobacco bag were showing. Sam rips it out and says, 'We have to do it again.' Another hour passes while the posse returns to their starting position two thousand yards away and we shoot it again. Sam was stalling again. I could have been out there with the posse completely nude, and you wouldn't have been able to tell—much less could anyone see those cigs."

Peckinpah would often arrive late to location, sometimes an hour late. The director was again pushing for time. About to film the Wild Bunch in a steam room, he told Kazanjian to seek out Carrere, who was prepping another location. Kazanjian jumped in a car and made the long drive over dusty roads. "I said to Eddie, 'He wants to see you.' 'Why?' 'I don't know.'"

They both drove back in different cars.

"Eddie gets out of his car, we walk in. And in this steam room set is a little table. Sam says, 'Eddie, I want it moved from this wall to that wall.' About four feet away. Sam did things like that because he needed time to figure out how to shoot the scene."

CUTTING THE CORD

Peckinpah and company planned to film another shoot-out on a bridge at the Río Nazas location, south of Torreón. When the posse pursues the

96

Wild Bunch, explosive charges set by the latter dump the former, five men on five horses, into a fast, deep river. A dangerous stunt. Special effects supervisor Bud Hulburd had been shipped out specifically to oversee construction and operation of the bridge's center section. Hinged on the side so as not to be seen by the camera, the center section could be swung down like a trapdoor to let fall the riders.

Fred Gammon was now 1st AD. Kazanjian was in charge of the stuntmen, but the first day was a bust, because the river current was too strong, about 16 mph. Conditions improved the following day, and the 2nd AD got the stuntmen and their horses ready. Peckinpah, however, concentrated instead on insert close-ups of the fuses burning. The director finally called for the stunt, but each time Kazanjian moved the stuntmen and horses into position on the bridge, they'd be waved off minutes later, over and over again. The stuntmen grew apprehensive and jittery.

One of the stuntmen, Joe Canutt (the double for Lyle/Oates, son of famed pioneering stuntman Yakima Canutt) lodged a complaint when he learned that the charges to blow the bridge were much larger than necessary, something Peckinpah had specifically requested. Canutt and his stunt colleagues, top-notch professionals who knew their jobs, were also worried about the planned explosions in and around water; due to the increase in water pressure caused by the explosions, there was a danger the stuntmen would have their ears blown out. Production eventually reduced the size of the charges above, and eliminated those below the water line.

"Sam was again stalling and stalling and stalling," Kazanjian says. "I had five stuntmen on the bridge sitting on horseback, very nervous. The wind was blowing and we thought we were going to lose the bridge, and the water was raging, and Eddie Carrere was going crazy. You had stuntmen sitting on the bridge for hours, then coming off and getting back on again, on and off, and the longer they waited the bigger the stunt was becoming in their minds. Finally, it was too dark, so we didn't shoot that day."

The next day was a Sunday, an overtime day. At last the six cameras were primed to film the stunt, three on shore, three on barges secured by cables in the river. Peckinpah and Ballard stood on one of the barges. Canutt and the other stuntmen mounted their horses and took their places. On "action," the charges exploded and the trapdoor swung down, plunging horses and riders into the swiftly moving river. One of the riders was knocked out and had to be fished unconscious from the water, but none of the stuntmen were seriously injured. The only "casualty" was one of the cameras.

After the take, with enough footage in the can, the barges were hauled to shore. Crew were pulling the cable attached to the one carrying Peckinpah and Ballard, when a voice called out, "Cut the cable! Cut the cable!"

"Who said that?!" Peckinpah shouted.

"That was Howard!" one of the crew shouted back.

Peckinpah didn't say a word, but grinned, then smiled.

In an odd way, Kazanjian had found the right note.

He then negotiated with the stuntmen for their pay. SAG set their normal weekly rate, overtime, and meal times, but special stunts called for separate negotiations. Everyone was happy with $2,000 apiece, which was a pretty good haul at the time.

Another day's shoot took them to a river the Wild Bunch were to cross on horseback. Holden, Borgnine, Oates, Johnson, and Sánchez were filmed approaching the river, then stuntmen doubles took over for the crossing: Tap Canutt and his brother Joe, and their crew. It went well, but Peckinpah then asked for heavy rocks to be put in the saddlebags so the horses would really have to struggle in the water. On the second take, a few of the horses nearly drowned.

A master shot and close-ups were scheduled for second unit work. When the second unit returned at the end of the day, Kazanjian asked if they'd obtained the shot. They did, in one take, but without the rocks, "a secret not to be revealed to Sam," he says.

MORE CLOSE CALLS

At the location for the village of Angel (one of the Wild Bunch, played by Jaime Sánchez), El Rincón del Montero, Peckinpah found his villain.

He cast Emilio "El Indio" Fernández Romo, perhaps the most famous actor in the history of Mexican movies, as General Mapache. The son of a European father and a Native-American mother, Emilio Romo had symbolized Mexico for a generation, thanks to a machismo formed in the revolution of 1910 to 1917 and his status as a devout nationalist.

The legendary Romo invited Kazanjian to his home. "I was scared stiff," the assistant director says, "because he was the same character in the film, completely crazy—at home!"

It was Romo who suggested a shot in which ants attack a scorpion; Peckinpah wrote it into the script as the film's opening. The ants had to be shipped from the United States, thousands, in a glass jar. The imported ants would attack scorpions; the native ants wouldn't.

Romo also suggested local actors Jorge Russek and Alfonso Arau play lieutenants Zamorra and Herrera. Peckinpah agreed, also casting Mexican film director Chano Urueta, who was in his eighties, as Don Jose, a kind of wise man. His line, "We all dream of being a child again, even the worst of us. Perhaps the worst most of all," underlies much of the film.

One morning, the hotel where most of the crew and a few of the cast were staying ran out of water. Kazanjian scrambled to find out why. He discovered that on the next day's location, about hundred yards away, Peckinpah had ordered a little pond made and filled. No one could shower or have tap water for two days, but the director was able to film local boys jumping and splashing in a pond in the background of his scene, because art director Carrere had dammed up the hotel's water supply.

Peckinpah continued his ways. Kazanjian recalls, "There was supposed to be about twelve goats in a scene the following day to be shot out at our Dinamita location. I asked, 'Sam, do you want white goats or black goats?' By now I've learned. He says through his teeth, 'White goats.' I got both colors. The next day, he says, 'Bring the goat herder in; I want seven white goats and I want seven black goats.' I said, 'Coming in.'"

Actor Ben Johnson became kind of a father figure to the 2nd AD, which helped dissipate the insanity. "I didn't need a father figure, I had one back home," Kazanjian says, "but he was that guy on this location,

The bridge sequence in The Wild Bunch *(1969) was shot on location at Rio Nazas south of Torreon, Mexico. Here, the bounty hunters (Robert Ryan's group) are closing in on the Wild Bunch. The bridge, set with dynamite earlier on by the Bunch, is blown up, plunging the bounty hunters and their horses into a rapidly flowing river—a very dangerous but well-timed stunt.*

100

Director Sam Peckinpah while working on The Wild Bunch. *"Of the fifty pictures or so I took during the shoot," Kazanjian says, "not one is with Sam or of Sam. One didn't take pictures of Sam. You couldn't get caught with a camera and not be 'working,' and you couldn't go up to Sam and ask for a picture with him." Not surprisingly, Peckinpah fired the unit photographer about halfway through the picture.*

one of the nicest actors I would ever meet. Ben and I spent time talking between shots when we had time. Ben would tell stories about John Wayne, but would never talk about himself. He told me about his ranch, about growing rice, and how important it was for someone like me in our business to have a job they could fall back on when not working. I should have listened!"

A few of the other actors were having problems with the director. William Holden threatened to quit because of Peckinpah's verbal abuse of the crew. Robert Ryan's contract allowed him to return to the United States for a period of time to campaign for Senator Robert Kennedy. As soon as he flew back to the States, however, Peckinpah recalled him. Kazanjian had to get Ryan back to the location, dressed and made up with a mustache that was uncomfortable to wear. The actor was more or less consigned to a hot dressing room all day, waiting to be called to set. "Ryan would ask me what scenes he was to be in and I always replied he was not on the call sheet to work, but on 'H' for 'Hold,'" Kazanjian says. "We both made a deal that he wouldn't put his mustache on until he was called, but he did get dressed. Sam always asked me if Ryan was ready. It was about ten days of that. Sam could be at times a mean bastard, and he wanted Ryan there. But Ryan was a great guy. I got along well with him, if not all the cast. But I did feel a bit distant from him at times because of his stature in the business."

Other sources say that Ryan finally had enough and threatened to punch out the director. Ernest Borgnine also promised to "beat the shit out" of Peckinpah on one dusty location if the director didn't improve conditions. Everyone was having trouble breathing. Borgnine also railed against Peckinpah's tardiness. Early on, when the actor realized the director was handing out live ammo to fifty Mexican army extras, because he thought real bullets looked better in their bandoliers, Borgnine left the set in protest. He returned to his room and swore to stay there until he was notified that all the live ammunition had been returned. The 1st AD was given that task, but not all of the cartridges could be found; afterwards, gunfire could be heard sporadically at times.

Decades later, Borgnine would remember Peckinpah as a "wonderful" man who "loved actors" and would spend hours talking to them about their characters. Kazanjian says: "Borgnine himself was a wonderful man who I think would never say a negative thing about someone. Borgnine just seemed pleased to be working with other great talent, such as Warren Oates, who was fun to be around. He often was smiling with a joke to tell."

MAD PIKE

Production filmed the posse bedding down for the night at the Perote Winery. At El Romeral they shot Sykes (Edmond O'Brien) waiting with horses for the Wild Bunch after the robbery. After another night of carousing, some of the bunch hadn't learned their lines. Peckinpah, annoyed, read them out loud, lectured his cast, and gave them an hour to learn their lines while he planned the shot. "Edmond O'Brien was a quiet professional who had a long list of fine credits," Kazanjian says. "He was the eldest of the actors but just two years older than Ernest Borgnine. Ben Johnson and William Holden followed, one year younger than Borgnine."

At the Sonora location, production geared up for another set piece shoot-out, in which the Wild Bunch robs a train of its weapons shipment (in order to hand them over to General Mapache). One of the gang members was supposed to throw the engineer from the moving cab, but the stuntman double, instead of sailing free over the side, grabbed one of the handrails to ease his fall, miscalculated, and cracked his head against the coal car.

Then bad blood between Holden and Peckinpah came to a head. Kazanjian didn't hear exactly what they said to each other, but Peckinpah shouted something from beside the train track where he sat in his director's chair to the actor, who was in the locomotive engine cab. It was hot and it was tense, and suddenly they weren't talking. Kazanjian was immediately drafted as their go-between.

"What's happening?" Holden yelled between takes after a long time sweating in alone in the cab.

Kazanjian delivered the question to the director, who yelled something back. And so it went. "Sam was stalling again," says the 2nd AD.

103

"What am I supposed to be doing?" Holden shouted.

At this point star and director were close enough to hear each other, yelling back and forth, yet the farce continued. "You tell Holden," Peckinpah roared, "that I'll tell him when I decide what he should do."

With tensions at a maximum the following morning, they prepared for a big stunt on the rail spur south of La Goma. Down the line, Peckinpah was sitting on a camera crane to film Holden driving the train. He insisted that his actor drive the locomotive himself and bring it in full speed, before sliding to a stop next to a wagon (in which they would stash the stolen weapons). Warren Oates was put on a flatcar in front of the engine. Out of view of the camera, not far beyond where the train was supposed to halt, was a small bridge upon which another flatcar was parked with production's generators, spare lights, cameras, and other valuable material.

Kazanjian watched as several takes failed to satisfy Peckinpah, who wanted Holden to drive the train faster.

The sun reached its apex and the temperature soared.

On the following take, Holden, fatigued and/or pissed off, went full tilt. He drove the train at a great speed, pushing the flat car with Oates ahead of him, barreling down the tracks, then put on the brakes—too late. The wheels locked and sparks flew. Oates saw the gap between his flatcar and the production flatcar decrease alarmingly, and took off for the comparative safety of the engine behind him, while crew bolted from their haven under the bridge, afraid of an explosion or worse.

The two flatcars collided with a crash. The heavily laden production flatcar bounced into the air and came down with a huge thud, almost falling off the trestle.

Kazanjian ran down the tracks to survey the damage.

"Warren was laughing his head off," he says. "I do think because he was stunned."

Fortunately, no one was hurt. The engine's cowcatcher was bent out of shape. But it did mean a lengthy report to fill out at the end of the day for the 2nd AD, which he dutifully sent off to the studio.

The whole sequence, including Borgnine's character falling between the rail cars, took about six days to shoot.

ABOVE: *What production called "The Grand Canyon" for* The Wild Bunch *was actually in Mexico just outside of Parras. Aboard a Titan crane, Kazanjian checks shot parameters before setting the scene's background extras, protected by a grip and held in by a seatbelt should he risk falling ninety feet to the canyon floor.*

FOLLOWING SPREAD: *What became the famous "walk" of* The Wild Bunch, *much imitated for the last fifty years in movies and TV: Ben Johnson (Tector Gorch), Warren Oates (Lyle Gorch), William Holden (Pike), and Ernest Borgnine (Dutch) stroll over purposefully in a long shot to confront the sadistic General Mapache—in what is a prelude to the final cathartic bloodbath.*

CHANGING TIMES

Late in the story, Freddie Sykes (Edmond O'Brien) is shot in the leg by Deke's posse. At the very end of the picture Sykes rides up to the hacienda and speaks with Deke (Ryan). On that day, Peckinpah told wardrobe that the bullet wound, blood, and wrapping were on the wrong leg. "I told Sam they were right," Kazanjian recalls. "It was another example of Sam's inconsistency, what we call a 'mismatch.' Crayton Smith, the script supervisor who tracks these matches, remained quiet. Who was right? The director, because he gets what he orders. Sam shot the scene as he wanted it. So Sykes gets shot in one leg, and a few minutes later his other leg is bandaged."

Much more gunplay and continuity headaches were in store, as Peckinpah, Kazanjian, the stars, crew, and hundreds of extras in uniform or in period garb converged on the Hacienda Ciénega del Carmen, in the desert between Torreón and Saltillo, for the film's bloody, super-violent shoot-out between the Wild Bunch and Mapache's army. To reach the remote location, the production company had to put in an eighteen-mile dirt road from the main road to the small town. Crew then hauled over equipment, generators, lights, and sundry supplies of all kinds.

That eighteen-mile road took nearly an hour to drive because of the slow speeds necessary to navigate it. Kazanjian often rode with Crayton Smith in an old car. So much dust from the dirt road would come up through the floorboards that they'd arrive at the location so dusty they couldn't see the color of their jeans anymore (rumor was that the first set of drivers had newer and cleaner cars, but charged more, so production manager Faralla had fired them and hired the older cars to save money).

Act I of the shoot-out was relatively simple, what would become the famous "walk" of the Wild Bunch toward camera. The buildup before the slaughter. "Much of the walk was with just the Wild Bunch," Kazanjian says. "When they entered the courtyard Cliff Coleman and I staged and directed the extras."

The script had described their arrival at the camp only briefly, covered by Pike's line, "Let's go." Peckinpah improvised much of the setup on the spot. "'Cliff, wait a minute,'" Coleman recalled Peckinpah saying. "'I wanna do a walk-thing.'"

Kazanjian and Coleman helped the director form a drunken group of singers and to layer in other business. The camera was moved farther back to prolong their approach.

The following shoot-out—what was referred to as "The Battle of Bloody Porch"—is triggered when the Wild Bunch demand the release of Angel (played by Jaime Sánchez), who is already half-dead—and General Mapache sadistically cuts his throat. The first take of the deed didn't come off, for it was a tricky shot. Romo wielded a rubber knife while a crewmember off-camera handled a tube of blood that fed into a special prosthetic on Sánchez, who had to react on cue, but didn't. The next take went better.

Peckinpah and Ballard shot the ensuing bloodbath, which revolved around a Gatling gun, using five cameras. They took eleven days to film the innumerable stunts, explosions, and general mayhem. Crew wired the courtyard with over ten thousand squibs and used a kind of large switchboard to detonate them on cue. Each charge was timed to go off with the action of an extra. "It was painful to get it done right," Kazanjian says, "and Sam was insistent about what he wanted, and rightfully so."

Tempers flared.

Renowned makeup artist Al Greenway was told to pack up and leave for "whatever reason," Kazanjian says. "He said fine and closed his makeup case and large wooden flat box, which had hundreds of mustaches, sideburns, chops, etc., including those of our principal cast members. Needless to say, he ended up remaining until the end.

"Holden, Ryan, Borgnine, and the others were under a great deal of pressure in the chaos. Crew, cast, and myself had never seen or worked on a film with squibs filled with black powder and fake blood. Blowing holes in people was something we all had to get used to. The Wild Bunch cast was great to work with and I'd seen them every day for months. I loved them. And when I saw them die on that location, I got a chill."

Borgnine said in 1969, "When we were actually shooting, we were all repulsed at times. There were nights when we'd finish shooting and I'd say, 'My God, my God!' But I was always back the next morning, because I sincerely believed we were achieving something."

At the end of these hard days, Kazanjian drove a red Plymouth Barracuda to deliver the call sheets. "On one occasion, I was driving from the hacienda on the long dusty road after the long day's shoot with Cliff Coleman. The slow-moving vehicles in front of us were churning up dust, which got to Cliff. He said, 'Stop!' Then reached over with his long arms and opened my door and pushed me out. He climbed over to the driver's side as I ran around and jumped in the passenger seat. He gunned the car, veered left, and drove over the dirt barrier on the side of the scraped road and proceeded to pass the vehicles in front of us. Avoiding cactus plants, we'd only passed two vehicles before Cliff hit a rock and broke the pan. The car came to a dead stop. Leaving the Barracuda, we jumped in one of the follow vehicles. I reported the breakdown to Faralla and never saw or heard about the vehicle again."

Several of the American crew returned to Los Angeles because of illness, two with a fungus in their lungs due to the dust and foul dirt in the air. Kazanjian attributed it to production's horse corral that housed the Mexican army's fifty horses just a few feet from the eating area at the Hacienda Ciénega del Carmen. "The manure from the horses built up so high in the corral that I joked the horses would soon be able to step over the corral fence," he recalls. "When the wind picked up, which was often, all this dry manure would blow around."

Although filming the finale, they were only about halfway through principal photography and already four days behind schedule. They slipped another day due to the shoot-out's complex setups. A kind of walk-through facility was set up so that extras already killed could have their clothes dried out and painted and then put on a fresh outfit and be killed again. Gordon Dawson, lead wardrobe, was kept busy with his crew, cleaning and patching costumes.

"We wanted to show violence in real terms," Peckinpah said in 1969. "Dying is not fun and games. Movies make it look so detached. But there is a very, very thin line, and I think we operated as close to it as we dared. We hope that, for most audiences, we stayed on this side of the line. But I am willing to admit that we may have passed over it at some point. We feel the violence is a catharsis, a release, but sometimes the line is hard to find."

"*The Wild Bunch* was movie violence," Holden said in 1978. "People know it's fake blood and special effects. I'll be a sonofabitch if a movie like that even touches the sort of violence you see on the TV news, from Beirut or Zaire."

The times were violent—Vietnam, assassinations, riots in the streets—and the movie reflected some of that.

The company moved back to Torreón for the last few weeks of production.

Cliff Coleman was also fired; once again Faralla did the firing. The studio dutifully sent over another first assistant director, who had conveniently just finished a picture in Mexico, Fred Gammon.

"I don't ever recall Bill Faralla out at the set while we were shooting," Kazanjian says. "But often we would see him in the mornings while actors were getting into their cars, and crews loading on the bus. One day while I was on the bus checking the crew and just about to instruct the driver to leave, Bill walked the length of the bus looking up at the windows; the gaffer said under his breath, but loud enough for some to hear, 'I wonder who is being fired today.'"

Over 70 percent of the crew would be dismissed on *The Wild Bunch*. Peckinpah was the eponymous "wild" man.

| Wild Eats

| As Kazanjian approached the door to the caterer's kitchen at Torreón, he saw frozen chickens thawing out in the sun. "That disturbed me," he says. "In the kitchen I told the cook we would be breaking early. He said he wouldn't be ready. To the side of the stove I saw a pot. I looked in and asked the cook what this was. He said 'rice.' I asked what all the black spots were. He came over to the pot and swished his hand over the top and at least two dozen flies flew out. When I returned to the set, I told Peckinpah's assistant the cook would not be ready early. I also told Crayton Smith not to eat the chicken. The next day many of the crew fell ill."

At one lunch, "filete" (steak filet) was served with guacamole. Kazanjian had never heard of or seen guacamole before. "While picking at the meat my mouth began to burn, because a bit of the dip had touched it. I drank quickly from a bottle of water, and Lucien Ballard asked what was wrong. I said the meat was burning my mouth. Lucien said I should eat the guacamole to soothe the burn."

Ballard didn't mention that the dip was filled with hot peppers.

"My mouth lit on fire, I got hot, begin to perspire, and Lucien said to eat more. I jumped up and ran a block to the production office where Morrie, the accountant, asked what was wrong. I couldn't speak, but pointed to my open mouth. Morrie helped me with salt and a swig of beer to cool the burning. It helped, but I lost my voice for several hours thereafter. (Even today I cannot take any food spicy or hot.) The upside was the crew at our table was able to laugh about it."

TWO CLASSICS

Peckinpah wrapped his movie, and Kazanjian's last day in Mexico was July 2, 1968. One of the few to make it through the entire shoot more or less unscathed and employed, he returned stateside. He hadn't seen the last of the director, however, who asked Kazanjian to help shoot some inserts: low-angle shots of the leads against neutral backgrounds, which were cut in.

Not long afterward, he was walking down one of streets on the Warner Bros. lot between soundstages when Peckinpah passed by in his Porsche. He spotted Kazanjian and, displaying his gentle side at last, stopped the car, got out, hugged him, and thanked his 2nd AD for a job well done.

Upon seeing the final film Kazanjian found it "a bit violent," but Peckinpah declared this film "closest to me."

He invited Jay Cocks, film critic of *Time* magazine, to see it. Cocks brought his friend, director Martin Scorsese. They sat in an empty Warner Bros. screening room with only two other critics, Judith Crist and Rex Reed, to watch the movie. "We were mesmerized by it," Scorsese says. "It was obviously a masterpiece. It was real filmmaking, using film in such a way that no other form could do it; it couldn't be done any other way. To see that in an American filmmaker was so exciting."

Cocks would remember that he and Scorsese "literally turned to each other at the end, stunned. We were looking at each other, shaking our heads, like we had just come out of a shared fever dream."

Audiences and other critics would have mixed reactions. "With *The Wild Bunch*," Peckinpah said, "people get involved whether they like it or not. They do not have the mild reactions to it." The *Variety* review was critical: "Film at 145 minutes is far over-length, and should be tightened extensively, particularly in first half. After a bang-up and exciting opening, it appears that scripters lost sight of their narrative to drag in Mexican songs, dancing and way of life, plus an overage of dialog, to the detriment of action."

Peckinpah was nominated for best director by the Directors Guild. As the only assistant director who had survived, Kazanjian was invited to the awards banquet in early 1970. He asked USC classmate George Lucas and his wife, Marcia Lucas (they were married in 1969), to join him and Carol, Howard's longtime girlfriend, for this special event. "We were seated way out near the exit, because who were we?" Kazanjian recalls.

"That's where I met Howard and Carol," Marcia recalls.

Peckinpah lost to John Schlesinger for *Midnight Cowboy*, but his film did beat *Butch Cassidy and the Sundance Kid* into theaters, on June 18, 1969. The latter movie was more entertaining and upbeat, with a hit song and an unhappy ending—but bloodless—and when it opened a few months later, its box office returns eclipsed those of *The Wild Bunch*. In the decades since, however, both films have been heralded as two of the greatest Westerns ever to emerge from Hollywood.

CHAPTER 6: *Vagabond Celluloid*

T he studio assigned Kazanjian to work for about six weeks on *Once You Kiss a Stranger* (1969). On set he was impressed with the speed of Jacques Marquette, "one of the fastest DPs I've worked with. He always had a smile or joke while he quickly lit a scene and got his camera in place." Marquette's work went back to the 1950s where he had to be fast in order to make low-budget films such as *Attack of the 50 Foot Woman* (1958) and *The Brain From Planet Arous* (1957), as well as many TV shows.

In December 1968, Kazanjian moved on to another Warner Bros.-Seven Arts production, *The Great Bank Robbery* (1969). Its director, Hy Averback, knew Kazanjian from *Toklas* and "upped" him to first assistant director, which was reported in industry trade papers: "The promotion was made after first assistant director Jack Cunningham was released so that he could take on production duties at 20th Century Fox Studio on *The Undefeated*" (an action-adventure film starring John Wayne and Rock Hudson).

The story of *The Great Bank Robbery* concerned three bumbling teams who are attempting to rob the same bank in an Old West Texas town; its cast featured Zero Mostel, Kim Novak, Sam Jaffe, and Elisha Cook Jr., among others. On the thirteenth of that month, production photographed their stars escaping in a "Balloon Basket" on Stage 5, followed by full flight with a hundred extras at Disney Ranch. "Kim Novak was a delight," Kazanjian says. "In the scene where she rides naked on a horse as a diversion, like Lady Godiva, except with her breasts covered by single flowers, she gave me one of the flowers afterward."

On location in Sonora, Kazanjian was nearly attacked by irate stuntmen when he informed about a dozen out of two dozen that they and their horses were no longer needed on the picture—after only a single day's work instead of the promised week. "I had to say, 'You're staying, you're going, you're staying,' because that was the job given to me," he says. "Needless to say, the riders were not happy." Kazanjian thought it better to back away after giving them notice. Mike Lally, a stand-in and a one-time early union leader for extras, went over to the disappointed stuntmen and suddenly everything was fine.

That night at the hotel, Lally called Kazanjian into his room and showed him a small gun. "That's what did the trick with the stuntmen," he told the AD, who recalls that Mike added, "'I'll protect you.' I don't really believe he threatened the stuntmen with a gun. Just words. *The Great Bank Robbery* was a challenging picture, but a fun one."

After wrap, Kazanjian was moved onto *The Arrangement* (1969), to work with the celebrated and somewhat notorious director Elia Kazan. Kazan was famous for his Brando pictures and his stage work, but controversial because he'd named names during Hollywood's Blacklist period, which had been broken only a few years before.

The romantic drama had an all-star cast—Kirk Douglas, Faye Dunaway, Deborah Kerr, Richard Boone, Hume Cronyn, Carol Rossen, and others—and on January 15, 1969, Kazan, Kazanjian, and company filmed Boone in his character's bedroom set on Stage 18. "Kazan was a brilliant filmmaker and we had a great crew," Kazanjian says. In particular he noted DP Robert Surtees, with whom he'd already worked twice, a veteran of *Ben-Hur*, *The Graduate*, and many others. "And you had Kirk Douglas, who was Kirk Douglas. He was known to be a difficult actor. You had to be careful how you asked him to come to the set. You had to make sure that when you asked him to show up at a certain time that you were really ready for him."

For Kazanjian, it was a less pressure-filled job than others, for Kazan had already filmed about half the film in New York with an East Coast 1ˢᵗ AD named Burtt Harris, with whom Kazan had worked before. Kazanjian was there only to help the director finish the picture and liaised with studio associate producer Charlie Maguire, another mentor to the younger man. Kazanjian was West Coast DGA covering for Harris, an East Coast AD.

115

"No matter how long one has been in our industry, we learn something every day," Kazanjian says. "Sometimes through mistakes, but usually working with top filmmakers. On *The Arrangement*, a second unit was to be handled by Charles Maguire and myself. The scene called for a small car, driven by Kirk Douglas, to be sandwiched between two semitrucks, after going under the belly of one of the trucks in a tunnel in downtown Los Angeles. We were to film from an insert car. Charlie and I planned on twenty nondescript vehicles to fill out the background of the tunnel. On the call sheet, art director Malcolm C. Bert noticed the requirements we'd listed and called me into the art department at Warner Bros. where he'd laid out the tunnel on a piece of long white paper. He'd crafted movable paper trucks and cars, and he told me no matter where the camera might be on the insert vehicle, I would never see more than seven vehicles.

"I told Charles Maguire this. We looked at each other, and decided to go with ten vehicles, not twenty. Afterward in dailies, with all the camera angles, we never saw more than five cars, which really did fill the tunnel visually. From that day on, on all productions, I've worked very closely with the art department. I've saved tens of thousands of dollars that way by not spending on things the audience would never see."

The movie was not one of Kazan's great successes, but he and Kazanjian got along well. "I'd talk with Kazan between takes, but after explaining the next setup to the crew, he would usually go to his dressing room on the stage and type. He was modifying the script all the time. I must admit I was a bit frightened of Kazan; to this day I don't know why.

"I saw him once later on a sidewalk in New York," he adds. "I was with my dad, and Kazan said, 'Can I take you to lunch?' We had lunch and he was great."

WONDERFUL WORLD

At this point in his career, Kazanjian was a known expert at his job. He could move from studio to studio, if required. At the end of *The Arrangement*, Warner Bros.-Seven Arts was doing very little, and John

Bloss, head of physical production at the Walt Disney Studios, asked the 1ˢᵗ AD to come over. Kazanjian was also asked by Metro-Goldwyn-Mayer and 20th Century Fox, but Disney, Warner Bros., and Universal were closest to his home in Pasadena, with less traffic to fight. Because time on the lot averaged from nine to fourteen hours a day, one had to factor in the commute.

Kazanjian made three TV movies in a row at Disney: *Smoke* (1970), starring Earl Holliman and Andy Devine; *Secrets of the Pirates' Inn* (1969), with Ed Begley, Paul Fix, and others; and *Menace on the Mountain* (1970),with Pat Crowley, Albert Salmi, and a young Jodie Foster. On *Smoke*, Kazanjian worked with a teenage actor named Ron Howard, who broke his jaw while playing baseball. Production had to shut down while Howard recovered. On *Menace*, Kazanjian made sure seven-year-old Jodie Foster was properly looked after, and on time. Kazanjian says, "Jodie was a sweet little girl, and she had to have a teacher and her mother there. Child actors are often in 'school' until they come out on the set.

"I learned a great deal at Disney," he adds, "including how to use sodium vapor in the special effects department." (A sodium-vapor screen was similar to blue- or greenscreen—a white screen that shone blindingly yellow due to the intense backlighting of the sodium-vapor lights; the process had been used to a great extent on the studio's 1964 film, *Mary Poppins*.) "Disney Studios was a wonderful place to work. The parking lot had easy access and it was a very short walk to the Animation Building where I had my office on the first floor. I was told Walt Disney built the main building during the war and designed it with three major wings to accommodate a hospital if needed. Each office was a decent size. The lot was rather small compared to other major studios' and I enjoyed walking around and exploring during my lunch time. Zorro Street and a small jungle area still existed, along with three good-sized soundstages and the sodium vapor stage. At the carpentry shop, one could find workers making props and sets for Disney World while trucks were loading teepees for transport. The makeup department was headed by Bob Schieffer, with whom I'd worked with on *Camelot*.

"Walt himself had passed, but on occasion Roy Disney Jr. could be seen in the Animation Building." (Roy Disney Jr. was the son of

117

While shooting The Great Bank Robbery *(1969), Kazanjian discusses the next day's scenes and call time with the great Kim Novak (Sister Lyda Kebanov, "Forger") on location at the Disney Ranch, circa 1968.*

Walt's brother, Roy, cofounder of the Disney studio.) Kazanjian would be offered a second assistant director job on *The Black Hole*, which had a long gestation period before coming out in 1979, but turned it down and left Disney.

THE PLOT THICKENS

Meanwhile, up north in San Francisco, Francis Ford Coppola and George Lucas had formed their own production company, American Zoetrope, in 1969, financed mainly through a deal with Warner Bros. for seven films. In the fall of 1969, Kazanjian moved to another studio to work on *The Christine Jorgensen Story* (1970), a United Artists picture being shot at Paramount. Its controversial story was about a sex-change operation and its implications. When he could, Kazanjian would fly up to visit his friends' hip digs on Folsom Street. The three remained close. Coppola was working on various projects and Lucas was writing his feature version of *THX 1138* (1971).

"George and Francis ran away," Kazanjian says. "They ran away because they didn't believe in Hollywood and the way Hollywood was making films, the union films, the mandatory crews, the power of the executives above them. It was about getting away from Hollywood and saying, 'We can do it on our own.'"

Lucas asked Kazanjian to be his 1st AD on *THX*.

"He knew I'd worked with a lot of great actors," Kazanjian explains, "and he knew the story he wanted to tell and where he wanted to put the camera. George literally said, 'Howard, you know how to direct actors, I know what I want to do with the camera.' I accepted the job, but George decided to shoot it nonunion and I was unable to work in a nonunion capacity. I was also conflicted schedule-wise with the show I was on, *Christine*."

Marcia Lucas recalls, "Francis joked, 'I got the Warner Bros. multipick pack. I'm going to make ten movies for a million dollars and one of them will hit.' George was going to make the first one, *THX 1138*. When he made *THX*, we had to start a film company and George was saying we need business cards, we need stationery and everything,

119

so he said, 'Make a logo for Lucasfilm. Make it like the Bekins moving company logo.' So I sat down and made the Lucasfilm logo. And then I didn't want to be a corporation. I said that in England corporations are limited. I said, 'Lucasfilm Limited sounds so good together. It flows together.' George and I were partners." (Kazanjian maintains, however, that the Lucasfilm logo is a copy of the Warner Bros. logo and once spoke to Lucas about it.)

The director of *The Christine Jorgensen Story* was Irving Rapper, whose long career in the business stretched back to dialogue coach on *The Adventures of Robin Hood* (1938), director on *Now, Voyager* (1942) with Bette Davis and Paul Henreid, and many others. Among the crew was DP Jacques Marquette, whom Kazanjian knew from previous assignments. "Irving's set was so quiet," Kazanjian says. "If a cat walked in with cushioned pads under its feet, he would scream, 'Quiet!' He taught me a great deal. Any set I've ever run since has always been quiet. People can talk quietly, move the lights, but I don't tolerate screaming or yelling. I don't tolerate bells going off; I don't tolerate, 'We're rolling! Speed!' None of that. All the soundman has to say, quietly, is 'Speed.'"

He adds, "Irving Rapper was seventy-one at the time, but I didn't know it until years later. He had the energy of a younger director. Hollywood tends to frown on filmmakers over fifty, but I believe with years of experience on countless productions, one tends to know more than those under thirty. One must not only be creative, but also understand how, physically, to make films and how the industry works from administrative, legal, accounting, and distribution on down."

Upon the film's release in June 1970, the critic for *Variety* wrote: "Everything about *The Christine Jorgensen Story*—the title, the performance of John Hansen in the title role, Irving Rapper's direction, and the script—has the style of a 1930s melodrama to the point of being camp. It is frequently unintentionally funny. However, the basic facts and drama of George Jorgensen's sexual transformation by surgery and hormones have enough curious interest to probably attract profitable audiences for a sensationally exploitable programmer in multiple release."

That same year Kazanjian married his longtime sweetheart, Carol, and they took a few weeks off.

Howard spent the latter half of 1970 on *The Fifth of July* and *Decisions! Decisions!*, a 1971 TV movie for Motion Associates West. A mutual friend of Lucas and Coppola, John Korty was to direct *Fifth*, one of the seven films that Warner Bros. was financing for American Zoetrope. Korty was a Bay Area independent filmmaker and, not coincidentally, an early inspiration for Zoetrope. Consequently, Kazanjian spent more time up at the Zoetrope offices, where Korty was plotting out how to shoot his story about the assassination of the president, vice president, and the speaker of the house—and the collateral fallout. "The log line would have been something like, 'What would happen if such a thing occurs!'" Kazanjian says.

Kazanjian would often spot Coppola holed up with writer Mario Puzo in an office working on the adaptation of the latter's novel *The Godfather* (1972). Coppola was "excited" about his project and again asked Kazanjian to be his 1st AD, but DGA rules again intervened: A West Coast DGA member could not work within the jurisdiction of the East Coast DGA, and Coppola planned to shoot his gangster epic on the East Coast.

By then George Lucas was in postproduction on *THX*. He would edit during the day in the attic of his rented Mill Valley house; sound designer Walter Murch would take the night shift. At times Lucas would ask Marcia, who was working as his assistant editor, her opinion on scenes. "He was on the Steenbeck and I was on the bench," she says. "And I'd walk over and there was, for example, this scene in the white prison, the limbo prison. It went on and on and on. I was bored out of my mind. They were spouting philosophy and I said, 'I just don't feel anything for these characters. I'm not really rooting for them. For some reason, I'm not emotionally involved with them, but I like what you've done. You're a brilliant filmmaker, but it's not my cup of tea.'

"George said, 'You don't get it, Marcia. It's so easy to make people care about characters.' I said, 'Well, if it's easy to do, maybe you should think about it.' He said, 'I know how to create a villain. I have a cute little kitten, and this man comes in the door and he picks up this kitten, and he breaks its neck, and he throws it away. I've got an instant villain. This isn't brilliant filmmaking. This is just B-movie stuff.'"

121

In October, Korty and Kazanjian flew to Washington, DC, to shoot the film's opening titles and run-bys (one setup was on 17th Street). While there, the director was suddenly asked to fly back to Warner Bros. "A few days later we got word that the film was canceled," Kazanjian says. "We never knew why. I suspected Washington, DC told Warner Bros. to put it on ice."

BRIEF ENCOUNTERS

From April to July 1971, Kazanjian was hired on another Disney picture, *Now You See Him, Now You Don't* (1972), starring Kurt Russell, Cesar Romero, and Jim Backus; Russell was one of the studio's young stars, and the film was a sequel to his *The Computer Wore Tennis Shoes* (1969). When another picture at Disney didn't "go," its 1st AD, who was the son of one of the five key Disney executives, stepped in and Kazanjian moved back to the 2nd AD position.

Kazanjian worked with special effects crews in postproduction to create Russell's invisibility. His invisible footprints were made to appear in sand; more invisible prints were concocted via a marionette process; another method made use of an elevated stage—sand fell away from the floor to form footprints; yet another technique was to film an actor wearing shoes painted blue (early bluescreen) later to be eliminated via visual effects. The idea was that by alternating techniques, the audience would never be able to figure out how it was done. Arthur J. Vitarelli was second unit director, another top-notch technician who passed on his wisdom and knowledge to the assistant director.

Kazanjian next worked for a few days on director Sidney Lumet's *Child's Play* (1972), staying at a lousy hotel room while scouting locations in the rain. Its associate producer, Hank Moonjean, with whom Kazanjian had worked on *Cool Hand Luke*, had asked for his old friend to be the 1st AD on Lumet's picture. "I had very little prep time in LA, flew to NYC, met Lumet, scouted for a few days—and then was sent home! It was the same story again: West coast DGA ADs could not work on the East Coast."

Kazanjian labored mostly at Disney from late 1971 to early 1972. Lucas's *THX 1138* came out and was a significant flop in the spring of

122

1971. So much so that Warner Bros. pulled out of its deal with Zoetrope. "*THX* went in the toilet," Marcia Lucas says. "But then George said, 'I'll show you that I can make a movie with characters you're going to care about.' I had challenged him, and Francis challenged him, too."

In the spring of 1972, Coppola's *The Godfather* was released and became a huge box-office and critical success. The Kazanjians stood in line to see it. "Many years before, I saw *The Sound of Music*, which was a huge hit for Fox and saved the studio," Kazanjian recalls. "While we were standing in line, I said to Carol, 'A filmmaker is really lucky if they have one big blockbuster in their lifetime.'"

Lucas asked Kazanjian to do his next film, one with characters to care about—titled *American Graffiti* (1973); Coppola was producing. Marcia recalls: "This executive at Universal said, 'We really like this; we're ready to make this movie, but you need a strong producer.' They gave George a list of producers who would be acceptable and one of them was Francis, because of *The Godfather*. George said, 'I owe the guy. He gave me my shot at my first movie. So I'll let Francis produce it for me.' Francis was the executive producer. Gary Kurtz was the hands-on line producer."

Lucas would write the film with his USC schoolmate Willard Huyck and his partner, Gloria Katz (a UCLA alum), who worked mainly on the Steve-Laurie (Ron Howard-Cindy Williams) relationship scenes. Kazanjian agreed to be Lucas's first assistant, for the film was planned as a union picture. But the feature he was working on at Disney was delayed and he ended up passing on *Graffiti*. "Once you commit, you commit," Kazanjian says. "I believe very strongly, whatever I do, if I make a commitment, I'm going to stick to it."

Howard Koch Jr. (now Hawk Koch) asked Kazanjian if he would help backstage at the 44th Academy Awards in April 1972. His father, Hollywood veteran Howard Koch, was producing. Kazanjian attended the all-day rehearsal, during which the presenters practiced their speeches either from the left, right, or middle of the stage. In the audience section of the Dorothy Chandler Pavilion, life-size pictures of key actors, producers, or directors were in their assigned seats so the TV crew could also rehearse. Kazanjian's job was to work with the camera crew on the right side of the stage near the Green Room and help point out where people were seated.

On April 10, 1972, in his rented tuxedo, officially designated as "Program Participant," he worked the show. He recalls, "The highlight of the evening was seeing Charlie Chaplin being wheeled out backstage to his position onstage, waiting for the curtain to rise and his introduction. Wow!" Chaplin, eighty-two, was being given an honorary Oscar. Kazanjian had previously seen all of Chaplin's films that were available and regarded him as one of the greatest talents of all time. When Chaplin appeared on stage, he received an astounding twelve-minute standing ovation. It was an historic moment in Hollywood—the iconic Chaplin had outlasted the fear of communism in the United States, for which he'd been more or less exiled, and was making a triumphant return. "Oh, thank you so much," he said at the podium. "This is an emotional moment for me, and words seem so futile, so feeble. I can only say thank you for the honor of inviting me here. And you're wonderful, sweet people. Thank you."

Up north, *Graffiti* was in post. Marcia saw the footage. "George was good at low-budget filmmaking," she says, "because he shot two cameras on everything. It saves time. You don't have to relight the set, move the camera, and set up for over-the-shoulder or close-ups, and so he made this movie about cruising teenagers one night in a small town. Visually, George has a great eye. If George hadn't been a director, he would have been a cinematographer. He could always make everything look fabulous."

Verna Fields had started editing while Lucas was shooting, with Marcia Lucas assisting, but it was Marcia who primarily edited the film in post after Fields went on to another movie. "I made this deal with George," she says. "The day you wrap, you have to let me start editing. George would also do some cutting, and we were doing a lot of work. It was a great film, but I had to restructure it to make the story work. I'm not an intellectual film editor. I'm a very intuitive film editor, and I really care about character and story, and I really care about pacing and timing, and if I get bored—I'm here for two hours in the dark to be entertained, and if I get confused or I get bored, I'm unhappy and I

124

get twitchy because it isn't working for me—I want it to work. My whole thing was every movie I worked on had to work. It had to work. *American Graffiti* had to work."

Released in the summer of 1973, *Graffiti* was Lucas's first big hit, a surprise bonanza. Marcia Lucas says that its success made the Lucases feel "on top of the world. Yay! Yay, we did it! We made a good movie. It was the sleeper of the year."

For the rest of 1973, Kazanjian was at Universal Studios working on TV movie/pilots for *Partners in Crime* (1973), starring Lee Grant and Lorraine Gary, who was married to Sid Sheinberg, president of Universal; and *Griff* (1973), starring Lorne Greene. *Partners* was directed by Jack Smight, who proved difficult.

Production had scheduled a move from a studio stage to a restaurant on Lankershim Boulevard. Kazanjian told Smight that the crew would pack up, break for a mandated lunch, then move to the restaurant exterior for a location scene. Smight went to lunch with Lorraine Gary and Sid Sheinberg, number two at Universal, at the restaurant.

When the trio exited the restaurant after their hour-plus lunch, Sheinberg saw the crew unpacking and setting up for the shot and asked Smight what was going on. Kazanjian remembers, "Jack, rather than tell the truth about the move and the crew lunch, said, 'We're waiting on Howard Kazanjian, as usual.' Not long afterward, I went to see Dick Bernie, who was head of TV production, and he looked up from his desk, smiled, and asked, 'Did you get the knife out of your back yet?' Sid had called his office and complained about the delay." It was the kind of petty lie that could ruin a career.

Toward the end of the year, Universal called him in for a day on a young filmmaker's first theatrical feature film at the studio: Steven Spielberg's *The Sugarland Express* (1974). The director needed a 1st AD to organize a retake. In the film's story, a young woman breaks her husband out of a low-security prison to embark on a road trip to rescue their child before he's put into foster care. They end up kidnapping a young police officer and a huge flotilla of police cars follows them in a convoy that becomes national news (based on a true story). At one point, the couples'

TOP TO BOTTOM: *Hal Holbrook (Joe) and Goldie Hawn (Oktyabrina) shooting a night scene on the Universal back lot for* The Girl From Petrovka *(1974). Director Robert Ellis Miller is to the left of the actors listening to their rehearsal. Kazanjian is standing by the ladder with plastic snow on his head.* • *Kazanjian confers with producer Richard Zanuck on* The Girl From Petrovka; *Zanuck was one of the most successful producers of his generation (in partnership with his story expert, producer David Brown), with blockbusters* Jaws *(1975),* The Sting *(1973),* Planet of the Apes *(1968), and other movies.*

car, while stationary, is shot up by dozens of policemen, and Spielberg needed a close-up of the action.

"This is while Steven was in editing," Kazanjian says. "I went into the editing room with him and his editor, Verna Fields, to prep for the shoot. Steven wanted to show me the scene as it was. Then he asked the editor to run the end scene where the credits would eventually go. He ran the footage of the policeman, who had become friendly with the couple, sitting by a wide river. Steven held the handle of the Moviola and marked the footage saying, 'This is where the first credit goes, this is where the next credit goes.' He was watching for the best beat of what was happening and telling the editor exactly what to do. I was very impressed with that.

"The next day we went to the back lot where the art director had set up the car and shot several takes of the missing scene Steven wanted."

LAUGH-IN

Kazanjian moved onto *The Girl From Petrovka* (1974) in February 1974, directed by Robert Miller, primarily a TV director, and featuring Goldie Hawn, a huge star who had won a Best Supporting Actress Oscar for 1969's *Cactus Flower*. Hawn was cast as a Russian ballerina who falls in love with an American news correspondent, much to the dismay of the KGB, whose agents decide to sabotage their romance.

Production began by shooting exteriors in Vienna, Austria, before moving to Universal for most of the scenes. While coordinating their shoot in Europe from the studio, Kazanjian prepped for their return. "Goldie was one of the most delightful and fun-loving actresses I've worked with," Kazanjian says. "She was a delight, fluttering around and always smiling."

Things were a lot more challenging with veteran actor Hal Holbrook (Joe), whom Kazanjian would consider the second-most difficult person he'd worked with after Sellers. "That was because, as I understand it, he was having some family difficulties back in New York, while he was working long and tiring hours in Los Angeles." Another obstacle was DP Vilmos Zsigmond, who frustrated most of the crew by dominating the set and taking longer than usual to relight or adjust lights between takes. "Miller gave too much to Vilmos in the beginning," Kazanjian says. "I talked to him about it, but he'd already lost it; he'd given up. He gave in the beginning and couldn't take it back."

A brighter spot was Anthony Hopkins in a small role, who was easy to get along with. The film's producers were David Brown and Richard D. Zanuck. Zanuck had been head of production at Fox during the mid to late 1960s, with Brown his head of story. The two had become independent producers and had recently finished the Spielberg film, *Sugarland*; they planned to collaborate again. Kazanjian learned from them as he had from other veterans.

One day Holbrook complained that the real ice and plastic snow from an exterior set had been tracked into his dressing room onto a beautiful green carpet. Kazanjian recalls, "Outside the dressing room on the back lot at Universal, he starts screaming and yelling at me that it has not been cleaned. Like I'm supposed to clean the dressing room? A Universal Studios tour tram happened to drive by as Holbrook was yelling, and the tour guide says, 'See that? They're rehearsing!'"

It turned out the distracted actor had been tracking in the snow and ice himself.

JULY 1965 ■ 50 CENTS

AMERICAN
Cinematographer

The International Journal of Motion Picture Photography and Production

Photographing "The Sandpiper"

Kazanjian and friend Dennis Galling were invited to MGM to watch director Vincente Minnelli work. His secretary offered to take them on a tour, so they squeezed into Kazanjian's 1956 Thunderbird convertible and drove around the back lot. It was 1965 and the studio was being sold; bulldozers were ready to tear it down, but all the famous sets were still standing, from Esther Williams's swimming pool used in a series of musicals in the 1940s to the mansion in the more recent The Unsinkable Molly Brown *(1964). Later Minnelli invited the two USC film students on location to watch him shoot* The Sandpiper *(1965), starring Elizabeth Taylor and Richard Burton. "We went out to Carmel and spent two days there," Kazanjian recalls. "The crew was very gracious and answered our questions. And one day, when they were shooting on the beach, somebody took a picture for a magazine—you can see the camera crew and the director, and the two of us happened to be standing about fifteen feet or so behind the camera." (Minnelli wears a cap on left; the two USC students are closest to the ocean.)*

Twenty-three-year-old assistant director trainee Kazanjian on the set of the Four Star TV pilot High Noon, *circa 1965. The studio location shoot took place on the Western street of what is now CBS Studio Center (aka CBS Radford). Alf Kjellin directed, Peter Fonda starred.*

ABOVE: *A signed photo of star Paul Newman to Kazanjian. They worked together on* Cool Hand Luke *(1967), a Warner Bros. picture starring Newman as the eponymous Luke.*

OPPOSITE, TOP TO BOTTOM: *Paul Newman in the rain sequence where Luke looks to heaven. George Kennedy (Dragline) is left, crew are in far background.* Cool Hand Luke *began its shoot on location in Stockton, California. Months later, crew returned to Warner Bros. soundstages for the interiors. Stuart Rosenberg directed. • Newman and Kazanjian watch as the crew prepares the snapping turtle sequence on a cold Stockton day.*

ABOVE, TOP TO BOTTOM: *Shot in and around several cities in Mexico over a four-month period,* The Wild Bunch *(1968) was Kazanjian's first foreign location. Sam Peckinpah directed. The Titan crane camera over the "Grand Canyon"—actually a location in Mexico— where the Wild Bunch are met by Herrera (Alfonso Arau) to pick up the wagon and guns.* • *Kazanjian (far left) sets up extras in the headquarters of Mapache (Emilio Fernandez).*

OPPOSITE: *Kazanjian waits for instructions to give Ben Johnson (Tector Gorch). "Johnson was one of the true gentlemen of our industry," Kazanjian recalls.*

ABOVE: *Cast and crew wave goodbye on the last day of shooting the Warner Bros. picture* The Arrangement *(1969).*
Elia Kazan directed from his screenplay. Pictured are actors Kirk Douglas, Deborah Kerr, Hume Cronyn, and others;
Kazanjian is squeezed behind Kazan and Douglas, with associate producer Charles Maguire, who brought Kazanjian
onto the film. Maguire and Kazanjian would work again together on Raiders of the Lost Ark *(1981).*

ABOVE: The Great Bank Robbery *(1969) was another Warner Bros. picture. Kazanjian with bullhorn waits for extras to move onto the set with giant balloon. Shot at Disney Ranch over five days, the large, wonderful cast included Zero Mostel, Kim Novak, Clint Walker, Claude Akins, Akim Tamiroff, Larry Storch, John Anderson, Sam Jaffe, Mako, Elisha Cook Jr., Ruth Warrick, John Fiedler, Peter Whitney, Norman Alden, Grady Sutton, John Larch, and others. Hy Averback directed.*

FOLLOWING SPREAD: *Kazanjian and director Robert Wise discuss the next shot on location at the El Toro Marine Base for the Universal Studios picture* The Hindenburg *(1975, with destroyed* Hindenburg *in background). Wise holds a bullhorn and walkie-talkie; Kazanjian would use a bullhorn if necessary, but never liked working with walkie-talkies.*

ABOVE: *Production designer Henry Bumstead, director Alfred Hitchcock, and Howard Kazanjian look over the former's plans for the cemetery scene of* Family Plot *(1976) to be shot in Sierra Madre, California. Bumstead was a two-time Oscar winner for* The Sting *(1973) and* To Kill a Mockingbird *(1962). On the set of the Mrs. Rainbird home interior, shot on location in south Pasadena, California, all three men wear coat and tie, something Hitchcock requested of his crew on all pictures.*

OPPOSITE: *Hitchcock sits in his usual place immediately below the camera, in an alleyway set on location in Los Angeles (chosen to match the rear entrance of Grace Cathedral, shot earlier in San Francisco). Script supervisor Lois Thurman sits to Hitchcock's right, Kazanjian stands to his left. Note that the boom man is listening in on Hitchcock's conversation.*

FOLLOWING PAGE: *Hitchcock sits directly under the lens of the camera, a Mitchell BNC, while Kazanjian watches the action on the cemetery location in Sierra Madre for* Family Plot. *Storyboard artist Tom Wright is behind Kazanjian; prop master Bob Murdock has hands in pocket (left). Note that in this photo Kazanjian is wearing a vest, coat, and tie. Dress for the assistant director on a Hitchcock film was always the same, even in the San Gabriel Mountains on a very hot, dusty day. At the end of each day, clothes went directly to the cleaners.*

Chapter 7: *Man Friday*

"I could not tell you all the challenges that existed in setting up *The Hindenburg*," Kazanjian says of the 1975 movie. "One section of the script was only two inches long (2/8 page, in script language), and in that space, we used five sets, two of which had to be revamped into others."

It was a case of "be careful what you wish for," for the picture was to be directed by one of Kazanjian's all-time favorite directors, Robert Wise, whom he'd met at a fraternity banquet at USC. Wise was a master filmmaker and storyteller, capable of outstanding work in any genre: sci-fi (*The Day the Earth Stood Still*, 1958, and *The Andromeda Strain*, 1971); musical (*West Side Story*, 1961, and *The Sound of Music*, 1965); horror (*The Haunting*, 1963); Western (*Blood on the Moon*, 1948); film noir (*The Set-Up*, 1949); and so on. Wise said in 1998, "I've done every genre there is, and I approach each genre in the cinematic style that I think is appropriate and right for that genre. That's why I don't have a singular mark, but I justify that by saying that it's because of the number of genres I've done and the cinematic style that's proper for each one."

Unbeknownst to the crew, however, Wise's wife, Patricia, was ill and dying while they made the movie, and his pain would bleed into the production.

The film's story was based on events, real and fictionalized, leading up to the disaster of the *Hindenburg* zeppelin, which had gone up in flames while landing in Lakehurst, New Jersey, in 1937. For dramatic effect, writers Richard Levinson and William Link (of TV series *Columbo* fame) chose sabotage to explain the dirigible's explosion. Even at the time, and afterward, some authorities suspected foul play

129

as the cause of the conflagration that killed thirty-six people (instead of the more probable explanation: an electric spark in a couple tons of hydrogen). By placing a kind of detective onboard, the screenwriters were in familiar whodunit territory.

The *Hindenburg* was the pride of Nazi Germany, pre–World War II: a floating luxury blimp with flights from Frankfurt to the East Coast of the United States. In the script, when the Germans receive a warning that a bomb will destroy the zeppelin as it flies over New York City, they assign Luftwaffe Colonel Ritter to the airship as its security officer. The airship, of course, has many potential saboteurs aboard, from a German countess to a circus clown. Another investigator is Gestapo operative Martin Vogel.

"I was fascinated by two things," Robert Wise told the American Film Institute. "First the conclusion reached . . . that the *Hindenburg* was sabotaged by a young anti-Nazi crewmember who wanted to destroy this great symbol of the Nazi regime—not intending, of course, for it to blow up with people aboard. Second, I was fascinated by the whole era of lighter-than-air travel. When I read about what it was like to travel in a big airship—what the lifestyle was and how the passengers lived—I became completely captivated."

Wise cast George C. Scott as Colonel Franz Ritter; Anne Bancroft as Countess Ursula von Reugen; and Roy Thinnes as Vogel. Veteran character actor Burgess Meredith played card shark Emilio Pajetta. The cast was filled out by many well-knowns: Gig Young, Charles Durning, Richard Dysart, Rene Auberjonois, and others. It was a big-budget enterprise for Universal.

Once again Kazanjian would work with DP Robert Surtees. What he'd learned at Disney would help the 1st AD coordinate the film's many special and visual effects shots. Those effects shots, construction, and above-the-line costs inflated the budget. The studio wanted to cut it down by eliminating shooting time on one of the more costly sets. "They said, 'Instead of shooting eight days, you've got five days,'" Kazanjian recalls. "I said, 'The set still costs a million dollars. Take advantage of it. Shoot more in that set,' which we did."

TEMPERS AND FLAMES FLARE

Kazanjian ran the set as he saw fit: "I told Bob how I work, saying, 'This is how we're going to do it. No bell. When we're rolling, we're just going to say 'Rolling.' Wise agreed that it would be a quiet set. On the first day of principal photography, a crewmember was caught talking loudly during a rehearsal. Wise, as we had planned, bawled him out. That set the tone of the entire production. I'd used this method in the past and would in the future."

Production designer Eddie Carfagno (art director on *Ben-Hur*) had supervised construction of the huge sets, replicas of the zeppelin's interiors, and, in particular, the main passenger area. "The problem was you couldn't put three or four people in the same area of the interior catwalk where huge airbags hung on either side without the floor giving way," Kazanjian notes. "Why? Because the structure of the replica *Hindenburg* was built like the original *Hindenburg*."

Word got out that the set was unsafe. Kazanjian says, "OSHA walked onto the stage. I was sitting on top of this twenty-foot ladder because the *Hindenburg* interior set is supposed to be in the air. They immediately told me I couldn't sit or stand on top of a ladder. You have to be three feet down. And so it went, problem after problem, big and small." (Several changes were made by OSHA that day that affected the entire industry: for example, parallel platforms above six feet had to have a hand rail, middle rail, and kick board at the bottom floor level to avoid slippage.)

Kazanjian spent many evenings in the art department with Carfagno learning about the set pieces they'd be shooting. Certain sets would have to be altered, revamped during the night, or over a day or two, to be turned into other sets to save money. Kazanjian would have to make sure production was completely finished with one set before Carfagno transformed it into another. "Eddie was under pressure to make the changes and often came to the set asking if we were finishing that particular set that day," Kazanjian recalls. "Bob Wise had said to me, 'Look, just point me in the direction; I know how to direct.' I would do that with information I continually got from the art department and daily storyboards from Thomas Wright (who went on to be a director of many TV shows himself)."

131

The 1st AD had to deal with challenges relating to crew to sound to safety, to location to effects to actors. One day Kazanjian asked Wise if the next day's shoot in the lounge set required a nurse character; Wise said no. "The next morning we began shooting and Bob says, 'Where's the nurse?' 'You didn't want the nurse. The script supervisor was right here, we both heard you said no.' And he starts screaming and yelling at me in front of the entire cast. I told him later on, 'If you want to yell at me, if you want to fire me, fine. But take me to the side.' I said, 'Do you think Sid Sheinberg [the studio COO] would ever yell in front of people if one of his people did wrong? No. He'd take you to the side.' My assistant director called the nurse actor at home and she arrived ready just in time for the shoot."

Actor Robert Clary played Joseph Spah and had a short scene with Bancroft. "I am very close to [comedian and director] Mel Brooks," he told the *Los Angeles Times*. "When he married Anne Bancroft, I was very friendly with her, too. In the *Hindenburg*, we had a scene and I said to Anne, 'How's Mel?' and she said, 'Short.'"

The burning of the airship's interior was accomplished on Stage 12, at the time the largest soundstage in the US in square feet. To prepare, the stage's roof above the roof of the set had to be removed to let out smoke and heat; the fire department parked a truck outside, and a man was posted on the remaining roof with a fire hose.

They also burned up a replica of the zeppelin's nose, built on the same Stage 12. A half-dozen stunt artists wore fire-retardant gear in the flames. Airbags, supposedly filled with hydrogen, burned rapidly, and the stunt people had difficulty seeing because of the smoke. Wise could get only one master shot, but the flames did not, as reported elsewhere, come anywhere near destroying the soundstage. Kazanjian had made sure proper precautions had been taken and the burn lasted only about a minute, but they didn't have the budget to rebuild for close-ups.

The initial explosion of the zeppelin interior was captured by fifteen cameras, with fire companies placed strategically around the stage, rubber fireproof faces and air cylinders for each stuntman. Again production got only one take. The lounge could be made to tilt because it had been built on a large gimbal—it burned with stunt people jumping

132

out of the windows. "Was it frightening? Yes," Kazanjian says. "Was I a bit nervous? Yes. It is the sole obligation of the 1st AD to make sure every stunt, every action is safe."

PROBLEMS, MINOR AND MAJOR

The exterior of the burning *Hindenburg* and the reveal of its metal skeleton were shot at the Marine Corps Air Station El Toro, both inside and outside its twenty-story-high hangar. Actors running from the flaming airship skeleton, while flame effects cascaded to the ground, were also shot outside. Wise filmed the exteriors of the disaster scene in black-and-white because he wanted to intercut it with the famous documentary footage of the *Hindenburg* disaster (Wise had started as a film editor on *Citizen Kane*, etc.). (Marine Corps Air Station El Toro was located only about sixty miles from Universal Studios, but the money clock would start each day when cast and crew left the studio and would stop on their return. It was, therefore, more economical to treat it as a "distant" location, and lodge cast and crew on location and have the full day for shooting.)

The first take of an insert shot of three thousand pounds of water crashing down on a young actor, a minor, went well. But Wise wanted another for "protection." "Well, you don't do protection when there's fire and everything else floating around," Kazanjian recalls. "I said, 'Did you like that take?' 'Yes, but let's do another.' 'I can't let you; I can't let you do that to that child.' Bob was very upset with me again."

Moving inside the immense hangar, DP Surtees said, "I don't know how I can light the interior of this set. We don't have enough power."

On hand was Al Whitlock, matte painter and special visual effects supervisor, who suggested, "Let me do it." He discussed methods with Surtees, who then lit only the lower portion of the hangar to film the cast and extras. Wise shot it with the lens wide open, so that Whitlock could combine later the live-action plate with a matte painting in his lab to extend the set. Whitlock had been trained at Disney under master matte painter Peter Ellenshaw. For *Hindenburg*, he and his small studio department would create about eighty-five

Kazanjian on location at El Toro Marine Base for The Hindenburg *(1975), with DP Robert Surtees, three times Oscar winner, including one for* Ben-Hur *(1959). This was their second film together, following* The Arrangement *(1969).*

matte paintings to simulate the eight-hundred-foot zeppelin, its aerial journey, and its demise. Indeed, Wise had made sure Whitlock was on board before agreeing to do the picture. Wise had asked Whitlock: "Could we successfully put the *Hindenburg* in the air and fly it over the ocean, through all kinds of bad weather . . . then down past New York into Lakehurst where it explodes?" They could. "Al was confident," Wise said, "and excited about the project, so I went back to Universal and said that yes, I'd do the film."

The secret to Whitlock's work was to create original-negative in-camera matte shots whenever possible—no degradation of the image by using an optical printer. A few of the exterior trick shots created by Whitlock were filmed from the top of the hangar: for example, when the zeppelin drops its ropes and a dozen extras in German uniforms grab them far below.

"From atop of the twenty-story hangar, I hear on my walkie-talkie, *squeak, squeak, squeak*," Kazanjian says. "It's so far away, but it's Bob saying something. 'I'm coming down.' I wait at the bottom of the stairs for Bob to come all the way down twenty stories of stairs (there was no elevator). He grabs my ear and marches me way out in the field, and says, 'Are these German haircuts?' Well, the haircuts were pretty short and they're wearing caps, but he says, 'These are not German haircuts.' So we bring them in and give them all German military haircuts—but in the finished shot you can't see their hair *at all*. The people are too tiny for it to matter. Also, at the end of the day, the extras wanted more money—because the short haircuts meant they wouldn't be able to work for several days or even a week until their hair began to grow out."

For each day's effects shot(s), illustrator Tommy Wright brought in his storyboards. Wise followed them closely. "It was a very complex film, like a huge puzzle," Wise said in 1975. "As I was shooting, I referred to my sketchbook constantly, much more than I've ever done before."

"Bob had to approve them and usually did with no changes, then he'd tell the actors what to do," Kazanjian explains. "Tommy had worked with Bob several times before, but he kept telling me, 'Howard, you're being abused. Quit. Quit. Quit.'"

135

In addition to coping with a sometimes bully/director, and despite his commitment to safety, Kazanjian also became the center of a potential lawsuit. In one shot a little boy had been dropped into the arms of a crewmember on the ground from a height of ten feet. To sell the effect of fire cascading to the ground along with the child, small pieces of treated cloth coated in rubber cement had been lit, so when the boy fell it looked like he was surrounded by shards of falling flame. It seemed to go off without a hitch. However, the boy's grandmother had died that day, and his mother, who was with him on set, became very upset. After arriving home, she spotted a "burn" mark or her son's leg and called in OSHA. Kazanjian was blamed, as the assistant director, and threatened with legal action by local authorities.

"Universal said, 'Let's reproduce this on the stage,'" he says. "Because they were being sued, too; they redid the stunt and ran the film and the dailies several times and also in slow motion. You could see that it wasn't the fire—the kid had landed on the crewmember's belt buckle, which scraped his leg. I knew it wasn't fire, because I didn't let the fire fall on the kid. But those are the things you go through. The mother eventually calmed down."

On the bright side, Anne Bancroft was "lovely" to Kazanjian, and George C. Scott, who had won an Academy Award for his portrayal of Patton (which he refused to accept, on the grounds that he wasn't competing with other actors), was "a towering figure and you respected him. You kept your distance, but of course had conversations about call times and schedule changes and the like."

Patricia Doyle, Wise's ailing wife, passed away a couple of months before the movie came out. *The Hindenburg* received poor reviews, but was a successful spectacle. Its tagline promised to explain the mystery of the zeppelin's explosion, an historic event still very much alive in the general public's memory. Released on Christmas Day 1975, the movie performed well at the box office, helped by Whitlock and company's incredible effects. *The Hindenburg* earned back at least double its budget, but didn't make as much money as other studio-made disaster movies, such as 1974's *The Towering Inferno* or 1972's *The Poseidon Adventure*.

As the years passed, Kazanjian would run into Wise at events and in town. "He was genuine, he was warm, he was hugging. It was just that at the time he'd been suffering. That's our business. We go through it together, almost like family."

"In fact, Howard was very much like Robert Wise," Kleiser says, "a gentleman, quiet, efficient, reliable, all those things. He was really conservative and you could rely on him."

The Hindenburg was nominated for Best Sound, Editing, Cinematography, and Art Direction. It lost in those categories but won a Special Achievement Award for Sound Effects and Visual Effects. "*Hindenburg* is an incredible accomplishment to look back upon," Kazanjian said in 1975. "But it's behind me now. I've got to look ahead to the next project."

That next project would be helmed by another Hollywood legend: Billy Wilder.

BLAZES AGAIN

A Universal studio executive had suggested to Billy Wilder that he film a new adaptation of *The Front Page*. The stage play, written by Ben Hecht and Charles MacArthur, had already been adapted a couple of times for the cinema, most successfully as *His Girl Friday* (1940), starring Cary Grant and Rosalind Russell. Wilder, a former newspaperman in his younger days, agreed and financing was arranged. What appealed to him was the opportunity to do a period story, the tale of a ruthless boss and his star reporter in 1920s Chicago. "A reporter was a glamorous fellow in those days," Wilder said, "the way he wore a hat, and a raincoat, and a swagger, and had his camaraderie with fellow reporters, with local police, always hot on the tail of tips from them and from the fringes of the underworld."

"You couldn't set it at the present moment because journalism isn't like that anymore," said co-screenwriter I.A.L. Diamond in 1974. "In those days, guys would do anything to get a story and never more so than in Chicago."

The combo of Universal production chief Marshall Green; his second-in-command, brother Hilton Green; and Wilder himself resulted

137

in Kazanjian being assigned to the picture. The 1ˢᵗ AD was known to be cool and quick on his feet. Kazanjian joined up in April 1974. He was excited to work with Wilder, director of *Double Indemnity* (1944), *Sunset Boulevard* (1950), *Sabrina* (1954), *Some Like It Hot* (1959), and other wonderful films. However, the early 1970s had been a bumpier road for Wilder, with a couple of relative flops. "But Billy was very touchable," Kazanjian says. "You could meet with him one-on-one during preproduction."

The Front Page (1974) had a great cast, from stars Walter Matthau and Jack Lemmon, to costars Carol Burnett in a small role, Susan Sarandon, Austin Pendleton, and Charles Durning. (Note that Wilder's film was actually released before *The Hindenburg* because the latter had a longer post, due to its many visual effects.)

On set, Wilder and his 1ˢᵗ AD had to deal with a slow DP, Jordan Cronenweth. "Billy kept busy doing other things," Kazanjian says. "As long as Billy got the day's work done, he was satisfied. He was so sharp, so quick, talked fast, knew exactly what he wanted, worked very, very hard on the script. Billy would pace back and forth always thinking. Not often would I see him sit in his director's chair. I.A.L. Diamond would sit on the set all the time. Billy would look at him after a take, and Diamond would say, 'It's not "a." It's "an."'" He would not allow one word to be changed. Not one word missing or replaced with another. Except in a scene with a betting line: 'I'll give you odds of five to six,' or something like that. That was changed on set by Walter Matthau, who said it wasn't right. He was quite the gambler."

The 1ˢᵗ AD observed that Lemmon, famous for his role in *The Odd Couple*, shaved with an electric shaver twice a day, upon arrival and after lunch. Lemmon was always on time. The actor would play a piano that happened to be on one of the sets between takes. "Billy would not let us overlap our lines more," Lemmon told film critic Roger Ebert on set in 1974. "I think that would have made it better; I feel it's a piece in which you must overlap. But Billy, the writer, wanted to hear all of the words clearly, and he wanted the audience to hear the words. I would have liked to overlap to the point where you lost some of the dialogue. But when I talk about rapid-fire dialogue . . . The other day we had two pages of dialogue that took forty-five seconds. That's fast."

TOP TO BOTTOM: *Kazanjian stands behind famed director Billy Wilder (*Sunset Boulevard, *1950;* Some Like It Hot, *1959), who is looking over the shoulder of DP Jordan S. Cronenweth on the film* The Front Page *(1974), for Universal Pictures. • Billy Wilder (center) discusses a scene with cast and crew; famed comedienne Carol Burnett (Mollie Malloy) is on far right with hand on Charles Durning (Murphy); Kazanjian is in front of camera looking left.*

"Billy and Jack and Walter weren't getting along," Austin Pendleton (Earl Williams) recalled years later. "Both Jack and Walter said independently of each other: 'We're never gonna work with him again.' Billy was very clear with them all the time about exactly what he wanted them to play, and they had their own ideas. But he didn't want their ideas. I don't know if he had been like that with them [on their previous films together], but all of a sudden they'd had enough of it, or he suddenly was beginning to be that way with them, but they were unhappy. Billy was very sweet to me. He wouldn't print anything until he was happy with it, but he was very encouraging. And I got to know Carol Burnett, which was wonderful." (Burnett took advantage of time off from her very successful TV sketch show to play prostitute Mollie Malloy.)

Ebert recorded what he saw that day: "Wilder called for action. Lemmon sat on his chair back and nonchalantly exhaled cigar smoke into the thick air. The reporters raced to the windows. Searchlights searched and sirens screamed. The reporters raced back to their telephones and began shouting the good old standbys: 'Give me city desk!' 'Stop the presses!' 'Tear up the front page!'

"'Cut,' said Wilder. He patted in his pockets for another stick of gum. 'That was beautiful! That was terrific! That was nothing short of adequate!'"

While they were shooting, a fire broke out at Goldwyn Studios, where the director stored his art collection in an attic above a soundstage. "A lot of his art, millions of dollars' worth, all burned up," Kazanjian says. "Another person called him and said, 'Oh my God—all your Oscars are lost!' And Billy said, 'Who cares about the Oscars? I've just lost a Picasso.' And he rattled off more modern-day painters . . ." Pendleton would recall that when he asked Wilder about the tremendous loss, the director just "shrugged." (Enough of Wilder's impressionist and modern art collection survived, fortunately. In 1989, he earned $32.6 million at an art auction of his paintings held at Christie's.)

From Kazanjian's point of view, filming went smoothly. Wilder shot only what he needed, no coverage. He was one of those directors who cut in-camera. "After a master shot, Billy would say, 'Okay, coming in for a close-up. Pick up your line here,'" Kazanjian recalls. "In the middle of a sentence. He said he didn't want the studio interfering in editorial."

Only four days after wrapping, Kazanjian bumped into Wilder on the lot. The director informed him that he'd just turned over the picture, completed, because it had been precut and assembled during the shoot. "Billy invited me to a session with all the post cutters, sound effects, and so on. He told them what he wanted, where to put the music, a certain noise effect, etcetera."

The Front Page received a mixed critical reception, but was the first Wilder movie to turn a profit since 1963's *Irma La Douce*. It was becoming more difficult for older directors to make films that worked for younger audiences, which made up the majority of moviegoers.

"Years later I went to Billy's office because I wanted him to direct a picture I was developing," Kazanjian recalls. "And he said, 'Do you have the financing? Do you have the studio? Is it all going to be filmed on stages?' He was more concerned with it being on soundstages because he was getting older. As I was leaving and reaching for the doorknob, Billy asked me what I thought of a painting on the floor leaning against the wall. It was one of those multicolor no-subject paintings. I paused and didn't know what to say, other than 'interesting.' Bill said, 'The phrase is, "It makes a statement."' It did."

Following the *Front Page*, Kazanjian was to work with another older, even more legendary director, on his fifty-third film—the master of suspense, Alfred Hitchcock.

CHAPTER 8: *Heart of the Master*

B ecause Kazanjian had worked with established directors Wise and Wilder, Universal exec Hilton Green, who had previously been an assistant director on Alfred Hitchcock's *Psycho* (1960) and production manager on Hitchcock's *Marnie* (1964), nominated the young man to work with the venerable master of suspense. Hitchcock accepted, but it wasn't that simple. The director had a well-established team around him. He'd also recently recovered from a series of health problems. His longtime assistant, Peggy Robertson, and secretary, Sue Gauthier, had constructed a wall around the fragile director to frighten off undesirables.

"I kept wanting to see him," Kazanjian says. "After all, I'm the assistant director. I needed to meet with him. All I heard were excuses."

Under the aegis of Lew Wasserman, his one-time agent, now chairman of Universal-MCA, Hitchcock had a suite of offices that included a private theater. When Hitchcock was not in production, these offices remained empty with the exception of Robertson and Gauthier. In January of 1975, Kazanjian was given a room in the suite. Other offices would eventually house production designer Henry Bumstead and his art department, illustrator Tommy Wright, Kazanjian's 2nd AD Wayne Farlow, and, later, editor Terry Williams. A recent personnel addition was Alpha de Monte-Campbell, a woman who was handling Hitchcock's historical files and, on occasion, his fan mail. Monte-Campbell urged Kazanjian to keep pushing to see Hitchcock.

Weeks after building up the shooting schedule, boards, and budget, Kazanjian was washing his hands in the men's restroom, when Hitchcock walked in after viewing a film in his theater (the director also had a private restroom adjacent to his private office, but the men's room was closer to the theater). "Hitchcock just stared at me," Kazanjian recalls. "I said, 'Mr. Hitchcock, I'm your assistant director.' But I still couldn't get in to see him. Obviously, Sue and Peggy were not allowing entry."

Kazanjian knew that every morning Hitchcock sat outside Gauthier's office for a few minutes to see if anybody had called. "With his back toward the door, he could not see me. So one morning, I decided to walk in. I said, 'Oh, excuse me, Mr. Hitchcock, I just wanted to talk about the script with you.' He said, 'Come in.' He got up, and we went into his private office. From that day forward, every single morning of preproduction, I could go in whenever he was there. First thing, he and I would meet."

They would have coffee served in fine china cups, while Hitchcock sometimes reminisced about the business and his films. "Howard," the director explained, "I don't like directors who shoot the interior of a train with actors, and then put the camera out in a field to establish it moving through the countryside. How can the camera move from inside the train to the point of view of sheep in the field?" In his film *North by Northwest* (1959), Hitchcock had cut from Eva Marie Saint and Cary Grant inside the train to a camera half out of a train window for an exterior shot of the cars as they rounded a bend. "We could see the length of the train, but never had to leave it." (Eva Marie Saint would also recall Hitchcock insisting, even off set, that she drink her tea or coffee from a china or porcelain cup, not a paper one, because it was more in keeping with her movie character.)

Hitchcock screened films for Kazanjian to familiarize him with his work and methods. After each screening Hitchcock would question Kazanjian about what he had seen and learned. The director also invited Kazanjian to screen new films with him and Universal casting head Bill Batliner to discuss possible actors. In director Jim Goldstone's recent movie *Swashbuckler* (1976), they watched a scene shot from the POV of someone on the second story of a house. The characters hear a carriage pulling up outside on gravel. An actor goes to the window and looks down; from his POV a beautiful woman descends from the carriage, met by a handsome man. Suddenly the camera is at ground level to catch the two whispering to each other, before cutting back to the second story POV.

143

Again this violated Hitchcock's laws on point of view. "The camera must stay upstairs no matter what," he said.

"Psychologically, Hitch was right that the jumping camera had a jarring effect," Kazanjian says. "I'd studied Hitchcock films for years; now I was actually working with Hitchcock, and he had me view as many movies as possible in his private projection room. He would ask me questions and tell me stories about each film and sometimes about his cast, revealing their positives and negatives. 'Hoooward,' he would say in his slow deep voice, 'do you recall what color dress Kim Novak was wearing in Ernie's San Francisco restaurant?' referring to *Vertigo* [1958]. 'Green,' I said. 'No. *Emerald* green.' That alone told me a great deal about the level of detail Hitchcock expected. He went on to explain that no other person in the restaurant was allowed to wear green. 'Did you notice that as Kim Novak walked to camera, no other extra faced camera? Extras never walk toward camera. They walk away, or they crisscross.' Another lesson. Eventually, this would lead to a discussion of our film's wardrobe, characters, and even camera movement. At times Hitchcock would tell personal stories about the actors he'd worked with in the past. Often these stories would start with, 'Hoooward, did you know . . . ?'"

Hitchcock explained that in *Lifeboat* (1944) he'd filmed a plane crashing into the ocean from a POV over the shoulders of the pilot through the cockpit windows using rear screen projection—up to a few feet before hitting the ocean—at which point the rear projection screen was replaced by a paper screen and thousands of gallons of water were made to burst through it to simulate impact. Kazanjian was tutored on how to use a camera to mimic a person's gaze, how to frame shots to maximize anxiety and fear. The director would ask his first assistant about other films and arrange screenings if Kazanjian hadn't seen them. He would point out examples in his own films of high-angle shots and why and when he would use them. Hitchcock explained that he didn't like insert shots. He preferred to start on a telephone ringing and pan up to the person answering, or reverse that shot from character to a moving, closer shot of the telephone, a purse, or a gun, and so on.

The two often lunched together in the director's private dining room. Kazanjian could order whatever he wanted, but Hitchcock suggested the menu. The latter always had a hamburger patty with mashed potatoes or steak fries, or Dover sole from England with mashed potatoes. No salad or vegetables, and a cup of coffee. Dessert, rarely. "I always had the same," Kazanjian says. "Once he told me that fish must be caught by net and not by hook. I knew he wanted me to ask why, so I did. 'Have you ever seen a fish with a hook in his mouth?' Hitchcock twisted his mouth grotesquely as though there were a hook in it. Nothing further had to be said."

During one lunch, Kazanjian noticed a shipping box from England on the floor near their table. "This may have been a setup, as normally it would have been placed near the back-entrance steps to his car. The box was slightly torn, but soon the conversation came around to its contents. Hitchcock told me it was ten pairs of slippers. 'Ten pairs from England?' I asked. 'Ten' because Hitchcock's dogs chewed them up, so he always had a pair standing by."

Hitchcock requested through Hilton Green that his assistant director wear a suit and tie at all times. One day the director asked him, "Howard, does your mother know what color tie you are wearing?" Kazanjian learned from experience that Hitchcock objected to anything that wasn't dark black, blue, or deep brown. Conservative colors. "I'd smile, feel a bit awkward, and button up my coat and try to hide the full tie. This happened more than once."

The director explained that he wore suits of only three colors. "I was a bit taken aback as I thought they were all black," Kazanjian says. "But Hitch said, 'No, I have black, dark blue, and dark gray.' I never saw the dark gray or blue, or if I did, they were so dark they looked black. He also told me how he matched his coat with his pants. He opened the coat and showed me a double-digit number on the inside lapel; then he rolled his pants back at the beltline and showed me the same double-digit number."

Hitchcock felt it was dignified to wear dark suits and ties. He wanted Kazanjian to follow his good example.

Once Hitchcock sighed and asked if Kazanjian knew that he'd never won an Oscar. His pictures and crew had won several over the years, but not Hitchcock himself, though nominated six times. He'd made classics such as *Psycho, North by Northwest, Vertigo, The Man Who Knew Too*

Much, Dial M for Murder, Notorious, Rear Window, Strangers on a Train, and *To Catch a Thief,* to name only a few, but never received an Academy Award for Best Director. In 1968, the Academy had made amends by giving him the Irving G. Thalberg Memorial Award. One reason may have been that Hitchcock was a recluse, not a socialite. "He once told me that for many, many years he didn't invite anyone to his home. Consequently, Hitch was not invited to his peers' homes or anyone's home. Billy Wilder mentioned that long ago he'd been invited to Hitchcock's home. Hitchcock was sitting on the sofa and fell asleep at this own party. Billy said, 'We got up and left.'"

Kazanjian met the slipper-chewing dogs when Alma, Hitchcock's wife, brought them by before husband and wife left for their weekly dinner at Chasen's restaurant. The couple was always given the same booth at the established Hollywood eatery. Kazanjian recalls, "Tony Emerzian, the driver, would tell me, 'Can you believe it? I'm being paid by the studio to drive him, yet he gives me a $100 tip. Slides it in my hand once a week.'"

Hitchcock and Alma were very close. When her husband had been only an interstitial titles designer on silent films, she was already a respected film editor. She read every one of the scripts for her husband's films and gave advice. When she was ill for a spell during preproduction, Kazanjian says, "Hitchcock avoided talking about her condition. I never asked; I knew I shouldn't. It hurt him too much. He wanted to immerse himself in his work."

CAUGHT RED-HANDED

Their new film's working title was *Deceit.* Its script, written by Ernest Lehman (who'd written *North by Northwest,* among others), based on Victor Canning's novel *The Rainbird Pattern,* told a complex but comedic story about two couples—a phony psychic and her taxi-driver boyfriend; and a man and woman criminal team—whose paths intertwine. Originally the story took place in England, but Hitchcock didn't want to travel that far and for that long, so he'd changed the locale to the USA. Hitchcock and Kazanjian flew up to San Francisco to scout locations. At the United

146

Airlines desk at LAX, because they had to make sure they had seat belts large enough for Hitchcock on connecting flights, they were delayed.

Famously, the director didn't drive, partially because he was afraid of being stopped by the police for real or imaginary infractions. "He told me twice the story that when he was a young boy in England, I believe eight years old, he had done something wrong," Kazanjian recalls. "He never said what it was. His father gave him a note and told him to run it down to the constable. He took it to the police station, where the constable read the letter and threw Hitchcock in jail. This was a joke or a lesson. He was a bad boy and the father asked that he be put in jail for a short time. This scared Hitch for the rest of his life. Once when I asked him if he drove a car, he said he'd driven on occasions in his younger days."

The director, his production manager Ernest Wehmeyer, who met them at the airport, and his AD were driven from SFO to the city on Highway 1. Hitchcock told the driver they were late and to please hurry. Minutes later a policeman stopped their speeding limo. "We pulled to the side of the freeway and the driver rolled down Hitchcock's front-passenger window because he was worried about the traffic going by on the driver's side. The policeman looked into the window and rested his arm on the window ledge while speaking to the driver. Hitch looked straight ahead, never moved. From my view in the back seat, I knew he was sweating bullets. The officer asked the driver if he knew he was doing eighty. All the driver could say was that he was driving Mr. Hitchcock. The officer moved back a bit, took a look at Hitchcock, and then wrote a ticket.

"Five minutes later, we were on our way again and, after a beat, Hitch turned to Wehmeyer in the back seat next to me, and said, 'Pay the ticket.' The ironic thing was that we were in no hurry to get to Jack's Restaurant. We still got there, early, at 11:30. The master of suspense."

Hitchcock would eat only at Jack's or Ernie's (the restaurant which he'd re-created for *Vertigo*), in San Francisco. At the former they met production designer Henry Bumstead, a veteran of several of the director's films and two-time Oscar winner. "Hitchcock loved Henry Bumstead," Kazanjian says. "All who worked with this genius loved Bummy."

Unlike several Hitchcock movies that took place in very identifiable places, near or even on top of national monuments, the director had

147

decided *Deceit* wouldn't be tied to any specific locale. Kazanjian recalls: "Hitch said to me, 'I want to eliminate all reference in the script to where we are and people's names. Make those changes in the script.' I thought it would be an easy thing to do, but it wasn't. Sometimes you had to rewrite a paragraph, so I called on the script supervisor, Lois Thurman, to work with me, who made notes. Then we went back to Hitchcock. I don't know if he read it, but he said, 'Fine,' and the shooting script was printed. But I didn't like doing that."

By the time cameras were primed, actors hired, and budget approved, Kazanjian had become a kind of disciple. "You learn from all directors, but Hitchcock was the only one who worked so closely with me, and allowed me into his heart, into his past, and explained how to do things."

His apprenticeship was going to be put to good use.

Hybrid Help

Hitchcock and Kazanjian began the shoot on May 12, 1975. The schedule called for a few scenes to be filmed first at the studio before they went on locations in San Francisco before returning to the soundstages and a few more locations in the Los Angeles area. The cast had been set about three weeks earlier. Hitchcock had considered Angela Lansbury and Goldie Hawn for Blanche, the psychic, before deciding on Barbara Harris. He'd chosen Bruce Dern to play her taxi-driving husband, George Lumley; for the villainous couple, experts in ransoming their adult hostages, he'd cast Karen Black (Fran) and Roy Thinnes (Adamson). Coincidentally, Kazanjian had just worked with Thinnes on *Hindenburg*. Dern had played a small but important role in *Marnie*.

"I never thought I'd have a chance to work with Mr. Hitchcock," Karen Black told Roger Ebert. "I wonder how I'll like his sense of humor. I play a kind of a nice girl, not glamorous, looks good, dresses sorta nice, who'd like to be finished with stealing jewels and go back to painting, which is her real hobby, you see."

Studio sets were closed off to intruders of all kinds. On the set, "an atmosphere of the utmost courtesy and formality prevailed," wrote John

148

Russell Taylor, who was often present to gather material for his book *Hitch*. Kazanjian emphasizes: "No people running around, no raised voices or temperaments. Again, that is how I ran the set."

One of the first things Hitch and his team shot on a stage was Fran's mysterious appearance during a scene with a helicopter (prop) in which the ransomers receive their loot in return for their hostage. Taylor was surprised when the director wrapped the first few setups in one or two takes. "If you know what you want," Hitchcock told him, "and you know when you've got it, why do more?"

"Hitchcock would sit with me," Kazanjian says, "and explain why we were shooting a particular angle, why the script had been written a certain way, why a character reacted to this and not to that. I came to know every characterization of every actor. Assistant directors don't normally get involved in that. Hitchcock was very inspiring. Each day wasn't another work day, but a learning day."

Hitchcock would arrive at nine each morning, and Kazanjian would help him out of the chauffeured car, sometimes holding his arm while the director climbed the two or three steps to his dressing room trailer on stage. They'd then go over the day's shoot or whatever else the director cared to discuss, sipping their coffees. "Hitch would not tolerate anyone interrupting us for any reason. One time Peggy entered to ask a question, and he said in his usual commanding voice, 'Peggy, can you not see you are interrupting us?' I cringed, because we weren't talking about anything important, just old times, but it gave me the impression that we were a team. (Fortunately, I had Wayne Farlow as my 2nd AD who kept watch on crew and cast whenever I sat with Hitchcock in his dressing room.)"

On set, Taylor was impressed by the number of tricks employed in shooting the helicopter sequence; for some shots, Hitchcock used only a mockup of the front half of the copter against a black screen. A fake forest background extended only as far as the director had proscribed, for there was no use in spending more money for forest they wouldn't shoot. Taylor couldn't write in his book that Alma was ill again. Hitchcock left the set at times to attend to her, leaving Kazanjian in charge. He'd briefed his assistant, who completed the shots for the day. "But it really

149

OPPOSITE, CLOCKWISE FROM TOP LEFT: *Kazanjian sits in on a mock-up set of the Rainbird house interior at Universal Studios for a lighting test prior to production on* Family Plot *(1976).* • *Filming the scene on the staircase of the reveal of the diamond in the chandelier, Kazanjian (center) listens to DP Lenny South discuss the next shot.* • *On local location at the purposefully overgrown Sierra Madre Pioneer Cemetery are script supervisor Lois Thurman, 1ˢᵗ AD Kazanjian, John Steadman (graveyard worker), Alfred Hitchcock, Bruce Dern (George Lumley), and storyboard illustrator Thomas Wright.*

ABOVE, TOP TO BOTTOM: *Kazanjian confers with Hitchcock regarding a scene to be shot on location in San Francisco; DP Lenny South listens in.* • *Kazanjian sits with Hitchcock while an interior set is being lit in south Pasadena.*

was not me directing from my creative viewpoint, but from Hitchcock 'inside' me," Kazanjian says. "I'd been brainwashed to understand how he would direct the scene. I was his puppet. Each morning before we had our coffee discussion, I rehearsed the actors. Then with camera rolling, Hitch directed through me even though he wasn't present on certain days."

On location in San Francisco at night, Hitchcock stayed in his chauffeured car to avoid a howling, freezing wind. Before each take, he would roll down the window a couple of inches to speak with Kazanjian, but the noise from the running car made it "extremely difficult" to hear. "I'd point a finger to Tony and he would unlock the doors so I could jump in the back seat and listen to Hitch," Kazanjian says. "Then I'd go back and finish the scene. I was his body, because he was not that mobile. One must also understand he always believed, and said often, that once the script was finished, the hard part was done. Directing was easy. Of course, that was for effect."

A few weeks into the shoot, Kazanjian noticed that the entire crew was intimidated, even frightened of their director. Nary a one would approach or dare speak to him. Hitchcock was a man who had carefully crafted his own public image, largely through his weekly TV show, *Alfred Hitchcock Presents* (1955–1962): his "Good evening," his famous profile, his chosen theme music, his cameos in his own films, all had contributed to Hitchcock's self-conscious style. "And he did this all without a press agent," Kazanjian notes. "As a legend, he'd become untouchable. Crews were afraid to say hello or good morning to him."

Kazanjian therefore became the intermediary for questions posed by the crew to "Mr. Hitchcock." "I was having dinner with six crewmembers at Jack's one evening while we were shooting in San Francisco," he says. "Halfway through dinner the ladies' costumer blurted out, 'My God, you can talk with Howard.' Before that she didn't think she could talk with me."

On Tuesday, June 3, on the top of Nob Hill, Kazanjian rehearsed a crowd of about two hundred for a scene in Grace Cathedral during which Adamson and Fran kidnap the congregation's bishop (William Prince). (The cathedral is only a block or two from the Mark Hopkins hotel where Hitchcock had filmed exteriors for *Vertigo*.) It was the sixteenth day of filming and cast call was for 9 AM. "We'd scouted it before," Kazanjian says. "Hitchcock was familiar with the church and I think wanted to see it again and have dinner at Jack's. During the scout he'd already told me where he wanted his cast and where the kidnap would take place. Back at Universal Studios I'd made a drawing of the exterior and interior of Grace Cathedral. In red pen, Hitchcock had laid out the shots and angles he wanted. I was therefore able to tell the crew, before Hitchcock arrived, exactly where the cameras should be placed, and how to move the cast inside and outside the cathedral. When he arrived, all was set. The congregation was made up of local extras, and our set decorator, James Payne, had adorned the church with white flowers." (An exterior shot of the car racing away from the church, with a few of the congregation looking on, would be filmed later outside the back of the Presbyterian Church on Wilshire Boulevard in Los Angeles.)

Taylor was on hand and witnessed a few of the extras hamming it up, trying to get on camera, which annoyed the director. Kazanjian and his crew filmed what Hitchcock wanted in one or two takes, but Taylor heard Hitchcock muttering as he walked away, "That's what you would call directing idiots."

RECRIMINATIONS

Then Hitchcock fired Roy Thinnes. Hitchcock would claim that he'd always wanted to cast William Devane as the master criminal, but the actor hadn't been available. When Devane wrapped his starring role in the TV movie *Fear on Trial* (broadcast October 2, 1975), he became available and Thinnes was let go. "It's always horrible when any actor is dismissed or fired," Kazanjian says.

Taylor would cite Hitchcock as saying, "When I'm directing a film, *I'm* directing a film, not some actor." (Letters exist from Thinnes to Hitchcock suggesting ideas for certain scenes during preproduction; perhaps this trend continued on set.) Kazanjian was back at Jack's that evening at a table close to Hitchcock's when Thinnes walked up to the director and said something like, "You've dismissed me," or "Why did you dismiss me?" or "You did wrong." Hitchcock was speechless. "It was

153

a very difficult situation," Kazanjian recalls. "They looked at each other for a long while, and I do believe Hitchcock blamed the casting director, Bill Batliner, and eventually Roy left." Taylor would quote Hitchcock explaining: "But you were too nice for the role, too *nice*." (Italics are original; Taylor would also place the encounter at Chasen's after their return from San Francisco.)

"When Hitchcock related the story to me," Kazanjian recalls, "he said, 'Can you imagine Thinnes approaching me after he was dismissed?' Hitchcock did feel Thinnes was too nice, not sinister enough for the role."

Because of the actor change, they would have to return later to San Francisco for various replacement shots on location and inside Grace Cathedral. "When they're dragging the body [of the bishop] out to the car, that's all Roy," William Devane would say. "I think I worked about six weeks on the film, out of a ten-week shoot. It was quite an experience because, basically, you went to work at nine in the morning and you went home at 5:00, like you were working at a bank."

A Universal Studios press release, dated June 11, read, "Due to an artistic disagreement between Mr. Hitchcock and Roy Thinnes over the concept of the role, Thinnes asked for and received an amicable release."

Back on a Universal soundstage, Hitchcock sat while Kazanjian rehearsed the actors. "I'd say, 'Roll it,'" Kazanjian remembers, "and then, 'Action' and, when I thought the scene was finished, 'Cut.' There were times I'd automatically say, 'Let's do it again, but a bit faster, or slower,' etc. Whenever I gave direction, I would catch myself and look at Hitch. He never blinked and always supported me. I once went to Peggy and told her I was finding myself making decisions for Hitch and telling the actors what to do even in Hitchcock's presence. She said, 'He will tell you if you are doing wrong.'"

The only actor who bristled a little at the directorial chain of command was Devane. For one shot in a kitchen, Kazanjian asked Devane to say his line as he walked away, and then turn around. "It was one of the days when Hitchcock was trying to get a lot out of Karen Black," Kazanjian says. Devane wanted to walk, turn around, then deliver his lines and didn't want to take orders from an assistant director. "But that's screen time. I knew that Hitch wanted the pace to keep going."

With the crew and Hitchcock looking on, Devane objected: "My mother doesn't like to see me walk and talk at the same time. What will she say?"

"We'll shoot her!" Hitchcock nearly shouted.

"I was a novice," Devane would say. "I had very little film experience."

"Remember I'd been brainwashed by Hitch," Kazanjian reemphasizes. "He'd say, 'Why did I do this? Do you know why I have the camera here?' He taught me these things."

Hitchcock usually sat directly under the lens of the camera and would tell DP Leonard South: "Put on a 50," meaning a 50mm lens, or whatever lens was appropriate. Kazanjian adds, "And then he'd announce that the left frame would cut through the flower arrangement, the right to the edge of the door, a few inches above the actor's head; we're cutting through his second button on his shirt. Hitchcock knew his camera and lens. He was always right."

One problem for production was that a key elderly member of the crew was starting to forget things. When Kazanjian alerted head of production Marshall Green, "I got my ass ripped. Marshall screamed about how long this person had been at Universal and so on. I walked out dragging my tail. You learn. You learn that sometimes you need to keep your mouth shut. Sadly, months later it was announced this person had dementia."

A FAMILY AFFAIR

Hitchcock hardly ever attended dailies. "He told me it wasn't necessary, as he knew what he'd shot the day before," Kazanjian says. "Peggy told me I should see all the dailies, and if something was wrong, to bring it to Hitchcock's attention."

The opening scene of the film was to take place at a beautiful home in South Pasadena that Henry Bumstead had found. Here, matriarch Julia Rainbird (Cathleen Nesbit) would set up the story and put it in

155

motion by talking about her long-lost son. Hitchcock wanted lighting tests done, which production dutifully set up on a soundstage dressed to look like the rather dark Victorian sitting room. A camera crew shot with a stand-in made up as Rainbird. In dailies, Hitchcock didn't like what he saw. "He told DP Lenny South several times exactly how he wanted it lit: like a Rembrandt painting. We shot the next day, and the next and the next. We finally came close, but I don't think Hitchcock ever got exactly the look he wanted."

Kazanjian also found a camera movement problem with a challenging shot set up at dusk on a local location. The art department had already wrapped the portable set and chain-link fence outside a warehouse, but Kazanjian let Hitchcock know that what he'd carefully planned wasn't on film. During lunch Hitchcock viewed the dailies, agreed, and announced that they would reshoot it on a Friday evening, a week later. At the reshoot, Hitchcock said nothing other than telling the cameraman what he wanted. The camera operator who had failed the previous week felt "horrible," Kazanjian says, "and sat a few yards away on a street curb with his head hung low. No one had reprimanded him, but the next day he quit. The invisible pressure from Hitchcock caused this, and I felt extremely bad. Hitchcock wasn't upset, but the pressure just got to everyone."

At another nearby location, the Sierra Madre Pioneer Cemetery near Pasadena, they set up what would become a famous, complex overhead shot of cat-and-mouse intrigue during a funeral. Hitchcock didn't want a cemetery with manicured lawns. Its single older caretaker was therefore encouraged by production, in advance of their arrival, to do less than the usual upkeep so the cemetery would be noticeably unkempt and overgrown. "However, prior to our arrival," Kazanjian recalls, "someone kicked over and broke many of the headstones. Luckily, we'd brought in our own headstones." (As was usual, they didn't film any real names on the real headstones for legal reasons.)

Hitchcock turned to one of the extras looking into the grave, while filming the burial, and asked her who was being buried. The extra gave him the right name and reason. "I'd learned earlier that extras on a

Hitchcock film are not just bodies," Kazanjian says. "They need to know the situation, why they've been hired. I'd previously grouped the extras around the grave and explained why they were there as mourners and what character was being buried."

On stage they shot more of the taxi-driver/detective husband and his wife/supposed psychic. "Hitch loved Barbara Harris," Devane said. "He just loved her and would tell all these wonderful stories to her. I would sit around and hear all these wonderful stories, too. Never heard him tell the same story twice. The nice thing was that he understood the parent-child relationship, director to actor."

"One day Hitch was leaving his dressing room, walking to the set," Kazanjian recalls. "I'm right behind him, and Bruce Dern comes up. Now, he's taller than Hitch, so he puts his arm around his neck, and he was saying, 'Hey, Hitch. How are you? Did you have a good day?' And I'm thinking, *Oh my God . . .*"

Storyboard artist Tom Wright had laid out a sequence with a runaway car (when its brake lines are cut) in consultation with Hitchcock. They shot either directly through the windshield at Barbara Harris and Bruce Dern, or a reverse through the windshield over the hood of the Mustang to the road and curves racing towards them. After an establishing shot that included the hood of the Mustang, Hitchcock eliminated the hood and shot POVs of oncoming traffic. "He wanted you to experience the terrifying trip down the mountain road," Kazanjian says. "To show the near misses and almost running off the road or hitting the guardrail, he did not place the camera outside the car. Instead he shot a point-of-view from the passenger window angled down at the front tire nearly going off a cliff. As he'd explained, he kept the excitement within the vehicle."

Some of the chase was filmed at Angeles Crest Highway, in the summer heat. Cocooned within his requisite coat and tie, the 1st AD sweated out in the sun, while the director stayed cool in his air-conditioned vehicle.

One day Hitchcock asked Kazanjian to direct him in a commercial for Universal Studio Tours. "Tony drove us up the hill to the tour location and everything was ready, the camera crew, and they knew what they

157

10957 BELLAGIO ROAD, BEL-AIR, LOS ANGELES 24, CALIFORNIA

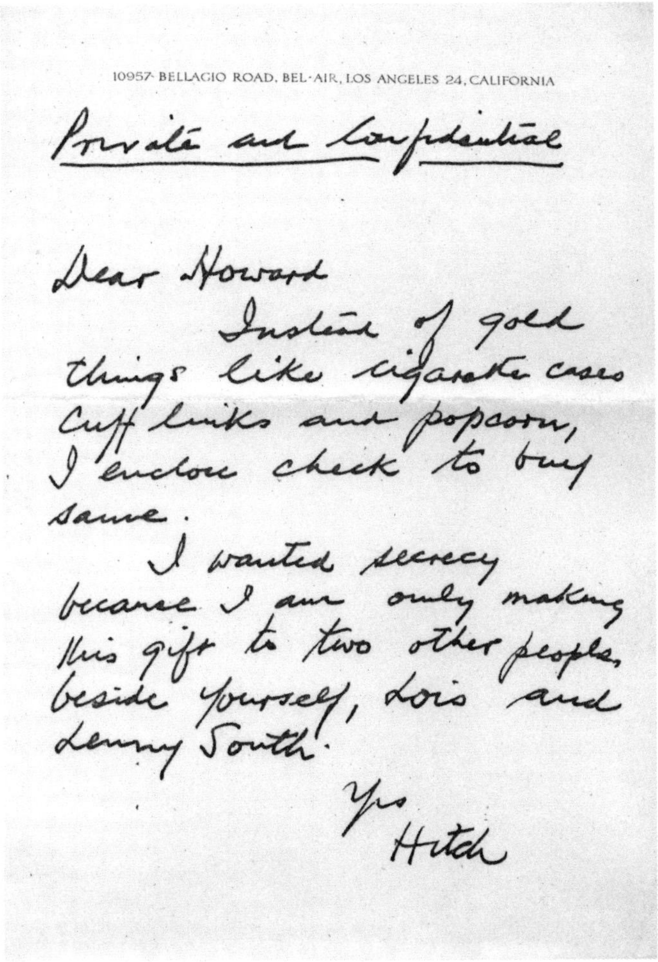

Private and Confidential

Dear Howard

Instead of gold things like cigarette cases cuff links and popcorn, I enclose check to buy same.

I wanted secrecy because I am only making this gift to two other people, beside yourself, Lois and Lenny South.

Yrs
Hitch

SEVENTH & OLIVE OFFICE
BANK OF AMERICA N.T. & S.A.
LOS ANGELES, CA 90014

ALFRED J. HITCHCOCK
10957 BELLAGIO ROAD
LOS ANGELES, CA 90024

№ 13709

July 22, 19 75

16-65
1220

PAY ONE THOUSAND and no/100 Only- DOLLARS $1,000.00

TO THE ORDER OF HOWARD KAZANJIAN

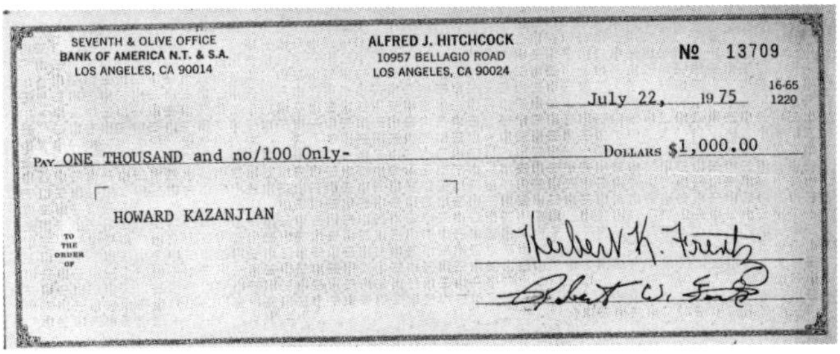

OPPOSITE, TOP TO BOTTOM: *Hitchcock gave a surprise birthday party to Kazanjian in "the pit," a semisubterranean stage at Universal (on right is 2nd AD Wayne Farlow). • Hitchcock tells a joke to Kazanjian, 2nd AD Farlow, and production manager Hilton A. Green on the set of* Family Plot *(note that on a Hitchcock set all executives are wearing suits and ties).*

ABOVE: *Hitchcock's letter explains his "secret" gift check of $1,000 to Kazanjian after wrapping* Family Plot. *Only two others received checks: script supervisor Lois Thurman and DP South.*

wanted," Kazanjian says. "But I became the one who said, 'Action,' and Hitch delivered the dialogue. He was a great actor, so I just watched him do his lines twice, and we drove back down the hill. This was one of two commercials I would see him make. Hitch wasn't thrilled about doing the commercials, but he had a great deal of stock in Universal." (They did another shot of the director on a tour tram with extras and one with his arms over his head like Superman. In the ad, Hitchcock would fly, sort of. A second commercial was filmed in front of the *Psycho* mansion on the Universal lot.) "He told me once, 'Howard, do you know that a little boy was born today that will never have to work?' It was the day his grandson was born."

Actress Karen Black married director L. M. Kit Carson on July 4, 1975, in Franklin Canyon Park. The invitation to the Kazanjians marked the time as "by dawn's early light." "I'm coming from Pasadena, so I didn't get there for the sunrise," Kazanjian recalls. "I got there shortly afterward, and they were having donuts. Later, for early lunch, hot dogs were served. The wedding was like a fair with cotton candy."

On July 26, production was on the set of Adamson's basement, where they kept their hostages, built on Stage 12. The only way to get to the floor of the set was via forklift. Kazanjian was informed by a security guard that he had a telephone call and ascended back up on the lift. When he returned, he found Hitchcock, production manager Hilton Green, DP Leonard South, storyboard artist Tommy Wright, and 2nd AD Wayne Farlow in the pit. Hitchcock had arranged a birthday cake for his protégé. "Cake, refreshments, all spread on two white linen tables," Kazanjian says. "In my entire career, my birthday has never been celebrated at work. But that's Hitchcock. To this day I marvel at Hitchcock taking a forklift ride.

"Most crewmembers felt Hitchcock was cold and unfriendly. I found him warm and fatherlike. There were times when he would pause and look at me with a slight smile. That was one of his ways of saying 'thank you.' Another way was when I would help him up a few stairs to his portable dressing room; holding my arm, he would give me a squeeze. That was his way."

On August 14, a blue page was inserted into the shooting script that gave the film a new title. The studio marketing department had abandoned "Deceit" because focus groups had said the word reminded them of extramarital affairs—and because Hitchcock also felt the word could refer to a bedroom situation of sex and deception. The film was rechristened *Family Plot*, a pun on the film's central mystery.

SOME RECOGNITION

Hitchcock wrapped *Family Plot* on August 18, 1975, about thirteen days over schedule, mostly because of the reshoots and the second trip to San Francisco.

A prominent magazine published a story written by someone who had visited the set, "that just ripped Hitchcock apart," Kazanjian recalls. "Said he was a drunk, that he was an alcoholic. I can tell you that Hitchcock, especially as he got older, kind of slurred his words, but he wasn't drunk. After Alma was very sick again, after the movie wrapped, he'd open his desk drawer and have a little glass of vodka late in the afternoon, but he was definitely not drinking while we were shooting. And he wasn't an alcoholic."

Special effects for the runaway car sequence also dragged a little when South had problems with the blue- or greenscreen. Despite the assistant director's warnings that the car wasn't lit brightly enough for the effect, when Kazanjian left production in September, they were still tinkering with it. Meanwhile, composer John Williams was writing the film score, but he and Kazanjian didn't meet. (Hitchcock and Kazanjian had screened *Jaws* during preproduction, which may have led to Williams being hired. This was the second film Kazanjian and Williams worked on without meeting.)

"More than anything, Hitchcock showed me that directing a film could be great personal fun without sacrificing artistic quality," Kazanjian says. "He is also the only director who really mentored me throughout the entire production."

The film was locked in editorial, scored, and mixed. Its last scene had Blanche (Harris) go into a kind of trance and find the film's

161

MacGuffin, a missing diamond, in a glass chandelier—making her partner believe she might actually be psychic. But in the film's last shot, Blanche looks directly at the audience, breaking the fourth wall, and winks. "Hitchcock said, 'After you see the movie you go home, open up the icebox, take out a chicken leg, and while you're eating it, you have *icebox* talk,'" Kazanjian says. "The scene and the wink were designed so the audience would go home and ask, 'How did she know that?' Hitchcock mentioned to me that Blanche might have overheard where the thieves had hidden the diamond while she was in the cellar hostage room; or she could have had a psychic moment, because it would've been very hard for her to hear, but maybe the intercom was left on. It created plausible deniability both ways. Hitchcock was saying to the audience, 'Work it out for yourself.' He did that by withholding the shot of her listening. He withheld that one piece of the jigsaw puzzle so you as the audience have to place it in.'"

On March 21, 1976, *Family Plot* opened the Filmex festival at Putt's Century Plaza Theatre in the ABC Entertainment Center, Century City. This black-tie prerelease world premiere was followed by a special "Filmex Society Salute to Alfred Hitchcock" at the Century Plaza Hotel (proceeds from the dual-event benefit went to Filmex). It was "a joint tribute to Hitchcock and to the American cinema," Arthur Knight, Kazanjian's former professor at USC, wrote in *Variety*. "In this Bicentennial year, I can't think of two American institutions more worthy of such a salute."

The review went on to say, "At 75, Hitchcock is still creative, still original, still enamored with the miracles that can be performed by the knowing juxtaposition of bits of celluloid. I don't think that *Family Plot* will ever be remembered as one of the great Hitchcocks . . . I am reminded more of the intimate, small scaled, black humors of *The Trouble with Harry* [1955]—a film that richly deserves exhumation and reevaluation. *Family Plot* is wholly without pretension. It was made to divert and entertain, and it does so to perfection."

On Monday, June 28, from 6:00 to 8:00 pm, the Kazanjians joined the Hitchcocks for a ceremony at Universal during which the Consul General of France and the French National Film Office

162

awarded the director that country's "Commandeur de l'Ordre National des Arts et Lettres."

For several months after the release of the film, Kazanjian dined occasionally with Mr. Hitchcock at his Universal office. The assistant director recalls, "One lunch he turned to me and asked me to call him 'Hitch.'"

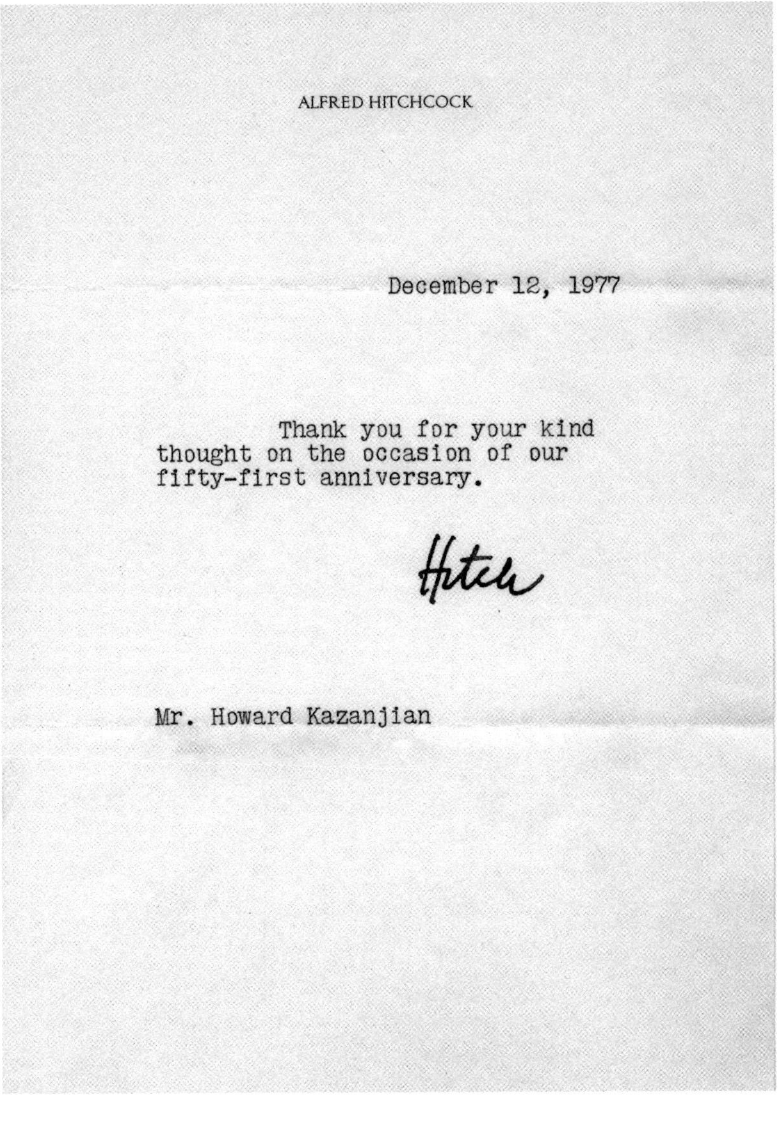

ALFRED HITCHCOCK

December 12, 1977

Thank you for your kind
thought on the occasion of our
fifty-first anniversary.

Hitch

Mr. Howard Kazanjian

Hitchcock's thank-you letter to Kazanjian. The two often
exchanged cards and notes in the years after Family Plot.

CHAPTER 9: *Joining the Rebels*
_____

K azanjian didn't go straight onto another film. "It got to a point where I said, 'I've had it. I've gotten the most out of being an assistant, I'm at the top, I'm quitting,'" Kazanjian remembers. "I said that to Hilton [Green]. But I also said, 'I'm not quitting the business— I'm quitting being an assistant director.' Hilton said, 'Don't leave. What do you want to do?'"

The former 1ˢᵗ AD told Green, also a former 1ˢᵗ AD, he wanted to direct and produce. Green told him to join the front office at Universal, "The Black Tower," the administration building built by Lew Wasserman. Kazanjian could assist Green and learn the ropes at the executive level. Kazanjian agreed and Universal elevated him to production manager, Green's assistant. Under Marshall and Hilton Green, the studio's top two production chiefs, he would assist on all theatrical films. Whenever Green was absent, Kazanjian, as production manager, would make decisions on production questions, budgets, and legal matters for all features in production. "Universal put the golden handcuffs on me: medical insurance, and so on," he says. "Working as an executive at Universal under Marshall and Hilton Green made the transition extremely smooth. I'd basically been doing much of the producing work as a first assistant director on several of my last films."

Kazanjian was being groomed to replace Hilton, and Hilton to replace his brother Marshall. He therefore turned down more offers to assistant direct, invitations from William Friedkin, who had just done *The French Connection* (1971) and *The Exorcist* (1973); and Mike Nichols, director of *The Graduate* (1967); and Elia Kazan on *The Last Tycoon* (1976). He also turned down George Lucas during this time, early 1976, when the director asked if he would be something like "unit manager" for a space fantasy called *The Star Wars*. Lucas's movie had just been greenlit by Alan Ladd Jr. at Fox. "When George pitched it to Ladd at 20th Century-Fox," Marcia Lucas recalls, "he said, 'I'm going to make a science fiction movie about the Dirty Dozen in outer space, which was George's original concept. He had all these despicable, crazy prisoners and miscreants, and they're going to get together and they're going to try to attack the Empire. He had everybody read [an early draft]. I mean everybody, all of his film school friends, and they all read it and everybody said, 'George, you need a gal. George, you need a woman in this movie.'"

Kazanjian had a meeting with Lucas and Gary Kurtz, who was producing, but he couldn't leave what promised to be a big job at Universal and people who were counting on him. He'd committed to it and didn't want to walk out. "George was offered several important pictures to direct after the success of *American Graffiti*," Kazanjian says. "But he chose to do his own thing and control his own destiny. Originally he wanted to remake *Flash Gordon*, but couldn't get the rights, so he decided to do his own Flash Gordon–type movie."

Lucas even gave up on his own project *Apocalypse Now*, in favor of *The Star Wars*. He'd cowritten the script for *Apocalypse* with John Milius, his old USC classmate; perhaps as compensation, he offered the writing job of *The Star Wars* to Milius, but that didn't happen. So Lucas went to work creating a universe populated by Jedi, evil warriors, and strange creatures called Wookiees. "My big malamute, Indiana, became Chewbacca," Marcia says, "because she used to sit in the passenger seat in my little Toyota Corolla station wagon, 3-speed on the floor. George always called her my furry copilot. When I'd gotten baby-crazy, George wanted to get me a puppy, and he loved these Alaskan malamutes. I looked at pictures of them, I said, 'Oh, they're so beautiful.'"

They found a breeder down on the peninsula and chose a puppy. Because the puppy was "Alaskan" Marcia wanted to find an appropriate Alaskan name. Not finding a place name to her liking, she decided to call the puppy an "Indian" with an "a" on the end—"Indiana"—and became the puppy's primary caregiver. "I wasn't going to name her

Nanook. That would be too cliché," Marcia says. "And George was close with her. He loved that dog. Indiana slept on our bed. Oh, she was a big furry lap dog."

For Kazanjian, office life soured after about six months. Lucas's offer had come at a bad time. Kazanjian might've accepted had Lucas asked only weeks later, for he was not at all happy doing a desk job. One day when both Marshall and Hilton Green were out of town at a USC-Notre Dame football game, director James Goldstone snuck in and offered Kazanjian a position as associate producer on his next Universal picture, *Rollercoaster* (1977). Kazanjian had come a long way since working as a trainee under Goldstone.

"I said, 'Let me think about it,'" he recalls. "Jim said, 'You can't think about it, you've got to make the decision right now.' He kept pushing and pushing. I knew Jennings Lang was the executive producer, the real producer on it, because he'd produced and I had worked with him on *The Front Page*. I called Jennings, and he said he'd let me run *Rollercoaster*, so I decided, 'Okay.' I threw off Universal's golden handcuffs and became an associate producer for Universal instead. I wasn't really leaving."

MARCIA STEPS IN

Lucas completed his script (with a dialogue polish by Huyck and Katz) and went on location to Tunisia to shoot out in the desert what was eventually called *Star Wars*. A freak storm destroyed part of the outside sets; his droids weren't functioning correctly; he was having problems with some of the crew and was worried about aspects of his film's story. "Of course, I had an editor-director relationship with George," Marcia says, "but I also had a husband-wife relationship with him. So, one night, we were getting ready for bed in Tunisia, after the day shoot, and George said, 'I can't believe this. I'm going to get laughed out of Hollywood.' The robots weren't working. The Jawas weren't working. He said, 'Nothing's working in my film,' and then he said, 'They go into the Death Star and everybody just runs out and jumps into the *Millennium Falcon* and flies away. Nobody's going to believe that.'

166

"He didn't say why, he just said that probably it's not going to work. I said I'd think about it. The next time we had a conversation around it, I said 'I have a good idea. What if Han Solo gets shot in the leg and Chewbacca has to carry him back.' But Peter Mayhew couldn't do that because he had bad legs. 'What if one of the robots get shot up?' 'No, no, no, no, the robots can't get shot up. My movie starts and ends with the robots.' I said, 'Well, what if Darth Vader strikes down Obi-Wan Kenobi?' He has nothing else to do at the end of the movie except stand in the war room with the rebels talking to Luke. George said, 'I think that'll work.'"

Marcia then sat at a typewriter at the hotel pool "writing this horrible dialogue," she says. " 'Once you were the master, now I'm the master.' And Obi-Wan says, 'If you strike me down, I'll become more powerful . . .' and I was just writing all of this silly dialogue."

In fact, Obi-Wan's statement about continuing in the afterlife—"If you strike me down, I'll become more powerful than you can possibly imagine"—was a result of Marcia's belief in "life after death," she explains. "I was born and raised Christian Science. I got out of the Christian Science religion when I was eleven or twelve, but I'd attended Christian Science Sunday school. Christian Scientists believe man is spiritual and not material. But I had to part ways with Christian Science because I believe we're spiritual beings in material bodies. We have material bodies that we have to take care of. So I didn't get along with them about not going to doctors, but that whole religion was a lot of 'we're spiritual beings' and I grew up with that. I'm a spiritual being, and so Obi-Wan was a Jedi Master and a spiritual being. That just made sense to me."

Back in the States, associate producer Kazanjian, Goldstone (primarily a TV director with a few feature film credits), production designer Bumstead, and unit manager Wally Worsley, scouted twenty-one parks in twenty-one days during *Rollercoaster*'s preproduction period. Many of the parks had two or three roller coasters, and they rode them all more than once, sitting in the front, back, and middle seats for the full experience. In Mexico City, the last stop before returning home, Goldstone and

167

Kazanjian climbed onto an old wooden roller coaster, which had more of a rocking feeling with better sound than the steel ones; Worsley and Bumstead chose to watch from the ground. As the script called for destroying a roller coaster, this location and ride was a possibility. "But as Jim and I rode the roller coaster, we could see boards shaking loose from their nails and a few flying off," Kazanjian says. "This was going to be a pass."

While flying back to Los Angeles, they could see fireworks going off in several cities celebrating July 4, 1976, the bicentennial anniversary of the United States. Before they started filming in September, Verna Fields (the Universal executive who seemed to be everywhere at this time, from editing Spielberg's *Jaws* to helping out on *American Graffiti* to, sort of, introducing Marcia and George Lucas) wrote a telegram to Kazanjian: "I know you'll be a wonderful producer, but I wish you any luck you may need. Love, Verna."

Rollercoaster was designed to fit into the disaster movie genre and to take advantage of a new sound system called "Sensurround," which had been used to great box-office success on *Earthquake* (1974) and *Midway* (1976). (The process made audiences feel low-frequency sounds in their guts rather than through their ears.) Goldstone cast George Segal and Timothy Bottoms as the hero and villain, respectively, and Richard Widmark, Henry Fonda, Helen Hunt, and Susan Strasberg in featured cameo roles. The poster promised that the movie would be "a suspense drama of the sort that Alfred Hitchcock does best." (A mad bomber targets hapless riders . . .)

Production selected a roller coaster at Ocean View Park, Norfolk, Virginia, and another in the same state. For the film's climax, they traveled to Magic Mountain (now Six Flags Magic Mountain) in Valencia, California, where the Great American Revolution roller coaster was filmed in action. While producing, Kazanjian met an eager young man from San Francisco named Louis G. Friedman. Friedman had made a dozen or so amateur short films as a kid and wanted to work in Hollywood. He'd tracked down Kazanjian through a cousin in the jewelry business. "We got along great," Friedman says. "Howard and I connected on several levels. We're both anal retentive neat freaks, which

CLOCKWISE FROM TOP LEFT: *For the disaster genre flick* Rollercoaster *(1977), Kazanjian test-rides the rollercoaster "Rebel Yell." • DP David Walsh sits with Kazanjian on location for* Rollercoaster *in Richmond, Virginia. • Director Jim Goldstone looks through the Panavision camera during an evidently pleasant pause, judging by the smiles of Kazanjian and 1ˢᵗ AD Andy Stone.*

is almost a prerequisite for doing physical management in film."

The producer couldn't offer Friedman a job at that time, but they stayed in touch.

MANUFACTURED STRESS

Both *Star Wars* and *Rollercoaster* were in postproduction simultaneously; Kazanjian would occasionally talk with Lucas, who was editing his film, among myriad tasks, with Marcia, Paul Hirsch, and Richard Chew. In post on *Rollercoaster*, the Sensurround process was married to scenes of roller coasters tearing along. Circa late January 1977, Lucas was down south doing post sound on his own film. "When we were mixing *Rollercoaster* at Goldwyn Studios," Kazanjian says, "George came in and watched us mix a little bit because he was having problems getting day mixing. He took over our room after we left for the day, so I would see George during that time. He was bouncing around several places, ILM, editing up north." ("ILM" was short for "Industrial Light & Magic," Lucas's visual effects facility in Van Nuys, not far from Los Angeles.)

Jennings Lang, who had become one of the more powerful executives at Universal-MCA, asked Kazanjian to be his assistant, but he declined. "Still Jennings was the first to tell people I had 'produced' two of his pictures for him, *Rollercoaster* and *The Front Page*," Kazanjian says. "Well, I really didn't. Solely from a production standpoint, I did, but not from a creative one."

Then a problem arose in relation to Kazanjian's credit. His original agreement with Lang had been a promised "Associate Producer" credit. "When the picture was finished," Kazanjian adds, "Jennings thanked me for the fine job done, but said another person (who may have given him the idea) had also been promised the Associate Producer credit, so I would have to share credit with him or take another credit. I didn't want to share, so we decided on Executive in Charge of Production. Then Marshall Green strongly said no. We wound up with Production Executive."

The mix-up rankled. At that moment Lucas asked Kazanjian for a fourth time to come join him. In March or April the old classmates lunched together, and Kazanjian says, "While we were both having a hamburger and a glass of milk on the noisy side of the studio commissary, like two little kids, he asked me to produce the sequel to *American Graffiti*. Now remember, I was to do *The Rain People* with Coppola and George; then I couldn't do *The Godfather*, couldn't do *THX 1138*, *American Graffiti*, or *Star Wars*. I told him that absolutely I would do the sequel to *Graffiti*, which would be a Universal picture. But George had to do something for me. He had to go see Ned Tanen, who had become president of Universal's theatrical motion picture division, and have him be the one that put me on the project. Let him get the credit! George agreed. He also said that he really didn't want to do the sequel, but if he didn't do it, Universal was going to do it without him. He owed them the film contractually. He said, 'It might be better if we did it together.'"

Lucas went to see Tanen. (Tanen happened to be the same executive who had taken *American Graffiti* away from Lucas and recut it, and who had also made it almost impossible to release *Graffiti*, getting into a famous argument with Coppola after a sneak preview. With Lucas watching, Coppola had offered to buy *Graffiti* from Tanen/the studio, who wanted to release it as a TV movie.) Tanen had also turned down *Star Wars*, but he'd had many successes at the studio and would be known for promoting young talent. A year earlier, he'd told Kazanjian that he would try to find a producing job for him. So when Lucas asked Tanen to make Kazanjian the producer on the *Graffiti* sequel, Tanen agreed, not knowing that Kazanjian had already verbally agreed to do it. Kazanjian had felt it was the right thing to do: Tanen and Universal would get the kudos for his promotion to full producer.

"Certain things had to be worked out at the studio," Kazanjian says. "Ned gave his blessing, and in a way, Universal thinks that they helped me to become a producer, which is fine. It was the polite thing to do. It wasn't me quitting, it was me just moving over to another Universal picture. But I knew what the future held for me at Lucasfilm, because George and I had discussed this." Even though the sequel was going to be a Universal picture, Kazanjian became at this moment a de facto Lucasfilm producer, about six weeks before *Star Wars* was to be released.

171

Lucas had suffered and fought for his space fantasy film, but thought he'd be lucky if it broke even at the box office; *Star Wars* had experienced many problems, and gone over schedule and over budget.

"*Star Wars* was a lock," Marcia says. "The work print was locked and we were waiting for visual effects to replace all the WWII footage when Marty Scorsese called me. He was making a film called *New York, New York* with Robert De Niro and Liza Minnelli and his editor, an older editor, had died of a heart attack. Marty asked me if I'd come down and help him. I said, 'I don't know; I think I've done everything I need to do on *Star Wars*—let me check with George.' George said, 'The film is great. We've locked the picture. John Williams is doing music. Effects are coming in. Yeah, you can go help Marty.'"

However, at a screening of *Star Wars* for Lucas's filmmaker friends—Spielberg, De Palma, Matthew Robbins, Hal Barwood, the Huycks, critic Jay Cocks, and a few people from ILM—"Brian De Palma came out," Marcia recalls, "and said, 'George, you gotta get rid of that Force shit. That's terrible. It doesn't work.' He didn't like 'May the Force be with you.' And he's a boisterous, loud guy. He didn't understand the black-and-white World War II temporary footage. He didn't get what that was all about—he just didn't get it."

According to Marcia, because Hirsch had been and would be De Palma's editor and because she was away cutting *New York, New York*, some edits to the film were made. She remembers: "I came back one weekend and we were having another screening of the film and all of a sudden, 'May the Force be with you' is cut out of the film three or four times—even when Harrison says it to Luke in the hangar before the big battle—Luke walks away and Harrison says, 'Hey kid, may the Force be with you'—they cut that out. Paul was the one who cut it out with George. I was really pissed. I distinctly remember having a fit: 'George, you cannot take that out of the film. You've got to put it back in here. It's got to be there. You've got to put it back in here.' That was a crisis. I said, 'It's going back in *there*, it's going back in *here*.' When all the pilots are getting into the planes, Princess Leia said to them, 'May the Force be with you'—that one stayed out, but I think all the others came back in."

Marcia Lucas felt that the sentiment had to stay because it was part of the film's spiritual side. "Oh, absolutely. Absolutely," she says. "The whole Jedi Knights, it was everything that they were about."

| Editing Run

| "George asked me if I'd cut *Star Wars*," says Marcia Lucas, "and I said sure, I would love to do it, because I wasn't pregnant. I have nothing to do. I'll work on the movie; so we started cutting." She began by reediting an assembly cut that had been kluged together by an English editor (who was not asked to complete the film). The film was in such "bad" shape that Marcia had to "reconstitute back to dailies." She recalls of the film's beginning: "That kitten thing George told me about—you can create a villain, have him kill a kitten. Well, the rebel officer in the ship was the little kitten Darth Vader kills by breaking his neck, so immediately you know Darth Vader is a bad dude."

Among other tasks, Marcia Lucas worked on problematic desert shots of the droids and R2-D2's capture by the Jawas. In the assembly, this moment had been edited as: the Jawas jump up and shoot the droid, which falls over; they then pick him up and carry him to the Sandcrawler vehicle. "I was looking at the dailies on it," she says, "and these Jawas are looking weird and I thought, *They should shoot him, then they should look and see if it worked. Then we should get big electric currents around him—then he should fall over slow and they should surround him.* When you're editing, you have ideas."

She also cut the laser sword fight between Obi-Wan and Vader. "George came to me a few weeks in and said, 'You have to work on the end battle. ILM needs that scene cut yesterday.'" That was the big assignment—the climax of the film. Richard Chew was also already editing, but they weren't going to meet the schedule, so Marcia

173

recommended bringing in Paul Hirsch, who had cut for their friend director Brian De Palma. George Lucas agreed and she got to work on the end battle.

At ILM, Joe Johnston and others were storyboarding this complex sequence—but their boards were to a large extent based on the cut Marcia was putting together using her husband's World War II 16mm footage (footage that he'd already cut together to give ILM an idea of what the space battles would look like). She recalls, "I kept having to make more and more dupes of this World War II footage, because I didn't have enough planes, enough POVs, enough explosions. Or enough planes going right to left, going left to right, planes going up, planes crashing. I was working with a shooting script and had the pilots in the cockpits, which they'd shot against the greenscreen. I had Tarkin on the Death Star. I had the rebel war room with the general and Leia and Threepio. Everything that was a special effects shot, I cut in from the black-and-white World War II footage, antiaircraft guns shooting at them . . .

"So, we had three editors and George would leave every Monday morning and go to ILM and be gone all week. Come home on Friday night or Saturday morning; I was left with the editors to edit it. I was kind of communicating to Paul what I thought was needed from certain scenes, and I'd tell Richard maybe this is what we should try to do with this scene, and I was stuck in that end battle. And then—I don't remember who came up with it—it might have been Paul or I might have said, 'I need a lot of built-in tension here. I need all the tension I can get because Darth Vader's on Luke's tail, and all his rebels are getting blown up,' and Paul said, 'If we had a time limit . . .' and I said, 'A time limit would be great.'"

They decided that the Death Star would be minutes, then seconds away from destroying the rebel base, the rebels, and the rebellion—a plot element that

174

Marcia realized could be manufactured completely in editorial—"because we had all the shots of the Death Star getting ready to fire up and destroy Princess Leia's planet of Alderaan. We have Tarkin watching the battle. We could create the tension from the footage we had. Then ILM made a visual [an illustrated graphic] that showed the Death Star rounding the planet to get in position to make the shot to blow up the rebel moon."

It was a huge effort to get it all to work—the X-wings, TIE fighters, Leia, the droids, the voice of Kenobi, Luke and Vader and the pilots in their cockpits, Tarkin, etc.—but they pulled it off, with ILM basing its shots on Marcia's edit. The end battle ultimately became one of the most seminal film sequences in the history of cinema, an almost musical piece that would withstand and even demand multiple viewings.

THRILL RIDES

Lucasfilm "South" consisted of two small offices on the Universal lot, left over from the production of *American Graffiti*, which Kurtz used whenever he was in town. His assistant Bunny Alsup was also his sister-in-law. The Lucases lived up north, in San Anselmo, Marin County, where they owned several satellite offices (located in houses and downtown buildings). Lucas's visual effects company, Industrial Light & Magic, as mentioned, was holed up in a warehouse in Van Nuys, not far from 20th Century-Fox Studios. Kazanjian made a trip up north to meet the Lucasfilm staff of about a half-dozen people. "The very first person I met when I walked in the door was Lucy Wilson," he says. "Lucy was number one, the first employee. She started in 1974, and was George's trusted all-around assistant. In the main house, 'Parkway,' Gary Kurtz had an office in the back, but he was never there. George had his office, which was the dining room. Lucy was in an enclosed sun deck porch area. The sound man, Ben Burtt, was in the basement. Above his screening room was George's writing room. It had a beautiful, stone fireplace. The theater was in Art Deco–style. He could show 35mm and 16mm."

175

Parkway was also home to Lucas's filmmaker friends, such as Michael Ritchie, who had recently directed *The Bad News Bears* (1976), and Carroll Ballard, who would direct *The Black Stallion* (1979). Across the bay was Saul Zaentz, whose Fantasy Films had produced *One Flew Over the Cuckoo's Nest* (1975) and was working on an animated version of Tolkien's *The Lord of the Rings* (1978); in San Francisco, Coppola was editing *Apocalypse Now*. The Bay Area filmmaking community was experiencing a creative boom. Lucas was also developing *Radioland Murders*, a screwball comedy set in the 1930s, with writers Willard Huyck and Gloria Katz, part of his three-picture deal at Universal. (The couple had helped polish scripts for both *Graffiti* and *Star Wars*.)

"Howard was nicest of all the producers and a breath of fresh air," says Lucy Wilson. Kurtz was liked overall by staff and crew, but had a mixed reputation with some. Sound designer Ben Burtt recalls: "When Howard came on board, suddenly there was this fellow that was very friendly and outgoing, who was much more personable right away. Howard was a different personality; it was much easier to make friends with Howard than it had been with Gary. Gary taught me a lot about the mechanisms of filmmaking, because he liked to explain things. Gary liked to share the technical information, and you listened. It was kind of a tutorial. I thought Gary was a great producer. But he was the boss. You always felt like you were on guard a bit with him, because he didn't give you a lot of feedback to let you know how things stood.

"Howard was much more engaged, asking you, 'How are you? What's going on? How's your family?' Always, Howard was, I felt, much more of a person I could talk to about the people on the crew, the social aspects of things we were doing. He was more interested in a relationship that you would normally develop, a friendship. He was closer to us in many ways."

"Of course, I already knew her, but I met Marcia again," Kazanjian says. "But it was mainly just Lucy and George. And then we had Duwayne Dunham and a few others who were hired to run errands and polish cars and do things like that, at least in the beginning."

176

Director Goldstone suggested that his core Rollercoaster team have their pictures taken with joke T-shirts stating their production "slogans/ mottos" as a gag, front and back. So while on location at Six Flags Great America in Richmond, Virginia, Kazanjian and a few identifiable crew posed for the shoot: (top row) Wally Worsley (unit manager; "over years of penny pinching"), Goldstone ("well, keep up your end"), Kazanjian ("the great Kazanjian"); (second row) David Sosna (2nd AD; "no cross too big or small"); L. Andrew Stone (1st AD; "if it's background it's got to be quality"); Peter Burrell (2nd AD, "our speciality is stand-ins"), to name a few.

177

"The company was really small and really brand new," Duwayne Dunham recalls. "It was already exciting. The whole Bay Area was making movies that were groundbreaking—it was an extraordinary moment in time."

"I was glad to see Howard," Marcia says. "I mean, I liked Gary Kurtz. Gary Kurtz did a good job. He did *Graffiti*. He did *Star Wars*. Gary got a little ego-ed out. Yeah, he did. You know, some of people get to feel like their self-importance is bigger than it really is."

On May 25, 1977, *Star Wars* was released on thirty-two screens in 70mm with stereo sound. Back in Hollywood, Lucas was still working on the mono version for the wide release and had literally forgotten about its limited opening. While eating a hamburger with Marcia across the street from Grauman's Chinese Theatre, he was shocked to see huge lines snaking down the sidewalk for his film.

"By the time we'd finished *Star Wars*, it had practically killed George, really," says Miki Herman, Lucas's production assistant at ILM. "He was like a hospital case. It was so much stress, so he went to Hawaii with Marcia after finishing the mono soundtrack, and they didn't even know that the film was such a success." On the island during the film's wide release, Lucas talked about an idea he had for an adventure movie with Steven Spielberg. Meanwhile, Fox telexed daily box-office reports.

By late June, *Star Wars* had become a phenomenon.

"I knew the movie worked and I felt it was going to be popular," says Marcia. "I felt it was going to appeal to a lot more than ten-year-old boys—but the international scope—it crossed over international lines, it was embraced by religions, it crossed races, everybody around this planet saw that movie, loved that movie. Who knew? Who knew that it was going to have that kind of impact?"

"I loved *Star Wars*," says Randal Kleiser. "I was in the theater when they showed it for the very first time—and when the spaceship came across the top of the frame at the very beginning, the audience screamed! It was so fun to be a part of that. It was very vocal. The crew was seeing it for the first time, and some of the public was there, and VIPs. It was one of the most amazing screenings I've ever been to because of the reaction to it."

"I didn't go to the premier," Kazanjian says. "I wanted to take my wife and stand in line and see it with a regular audience. It was incredible! The instant Darth Vader broke into the ship, the audience booed and screamed. It was soon after the picture opened, so I wasn't sure if the audience had already seen it, or if they just knew instinctively that the towering figure with 'the black hat' was the heavy evil one."

That same month *Rollercoaster* was released. Though not on a par with Lucas's film (nothing was), it did well. The *Variety* review read: "With an earthquake and a war under its belt, many felt Universal had exhausted the possible applications of its sound development, Sensurround. But now there is *Rollercoaster*, and the physical aural effect achieved by the gimmick is as chilling, frightening, and perversely appealing as, well, a ride on the Coney Island Steeplechase. Jennings Lang's production utilizes the device to its maximum and that alone should give the pic good word of mouth and sturdy legs."

But the new king of Hollywood and of movies worldwide was Lucas's quirky space fantasy—a true amusement park ride that teens and kids wanted to take over and over and over. *Star Wars* changed everything in the industry, from pace and storytelling, to visual effects and sound. Lucasfilm had a bright future—and Kazanjian was now a part of it.

TALENT SEARCH

On July 1, Kazanjian began preproduction on the untitled sequel to *American Graffiti*. Three days later, Lucasfilm—all seven employees, more or less—celebrated one of its first Fourth of July picnics, a concept dreamed up by Marcia Lucas. Gary Kurtz may have been there, but most of the time he was abroad, doing the legwork to line up crew and logistics for the *Star Wars* sequel. In Los Angeles, Lucas would squat in their small office on the lot while preparing his two sequels and *Radioland Murders*. "I must say Universal treated us very shabbily—and I was a Universal guy," Kazanjian says. "Eventually the studio gave us a three-office trailer, which was *still* too small."

"I stayed in contact with Howard, and then I had a call from him," Louis Friedman says. "He had been hired by George Lucas and they were going to shoot the sequel to *Graffiti* up in San Francisco, my hometown. So Howard asked me if I wanted to be his assistant and a PA."

Lucas told Kazanjian the basics of the story he had in mind. Like the original *Graffiti*, the sequel would follow several story strands: One would take place in San Francisco; another unfolded on the campus of the University of California, Berkeley. Though they doubted they could shoot on that particular campus, they planned to film on locations. No sets. Kazanjian, with art director Ray Storey (recommended by Kurtz) and unit manager Tom Joyner, went on several recces (scouting trips). Their primary base up north was at Parkway in San Anselmo. "It was the first studio production I had ever worked on, so it was very exciting," Friedman says. "It was up in San Francisco, a town that I was intimately familiar with. I went up there early on with Ray Storey, and helped lead him around in terms of places to see and people to meet."

Another story strand, that of Toad (Charles Martin Smith), would take place in Vietnam, so a suitable stand-in for that country had to be found. They looked at the Stockton and the Napa Valley areas and decided on the former.

Kazanjian also crewed up, interviewing dozens of people. Because Lucas, like Coppola, wanted to build up the San Francisco film community, Kazanjian's instructions were to hire as many San Francisco–based people as possible. Only Storey and Joyner, ultimately, came out of Hollywood. The producer knew that this tactic would create challenges down the road. A crew made up of locals would lack experience, for the most part. He had preliminary meetings with the two local unions as well, one on each side of the Golden Gate Bridge.

He was also on the lookout for a screenwriter, someone who understood both the *Graffiti* characters and their California milieu. Kazanjian read hundreds of scripts. "George and I had several meetings, both in Los Angeles and San Francisco, about what we wanted to do in the sequel," Kazanjian says. "We sat down and we started talking about concept. Eventually we came up with the idea that we would do two sequels. One, carrying the *American Graffiti* title, which Universal or

George wanted to call *More American Graffiti*—we were never really happy with the title—which would star Paul Le Mat [John] and be nearly all about drag racing and a new girl that he falls in love with, and Charles Martin Smith [Toad] in Vietnam.

"The second one was going to have some of the other characters—and Richard Dreyfuss [Curt]. Dreyfuss would be a conscientious objector and run away to Canada and become a journalist and write about the war. He'd write about whatever the other cast members around him were doing, women's lib, the 1960s. It would maybe or not have a title related to *American Graffiti*. We'd film the two movies back-to-back."

There was more discussion on whether the title should be "More American Graffiti" or "American Graffiti 2" and the former won out.

Lucas reiterated that he felt the writer had to be someone who'd been young in the 1960s and had experienced some of the things he wanted in the screenplay. Lucas didn't have the time or inclination to write the script himself. He was also going to hire a writer for the *Star Wars* sequel. Lists were made up. "We were open to recommendations," Kazanjian says. "Many of them were in the right age group; some were older. They came from all over the country, but we really felt it was better to get a writer from the Southern California area who had lived the *American Graffiti* life as opposed to someone who was raised in Brooklyn and never had a car or went to a drive-in. That isn't to say we didn't read those scripts or consider some of those writers. We did. We were also looking for comedy writers."

SERIAL ADVENTURES

With possibly two films to cast, Kazanjian made phone calls to actors' agents to see if they were available and "approximately how much money we were talking about," he says. "We did not want to do multi-multimillion-dollar pictures." The original actors were excited about the sequels. Ron Howard (Steve) and Cindy Williams (Laurie) were both starring on hit TV shows, *Happy Days* (1974–1984) and *Laverne & Shirley* (1976–1983), respectively, but production could schedule around them. They could be written out of a couple episodes if need be. One

181

of the finest casting directors in the business, Fred Roos, who had helped cast the original, came on board to advise on candidates for the new characters, which led to more interviews. Some were asked to read.

"We were able to get the complete cast back with the exception of Richard Dreyfuss," Kazanjian says. "He had recently been in *The Goodbye Girl* [1977] and was a big star and didn't want to be in a sequel. Even with George offering him the separate picture, he wouldn't do it." Harrison Ford said yes, though only for a cameo. With Dreyfuss out, the sequel concepts were reduced to a single film, featuring Paul Le Mat and drag races, Ron Howard and Cindy Williams, Charles Martin Smith in Vietnam, and Candy Clark (Debbie), who was promoted to her own storyline.

As of November, they had yet to find a writer. On the other hand, Lucas had hired Leigh Brackett, a veteran Hollywood scribe and novelist, to script the *Star Wars* sequel (her previous credits included *The Big Sleep*, 1946; *El Dorado*, 1966; and others). That film's treatment was dated November 28, 1977, and titled *The Empire Strikes Back*. "George talked to me about *Star Wars* episodes seven, eight, and nine way back in the beginning, when he was talking about episodes one, two, three," Kazanjian says. "Episodes four, five, and six were like World War II, he would say. The prequels were World War I. He didn't have an outline for episode six, nor had he figured out what seven, eight, and nine would be. At that time, he wanted to make a total of twelve."

Kazanjian attended the first meetings for *Empire* at the Universal offices with Lucas, illustrator Ralph McQuarrie, and ILM art director Joe Johnston, who were already busy drawing up concepts based on Lucas's ideas. "Ralph was the sweetest man that could be," Miki Herman says. "And he'd done a lot of things that he didn't really want to do for George, like matte paintings. He did anything that George asked him to do."

"Ralph was an extremely quiet and an almost shy person," Kazanjian says, "but friendly and extremely talented. He could almost walk past you and not be seen. Just after Ralph brought in some conceptual designs for us to look at and approve, George told me to watch and learn and pay close attention. He hadn't been happy with

182

Gary Kurtz on the first film. In fact, some of George and Gary Kurtz's closest friends told George it was a mistake to hire Gary back, so George insisted I be in every *Empire* meeting. George told me to get very involved because I would be producing the third *Star Wars* film. Gary, of course, did not know this. And George was building his empire at that time."

"There were two sides going on," Duwayne Dunham says. "There was Lucasfilm, which was starting to grow very quickly, and then there were the other movies. With George, we were working on the sequel to *Graffiti*, a little bit of *Empire*, and *Radioland Murders*. We were working on multiple projects at the same time, everything overlapped. It was just nonstop action."

Wanting to get in on that action and profit from Lucas's skyrocketing fame, Warner Bros. offered to rerelease *THX 1138*. They promised to put back scenes the studio had cut. Lucas agreed and asked Kazanjian to oversee the project, which included a new sound mix. He did as told, but the movie's fall 1977 rerelease didn't do any business of note. Universal was planning to reconstitute *American Graffiti* along the same lines; that studio also wanted to put back the scenes that had been cut and rerelease it.

Meanwhile Lucas was dropping hints about the adventure movie he'd pitched to Spielberg, who had been receptive. "George told me he had a secret project," Kazanjian says. "It's always good to let people know you have a secret project. Of course, with George, everything had to be secret. Later, he told me a little bit about some sort of action-adventure movie he had in mind." Lucas divulged more about his secret project as months went by, about things he'd already discussed with Spielberg in Hawaii. He asked Kazanjian to arrange evening screenings of old serials at Universal, because Kazanjian had access to the studio's projection rooms. "It became clearer what George wanted to do," he says.

Sometimes they'd watch only two or three serial episodes (depending on how long they were); other times they'd watch all twelve episodes of a serial, such as *Spy Smasher* (1942). Lucas told Kazanjian to screen more on his own, but didn't elaborate beyond that. Occasionally, director John Milius would join them, or filmmakers Hal Barwood and Matthew Robbins, if they were in town. "Some of our friends would come by, but there'd generally be only two or three in the theater," Kazanjian says. "I had to be there. If George was there, he'd say, 'That's an interesting effect; that's a good one.'"

Spielberg introduced screenwriter Lawrence Kasdan to Lucas. "Larry was going to write something for Steven and it fell through," Kazanjian says. "I recall the day that Steven introduced Larry to George and myself, we were in our office preparing *More American Graffiti* and talking about *Radioland Murders* as the next project."

Lucas eventually hired Kasdan to write his secret adventure movie.

MINI ARMAGEDDON

Preproduction on the *Graffiti* sequel ping-ponged between the Universal trailer and San Anselmo. To shore up operations in Los Angeles, Lucas purchased property from the Olson Farms Egg Company in January 1978 (after passing on an eight-story building in Glendale). The compound was situated across the street from Universal at 3855 Lankershim Blvd, North Hollywood. Carol Kazanjian, who was a real estate agent, had asked if the owners were willing to sell, and they were. (Universal had offered to purchase the property several times, but did not handle negotiations properly, reported Mr. Olson.)

The location, destined to be Lucasfilm HQ south, came to be known as the Egg Company. "It was a big brick shell and it had been the Olson Egg Company," Marcia Lucas says. "When I was growing up, my grandfather, one of the jobs he had, was egg candler at that same company. Candlers used to hold eggs up in front of flames to see if they were fertile or not. If you had a fertile egg, it didn't pass the grade. So when we bought that building, that's why it got called the Egg Company because of my connection with my grandfather, who worked there for the Olsons."

Before anyone could move in, Lucas planned to bankroll a massive renovation of its brick interior and exterior. Trailers were set up in the parking lot as temp offices, while the building was completely overhauled. "At that time, we were trying to construct Camelot," says Kazanjian (who knew something about the place). "George never used the term

184

'Camelot'; I did, and that was the direction we were going. If you're a historian, you know Camelot can't exist and it doesn't and it didn't, but we were trying. And Marcia was very instrumental in designing the Egg Company interior."

"George would go down to LA and work with the architects," Marcia says. "Then he'd get home, and moan and groan, 'They're not getting me. They don't understand what I want. They want everything to look like a prison. They want to do this real high-tech industrial look.' So I said, 'Give me a shot and I'll go down and meet with these people.' He turned it over to me and I worked with the architects and we did the interior design."

"Oh, together George and Marcia had incredible taste," Carol Kazanjian says. "Their taste dovetailed. They would have such and such furniture, then they'd have a Norman Rockwell painting; they matched all the furniture and coverings, everything. It was over the top. Marcia was also George's social ticket. She was intelligent, beautiful, and she loved people."

At an auction Marcia bought antique bevel glass doors, which were then used between the entrance and the secretary's office and lounge inside. "George and I were definitely on the same wavelength," she says. "I didn't want the metal railings. I made wooden railings. I didn't want these light fixtures in cages. It did look like a prison. I had them use green sconces with green shades. I painted the walls dark forest green to contrast with the light pine. And I could communicate to the architect and the designer who worked for the architect. She got it. She got me."

By that time, *Star Wars* merchandise, books and records and toys and so on, was ramping up, supervised by Charles Lippincott, who had masterminded the marketing and release of the first film in conjunction with Fox. Kazanjian knew him from the USC days and had worked with Lippincott when he was unit publicist on *Family Plot*. "It was really Charlie that got the merchandising going," Kazanjian says. "He was George's premier, head guy. And when we started expanding, Charlie was given the opportunity to pick one of those areas. George said, 'Charlie, you can be vice president of merchandise. We'll start that division.' But Charlie wanted marketing and PR. He said, 'I want it all, like I've done in the past.' I don't know if Charlie was stubborn or if he didn't understand the potential the company had. And so Charlie left the company. Charlie was not fired; he left the company because he wanted to do it all as he did on *Star Wars* when the company was small. Now George was thinking of a real company with a president, vice president, VP of marketing, VP of merchandising, and so on."

On one of the trips north, Kazanjian and Lucas went to visit American Zoetrope. The editing crew, headed by Walter Murch, was cutting *Apocalypse Now*, but Coppola was absent. A while later he arrived with his arm in a cast and a sling. It turned out that he'd recently pounded on a table so hard, to make a point, that he'd broken a bone. He invited them over to view a scene on a flatbed editing table and they watched Marlon Brando "pontificating," Kazanjian says. "The scene went on for a full ten minutes. Francis said he didn't know what to cut or cut away to."

Back down south, Kazanjian had Louis Friedman work with Kurtz to set up a video system to record auditions for *More American Graffiti*. "The Egg Company had not yet been converted into the Egg Company, it was still Olson Farms Egg, although they had moved out," Friedman says. "I went and rented some furniture, which we set up in an upstairs room. We put a Lowell light kit up, and I ran the video camera for all of the casting sessions. Fred Roos was there also. He brought in a few actors and actresses. Gary was a very technical kind of guy. I learned a lot from him, in terms of approaching something in a very pragmatic and technical fashion."

Some of the actors were put on tape twice, as Lucas narrowed down the choices.

"George talked to me often about his goals and how big he thought the company would be," Kazanjian says. "He was talking about himself as a filmmaker and the types of films he wanted to do after the *Star Wars* trilogy: personal, small pictures."

STRANGER THAN FICTION

In late 1977, Lucas was debating who to hire as president of his company. "George came to me one day and said he was down to two candidates," Kazanjian recalls. "One he described as a General Motors type, a Wall Street executive; the other was a robust, jovial executive. George couldn't decide between the two and he was asking me my opinion [laughs]. I gave him my opinion, but I hadn't met either of the individuals. My opinion was to go with the lower-key person, because I thought that's what Lucasfilm was all about. It's always been low-key, quiet, no pushing here. George picked the Wall Street type instead, who was Charlie Weber. Now, I'm not saying that was wrong; I might have done the same had I met the two. And then George suggested to Charlie: 'We need a vice president, so why don't you consider the man that was running against you?' And that's how John Moohr came into the picture."

Weber was the first president of Lucasfilm; John Moohr became vice president of finance and administration. Lucas made Kazanjian vice president of Medway Productions, the subsidiary for Lucasfilm's non–*Star Wars* movies; Kurtz was vice president of *Star Wars* Productions.

"George never knew how to interview people," says Jane Bay, who started as Lucas's executive assistant that fall. "He just had a gut feeling about people. In the beginning he went to his alma mater. He hired people that he had known at USC, so Lucasfilm was like a Northern California branch of the class that George and Howard were in, in LA. Howard was part of the beginning of the founding of the company. They were very close because they were schoolmates, they had a camaraderie that George didn't have with other people, not even with Gary. Howard and George had their own little connection that none of the rest of us had. I would say George was very close to Howard, as close as George would ever allow himself to be or anybody to be with him. Very close."

"I always had a very strong feeling that all of your employees need to be compensated," says Marcia Lucas, "especially when we got rich. Because *Star Wars* money starts rolling in and now we're going to make another *Star Wars* movie that we're going to finance. I said, 'If we're financing a movie, we need profit sharing for all these people that work for us.' And George said, 'Yes, I think we should.' I said one thing that's

Carol Kazanjian and Marcia Lucas during the early years at Lucasfilm's northern HQ, Parkway house, in San Anselmo, California.

going to have to happen with the profit sharing is not the CEO, not the CFO, not the producers, we're going to make this profit sharing depend on how long you've worked for Lucasfilm—that's it. If the janitor's been here longer, he gets a bigger piece of the pie. If the bookkeeper's been here longer, she's going to be getting a bigger piece of the pie. George said, 'You're right. We can do that. I don't have a problem with that.' See, George really has a good heart."

In more meetings on *More American Graffiti*, Lucas and Kazanjian talked about how to film their four stories, though a writer had yet to be found. "Most of us had seen the Vietnam War on television in the handheld-camera 16mm documentary style," Kazanjian explained in 1979, before the film came out. "We thought we would continue that for [our] Vietnam sequence and intercut stock footage with what we shot.

"One night George and I were standing in the trailers at the window looking out and talking about using a split-screen on the Candy Clark character. At that time we were talking about a 1.85:1 picture, not Panavision, not anamorphic. But then we were saying maybe the picture should be Panavision, because *Graffiti* was wide-screen and people like wide-screen and some of the stories would lend themselves better to wide-screen. So we talked about optically blowing up the Vietnam part to fit. I said, 'What would happen if we shot the drag racing in Panavision, Vietnam in 16mm, and shot each of the other two stories in a different aspect ratio?' George didn't say yes or no at that time. It was such a weird suggestion on my part."

THE SWINGING '60s
From January 23 to 27, 1978, Lucas and Spielberg met with their writer, Lawrence Kasdan, at a house in San Anselmo to brainstorm on the secret serial-style project. The idea was that Kasdan would take the transcripts of their taped conversations and turn them into a first draft screenplay (based on a Lucas treatment). Out of those talks, the hero's name changed from Indiana Smith to Indiana Jones.

189

"George had the basic plot in mind long before Larry Kasdan was hired to write the screenplay," Kazanjian says.

On the other hand, although Spielberg was part of the talks, he hadn't fully committed. He had no contract, only a deal memo. Nor did they have a studio deal.

More Lucasfilm story development took place when Leigh Brackett turned in her first draft for *The Empire Strikes Back* that February 1978.

By then the search for a writer on the *Graffiti* sequel had narrowed down to Bill Norton Jr. and Mary Kay Place. Norton had written a string of respected scripts, including *Cisco Pike* (1972), a film about contemporary youth culture. Mary Kay Place had written three episodes of the hit TV show *M*A*S*H* (1972–1983), which Lucas had liked. "In the back of George's mind all the time was Bill Norton and Mary Kay Place, as a team, to write the screenplay," Kazanjian said in 1979. "George really pushed for them. I was smart enough, I think, not to push for any particular writer or director. I had done my homework, reading dozens of writer's works, if not a hundred, and had a list of prospective ones that I would discuss with George from time to time. Many of the top writers on my list were only writers and not proven directors. But I also knew that George preferred writer-directors. Bill Norton certainly was one."

Lucas had heard that Place and Norton were occasional writing partners or living together, so he thought they might be a team. Kazanjian sent an offer to their agents, which was rejected. The agents made it clear that Norton preferred to write the script on his own. Lucas and Kazanjian talked to Norton, liked him, and read another of his scripts, perhaps called "Tijuana," about college kids in the 1960s. They liked how he handled his characterizations, the way he developed his plot and his dialogue. When Kazanjian offered Norton the assignment, the writer asked to direct as well. The producers told him that if his script was good, he could. (Mary Kay Place would eventually do a cameo as "Teensa.")

When the trio talked story, Lucas explained that because they didn't have Dreyfuss, the three main characters from *American Graffiti* would carry the film. Of course, the new stories would have to dovetail with the end of the first movie, which had told audiences that the Paul

Le Mat character (John) was killed in an auto accident; that Charlie Martin Smith's character (Toad) was missing in Vietnam; and that Ron Howard's character (Steve) became an insurance agent. The fate of the Candy Clark character (Debbie) was open.

Graffiti's story had taken place during a single night. "We didn't know how we could do the sequel in one night," Kazanjian says. "Eventually, George said we would do it on the same day over a four-year period. Bill really didn't like that, he thought it was impossible."

Lucas insisted. If approximately one and a half hours were divided into two-minute scenes, each anchored by two-minute songs, they would have twelve scenes for each story line, for a total of ninety-six minutes. That became the bedrock of script development. "We discussed each story from beginning to end, and then we put each scene on a three-by-five card," Kazanjian continues. "We broke it down and started shuffling the cards on a long table in George's office until it all came out perfect. The timing changed a little bit at the end. We had long discussions on when the picture should be daytime or nighttime. Bill wanted to take the day sequences into the night much earlier [in the film]. That was our most serious disagreement. It wound up that each story would go to night equally, but later in the picture."

The decision to film over a four-year period made the aspect ratio click in Lucas's mind: each year would reflect that time's filmic style. He had been mulling over Kazanjian's idea and decided that shooting each of the four stories in a different aspect ratio was the way to go. "I will take the credit if the movie does poorly," Kazanjian said at the time. "I'll take the credit if it does well. But it was really putting our two heads together and bouncing ideas back and forth. But Bill was a little disturbed about it. In 1964 they shot using very flat, very straight-type lenses, not too many dolly shots, or pans, or zooms, so we'll shoot the drag racing in that style, anamorphic wide-screen; 1965, Terry the Toad, we'll shoot handheld 16mm, 3-x-4 size, like newsreel footage; 1966, Candy Clark, split-screen, multiscreen; 1967, 1.85:1 aspect ratio long lens, 115mm, most of the time. We're going to have our problems now going optically 35, but that's my problem."

191

On March 1, 1978, the *Los Angeles Times* reported on the film's progress: "Movies, even sequels, don't always begin with the written word or a completed screenplay. At his headquarters in San Anselmo, George Lucas has been quietly 'supervising the writing' of the follow-up to *American Graffiti*. The script-in-progress is by Bill Norton Jr., who may also direct for Universal. Other unannounced news is that the movie will shoot this summer and already is partially cast."

Salaries had been worked out, and a budget fixed at about $2 to $2.5 million, according to Universal vice president Tom Mount, the studio executive overseeing the project.

"Places change," said Charlie Martin Smith (Toad) in the article. "But I don't think I look any older." (Smith had been eighteen in the original, six years before.)

Lucas told the *Times* that *More American Graffiti* was about the end of three eras: rock-n-roll music, political, and social. "It's an absolutely new movie," Norton said. "Everybody says that, but this one is. It's experimental, bizarre in the structuring, and unique in the style. George Lucas felt it wasn't worth doing unless we took chances and did something different."

Mackenzie Phillips, who played the unwanted adolescent companion (Carol) of John Milner (Paul Le Mat) in the original, was not going to be in the sequel, at first. "It happened after we saw the first or second draft," Kazanjian said. "We looked at it and saw a part for her. That was my suggestion, Bill loved it, and we checked with George, and George said okay." Norton suggested that she play the part of "Rainbow" as well. Phillips was costarring on another hit sitcom, *One Day at a Time* (1975–1984).

They also found a part for Bo Hopkins, one of the Pharaohs (Little Joe), before deciding not to cast any more people from the first film. "We had a very good story and we didn't want to change it to accept any other people," Kazanjian explains. Then John Brent, the sleazy used-car salesman in a scene cut from the first *Graffiti*, was cast late as a sleazy, pompous bar owner in 1966 San Francisco.

In progressing drafts, the story boiled down to drag racing; Vietnam; a flower child/hippie (Candy Clark); and a straight married couple (Ron Howard and Cindy Williams), in which Williams's character (Laurie) discovers the women's liberation movement. The whole would create a snapshot of America during the mid-1960s.

At the 1978 DGA awards banquet, on March 11, Lucas was seated at the "number one table," having been nominated for *Star Wars*. Spielberg was also at that table, having been nominated for *Close Encounters of the Third Kind*, along with the Kazanjians, whom George had invited. Marcia Lucas had to duck out in order to attend the Academy of Science Fiction, Fantasy, and Horror Films banquet. She returned with an award, while Lucas and Spielberg lost out to Woody Allen for *Annie Hall*.

"Steven was there with his girlfriend," Kazanjian says. "They even announced that it was the first time that two nominated directors were sitting at the same table. Later during the evening, George turns to me and says, referring to my inviting him to the DGA banquet when were just starting out—'I've paid you back.'"

COMBAT

That same month, Lucasfilm began organizing a future home for Industrial Light & Magic. The company rented, and eventually purchased, a large empty warehouse on Kerner Boulevard in the industrial zone of San Rafael, about twenty minutes from Lucas's home in San Anselmo. Around the same time, the Kazanjians purchased their own second home, in Larkspur, a quaint Marin County town. "It was high on a hill overlooking the shopping center below and the ferryboat landing and bay," Howard says. "We always felt like we were on vacation while in Larkspur."

Kazanjian was asked to reacquire ILM's equipment used for *Star Wars*. After that film had wrapped, a few ex-ILMers had formed a new company called Apogee and contracted to do the effects for a TV show, Universal's *Battlestar Galactica* (1978). Now Lucas wanted his equipment back, which Apogee was leasing, but which would take some negotiation. Consequently, the first group to occupy the building was the new crew for the *Graffiti* sequel. Kazanjian prepped the show and soon met Dick Gallegly, a production manager veteran of many studio and independent motion pictures and TV productions; Gallegly became the production administrator (manager) at ILM, later followed by Tom Smith, a producer veteran who would run ILM for several years. A few of the original crew, such as Richard Edlund, Dennis Muren, and Joe Johnston, also trickled northward to work on *Empire*.

The script for that movie, by Brackett, had proved unacceptable to Lucas, so he'd written the second draft of *Empire* himself. A complete rewrite, it was closer to a shooting script. (Brackett had been sick while writing her draft and, sadly, died only a few days after submitting it. Later Lucas brought in Lawrence Kasdan as co-screenplay writer to polish it; Lucas would take a "story by" credit.)

"George was writing," says Marcia Lucas. "Bill Huyck and Gloria Katz were in our kitchen one day at the Parkway house, and George was saying, 'I'm struggling with it.' And then Bill and Gloria said, I think as a joke, 'Well, maybe Darth Vader should be Luke's father.' I kid you not." It wouldn't have been a big jump in Lucas's mind. The original hero of his rough draft for *The Star Wars*, Annikin Starkiller, had a father named Kane who was half-man/half-machine. At one point in the writing evolution a General Ben Kenobi, mentor to Luke Starkiller, was also half-man/half-machine—so to make Darth Vader, who had started out in the rough draft as a completely humanoid character named General Vader, into a half-man/half-machine, now Luke's father instead of Annikin's, might have been something Lucas was already considering.

"I moved up north for *Empire* and started at ILM," Miki Herman says. "And I met Howard. He was very sweet, always cracking little jokes. He wore saddle shoes and plaid pants. That was my impression of him, that he was mostly a numbers man."

Kazanjian was also an experienced negotiator. "I found it interesting and educational to work with Eddie Powell, the union representative in San Francisco," he says. "Many of the jobs and skills of the ILM crew had no classification within the union. It was a challenge, but Powell was never a 'no' person. After all, there would be more employment and fringe benefits paid to the union."

194

Things were moving quickly. In May 1978, the restored version of *American Graffiti* was released in theaters, a kind of rerelease director's cut, which, in addition to the four restored minutes, included something else Lucas had fought for: Dolby stereophonic sound.

The bickering between Lucasfilm and Universal over equipment, such as the Dykstraflex, a motion-control camera built by John Dykstra and crew for *Star Wars*, became more heated in June. Lucas, through Fox, was also suing Universal and *Battlestar Galactica*'s producer, Glen Larson. Lucas felt that Larson's sci-fi adventure series was a rip-off of *Star Wars*. "He sued Universal Studios because not only were they copying *Star Wars*, they were using his ILM equipment," Kazanjian explains. "So it was up to me at a certain point to say, 'We now need the equipment back,' and get all of it up north. The interesting thing was that here George was doing the *Graffiti* sequel for Universal, yet suing Universal over *Battlestar*. I was being sent to meetings, as was Charlie Weber, with Glen Larson, trying to say, 'If you want to create a robot or a certain creature, don't copy us. Show us a picture and we'll tell you if it's okay.'"

Kazanjian also learned that month more about Lucas's secret project when Lawrence Kasdan submitted his first draft: *Raiders of the Lost Ark*. It was to be a rollicking, cliff-hanging adventure movie featuring archaeologist/hero Indiana Jones, who tangles with Nazis over an unimaginably powerful treasure: Moses's lost Ark of the Covenant.

"When Larry Kasdan delivered the first draft, the script was very close to the finished shooting script," says Kazanjian. "George gave some notes. You had to be a kid at heart, a comic book fanatic and a serial freak, to godfather a writer in creating characters and a story like *Raiders of the Lost Ark*."

Chapter 10: *American Split*

T he Lucases bought the first land parcel of what would become Skywalker Ranch in the spring of 1978. Before the purchase Lucas had again consulted Kazanjian on his choice between two opportunities. "I had not seen the property and George said to me, 'One is on Lucas Valley Road, and another one is gorgeous but less acreage' on some other road. Now I had not seen the place at all, but I said, 'Well, you have to pick the one on *Lucas* Valley Road!'"

Lucas did buy it; the development of the property, however, was going to be a financial strain on the company. Not only was Lucas financing *Empire* with his own money and a loan from Bank of America—now he was going to put millions of dollars into a project that his own executives were questioning. "No bank was going to lend him money on that facility," Kazanjian explains. "Mostly because he had a great challenge ahead of him to convince the Marin County Board of Supervisors to allow him to build. If it had gone bankrupt the only thing the land would've been good for would've been a Catholic school or a monastery. You couldn't divide the land. George was putting money there, he was putting money into his film, and he was putting money into a growing company."

Lucas had chosen the route of independent producer, with Fox distributing, though he had received other offers. Walt Disney Productions, for example, wanted to make a multipicture deal with Lucas. "It was an overall deal," Kazanjian says. "They weren't specific. They just wanted 'George Lucas.' Disney's son-in-law Ron Miller was running the company; I met with him and his assistant." Kazanjian took the offer back to Lucas, who wasn't interested. At the time, "he wasn't a fan of Disney's."

Lucas was always a fan of USC. Ken Miura, one of their former professors and associate dean of academic affairs, phoned Kazanjian one day to tell him about a parcel of land USC wanted to purchase—"if they didn't snatch it up in the next few weeks, they were going to lose it," Kazanjian says. "So I went to George, and George said, 'Meet with Ken and find out more about it.' We met at the restaurant Victoria Station near Universal Studios. I went back to George with what they wanted, and I got to tell you, just like that, George said, 'Let me get involved.' He took it over."

EXPANDING HORIZONS

Lucasfilm held its annual Fourth of July picnic at fledgling Skywalker Ranch. At noon, the small group had a BBQ for those with families and kids. "Duwayne Dunham arrived in a hot-air balloon, so that was a very interesting picnic," says Lucy Wilson. Dunham crashed the balloon but was unhurt. The evening was more of a VIP affair, with Coppola and Saul Zaentz and the like, lawyers, and Lucas's sisters and parents. Kazanjian recalls, "It was different dress and it was beautifully lit and in a different area with different food."

"We were like a family, the Lucasfilm family," Miki Herman says. "And Marcia was part of that, bringing everybody together. Harrison Ford would come. Steven Spielberg would come. Marcia always liked to play baseball. She was the head of the [softball] team. She was very athletic, and George just adored her. He really did."

The company's intramural softball league was her idea. Marcia also bought a sailboat for the employees' use—*The Seawalker*. "We used to all hang out together," Randal Kleiser says, "and I do remember one event which was when I went to George's house when he was living with Marcia in San Anselmo. They had an old-time oak refrigerator; they'd taken some of the panels out and put in beveled glass. Inside the beveled glass were stacks and stacks of TV dinners. I said, 'You know, George, now that *Star Wars* is a hit, you could probably get a cook.' He looked at me . . . 'Oh yeah, I guess I could.' They had not yet realized that they were ready for a transition. They were still having that college kind of lifestyle."

197

"George is a very stay-at-home person, a homebody," Marcia says. "I cooked dinner six nights a week. We went out to dinner one night a week. And then I'd go out one night a week and play softball at the ranch."

"I was in the Universal office for maybe two or three weeks before I went up to Marin," says Jane Bay, "which was a big change for me because I was an LA girl since I got out of college. And it took some adjusting, but it was such an unbelievable time at Lucasfilm. I was the secretary of the corporation and we had all these documents that we signed, and we felt like we were grown up. This was a big deal. I was just in awe of George and Howard, and the company that George founded. We were a little band of Indians in the middle of this huge phenomenon and it was overwhelming, because nobody had ever experienced anything like what happened with *Star Wars*. What happened was such a phenomenon, but we were not coping with the celebrity around *Star Wars* because George didn't want to be part of any of that. The fact that we were in Marin County shielded us from all that."

"Jane and I were really good friends," says Marcia. "She supported George. She loved working for George. She loved her job. She loved later being the queen of Skywalker Ranch, and all of the celebrities and so on."

That July, Howard and Carol also attended the wedding of Paul Le Mat and Suzanne Celeste de Passe, a producer at Motown and the discoverer of the Jackson 5. Diana Ross was the matron of honor and sang at the event. The bride's mother, Barbara Brown de Passe, was escorted down the aisle by Motown founder, Berry Gordy Jr. "In the middle of summer, we all had to wear tuxedos," Kazanjian recalls. "We had a brand-new Cadillac Seville, but because we were not in a limousine, the big bodyguards wouldn't let us park in the church lot. Needless to say, we had a long walk to the church."

After the ceremony in St. Alban's Episcopal Church, the wedding party adjourned to the Crystal Room of the Beverly Hills Hotel for a reception. The newlyweds then jetted to Acapulco for their honeymoon, while the Kazanjians returned to their home in San Marino.

Up north, Lucas eventually won permits and approvals for Skywalker Ranch. Work started on the immense, never-ending building project to turn a defunct dairy farm on neglected land into a kind of filmmaking utopia. Eventually, whole crews of woodworkers, carpenters, glassmakers, and craftspeople were employed on the immense task.

"The stained-glass windows and the handmade tile, Marcia was in all of that," Kazanjian says. "I sat in on many discussions between George and his designers, or just George and Marcia, where George wanted room for seventy-five employees at the ranch and Marcia was saying, 'You're crazy, George. It's gonna be one hundred and fifty; it's gonna be two hundred and fifty, and we have to prepare for that with the dining rooms.' 'No, I don't want that, we're not gonna have that many people.' Eventually it escalated far beyond what George ever, ever, ever imagined."

"George had all this money," Marcia recalls, "and he wanted to build a Northern California film facility. I was all for that because it was going to be young people and it was going to be artists getting together and writers getting together and all these creative people coming there to work and write and do sound mixes and record music. It was great. I was really in favor of it. He kind of made me a head designer on it." Marcia Lucas went to work on what would be called the "Farm Group": stone-foundation bungalows arranged in a circle, with one larger building equipped with a kitchen and several rooms, which formed an inn for those sleeping over at the ranch. Later she was in charge of the Main House, a large three-story Victorian-style manor. "George was going to put the recording stage and the editing suites on the right side of the Main House," she says. "But that was a dark place kind of in the forest and I didn't like the location, so I said, 'No, it needs to go on the left side.' I moved what became Skywalker Sound over to the other side of the valley, on the sunny side facing the lake."

Lucas told the celebrated Japanese film director Akira Kurosawa, who was on a rare visit to the States, about his film community plans during a meeting in Los Angeles. Kurosawa was introduced to Lucas and Weber by the translator, and then to "the current Lucasfilm 'family': the directors and producers of the sequel to *Star Wars* and *American Graffiti*"— that is, Irvin Kershner, whom Lucas had hired to direct *Empire*, Norton, Kurtz, and Kazanjian.

Kurosawa apologized for having not seen *Star Wars* yet, which had recently opened in Japan, but he had seen and liked *American Graffiti*. The

Americans asked Kurosawa many questions about his films; Kershner was the most "tenacious" asking about the telephoto lenses used on *Red Beard* (1965). They were surprised to learn that Kurosawa edited in the evenings after shooting. He explained, "If I didn't have the previous day's rushes fully edited, I couldn't set the pacing for the next day's shooting."

Up north, Kurosawa spent a few hours with Coppola, who showed him a few minutes of *Apocalypse Now*. "Irvin had always been a big fan of Kurosawa and Japanese films," Kazanjian says. "Kurosawa showed us storyboards of his proposed film and told us he did all of his own color storyboards. He signed a few posters to George and Francis. It was a short trip, then he returned to Japan."

FILM STALLS

Although Kazanjian wasn't directly involved, one of the more hilarious side stories of Lucasfilm's early days was developing back in Hollywood: *The Star Wars Holiday Special* (1978). "It wasn't originally supposed to be a TV variety show with comedians Harvey Korman or Bea Arthur," says Miki Herman, the show's Lucasfilm consultant. "It was supposed to be like Baryshnikov and Ann Margaret and really top talent. It would be a class act, but CBS kept wanting to make it longer to get more money."

Kazanjian *was* involved with preproduction on *Empire* as that ramped up down south and at the ILM facilities up north. "I broke the script down, I did the board," he says. "We had two boards, one was for shooting, and the second board was strips for budgeting and planning the special effects. I didn't break down how it was done, but I presented it and said, 'ILM, now you do the storyboards and figure it out.'"

Kurtz was spending most of his time in Europe and in England, where he had a home, scouting and supervising set construction. Lucas brought in Frank Marshall to supervise the physical production of *Radioland Murders*. Kazanjian would also oversee that film. Fred Roos recommended director Ted Flicker to do a rewrite. In July 1978, Steve Martin and Cindy Williams were discussed as leads.

"But ultimately the picture fell through and Frank was sitting without a job," Kazanjian says. "First George and then Ned Tanen wanted to put it on the (way) back burner. In fact, George very cleverly got me to get Ned to say, 'I don't like the script, let's put it on the back burner.' Because that's what George wanted. Either way, Frank Marshall had nothing to do, so George said, 'Rather than hurl Frank out the door, let's bring him in on *Raiders*.'"

Kazanjian arranged it. As Lucas's go-to guy, they grew closer. "We'd go to dinner and talk about nothing," Kazanjian recalls. "We talked about school, we talked about movies. George would see movies at the local theaters." With Kurtz away and Lippincott gone, Kazanjian would sometimes be drawn into licensing, because somebody had to coordinate the color of a character's costume with that of an action figure, or decide if, legally, a licensee could use an actor's face or name. If a *Star Wars* book included film credits, somebody had to check them.

Norton took longer than anticipated to write his screenplay for *More American Graffiti*, but when it arrived, Lucas and company liked it. "We really didn't have too many rewrites," Kazanjian says. "We loved it and we hired him as director; Marcia read the script and she commented directly to George; I never heard about it."

Shortly after Paul Le Mat returned from his honeymoon, they started filming the sequel to *American Graffiti*.

INDISPENSABLE STARS

Lucas had wanted his friend from USC Caleb Deschanel to be director of photography on the first film, but the DP hadn't been available. Since his student days, Deschanel had built up a reputation for innovation and attention to detail. He'd photographed a number of commercials and documentaries before Coppola had tagged him for pick-up work on *Apocalypse Now*. Thinking Deschanel was busy again, Lucas had looked at the work and styles of many cinematographers. He wanted someone who understood their goals, could light fast, work with a small crew, support the director, be part of the family, part of the company. "Then Caleb became available in the nick of time, only one or two days before we had to make a final decision," Kazanjian says. "But he was disturbed by the film's different aspect ratios and film stocks. He really wanted to shoot 35mm right up until almost the last day."

Kazanjian hired local Aggie Rodgers, a veteran of the first *Graffiti* (her first feature), to do the costume design. Another San Franciscan was Don Courtney, brought on for the special effects.

The idea was to shoot the movie in forty days, with each of the four sequences taking ten days or two weeks. Cameras rolled first on Ron Howard, Cindy Williams, Paul Le Mat, Charlie Martin Smith, and the others at a Fremont raceway, where the film's characters reunite for the only time in the story before dispersing to follow their own paths. Toad informs the others that he's going to Vietnam to fight in the war. "When Paul Le Mat was on camera, it didn't appear there was anything special to his performance," says Friedman. "But when you saw him in dailies—well, they talk about movie magic. The camera captured something different from what you capture with your own eyes and ears. That was the first time I became aware that the camera sees and records differently. It's not a one-to-one translation of the way you see it on the set, three dimensionally. That's part of what movie magic is—some actors like Paul light up the screen."

To keep interlopers away, the working production title of the sequel was *Purple Haze*. Kazanjian had anticipated problems with the complex drag-racing scenes due to their high-powered, finicky vehicles, as well as locations populated with children and animals. Most of the period drag-racers had been re-created; tires that "burned at the line" no longer existed; engines had to be built. "They're dragsters, rails, fuel-burning and gasoline blown or injected machines," Kazanjian said in 1979. "Very skillfully and carefully built with either Chevy or Chrysler Hemi engines. And each car was different. The heavy car, sponsored by the factory, was the fanciest-looking car, the best sheet metal, the best equipment, the shiniest chrome, and the biggest Hemi blown engine. Milner's car was a Chevy blown engine. We built four dragsters. We used and changed and modified many others."

The next year to be filmed was 1965, with Howard and Williams, mostly in a Marin County home for the location. Between takes Kazanjian reminded Ron Howard how years before the child actor had broken his jaw on the Disney production they'd both worked on. Louis Friedman says, "I remember saying to myself, *Ron Howard, he's working for two weeks and he's being paid a hundred thousand dollars.* I couldn't wrap my head around that."

That same afternoon Friedman remembers he and Kazanjian talking about how, once you start shooting, everybody is dispensable in making a movie except the actors in front of the camera. "I have to catch a plane to LA tonight and have a meeting with the studio tomorrow," Kazanjian said. "They have some issues they want to talk to me about . . . But, Louis, I can get on that plane tonight, and that plane could crash and I could die, and this movie would still get made."

SUMMER OF LOVE

A few of the 1966 scenes with Candy Clark and Mackenzie Phillips were filmed on location in and around San Francisco's Fillmore Auditorium, where Country Joe and the Fish played music for a set piece in the well-known rock venue; Country Joe and the Fish had come to prominence during the psychedelic late '60s and were still a popular counterculture rock group. "We shot all morning with Country Joe," says costume designer Aggie Rodgers. "We were at Winterland and having a huge lunch with lots and lots of extras everywhere. Howard came and sat next to me, and up comes Country Joe and the Fish. Joe sits across from me and begins chatting, because I'd gone to him earlier to clear his outfit. And he was very animated! For sure. He leaned over to Howard and said, 'Man, this is great—I'm peaking right now!' Later Howard asked me what Country Joe meant and I explained he was on acid. Howard was shocked. So much fun, but I don't think Howard got over that all day."

Kazanjian became aware of other drug-taking when Mackenzie Phillips, who was having personal problems, couldn't perform to expectations; her part had to be cut down. There were other difficulties behind the scenes. "I didn't have a great crew," Kazanjian said in 1979. "There were more sad moments than happy moments. I'm not a yeller, but I will never forget raising my voice at

WARDROBE FOR: Cop #1 PLAYED BY: Harrison Ford

CHANGE	SCENE NUMBER	NAME OF SET	DESCRIPTION OF WARDROBE
1966	18-20	Ext/D Haight Ashbury St.	black leather calif-hi- motorcycle boots navy blue button-up long sleeve shirt. narrow navy/blk tie black motorcycle leather police jacket zipped ½ way up. badge over left STAR white helmet w/ blk visor blk rim around bottom black leather chinstrap ear covers, extension at back of helmet to cover hair PD on BOTH HELMET SIDE, decal on FRONT Blk leather belt plain attached to bottom of jacket, has gunholster, ring holder, cuff pouch-RING, 2 ammo pouches. gold frame glasses w/ blk lenses- toothpick navy/blk calvary twill pants w/ jodphur style white stripe down outseam Pocket ticket book Rt REAR
#1		jacket-left pocket unzip rt pocket-down sleeves-unzipped	

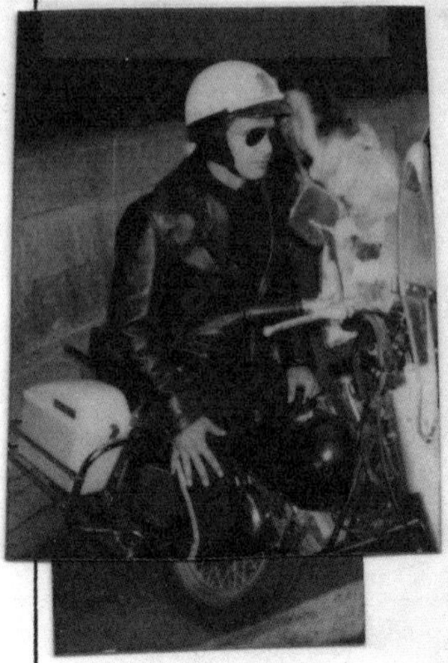

Costume designer Aggie Guerard Rodgers issued a costume prep sheet for More American Graffiti *(1979) explaining how "Cop #1"—Harrison Ford in a cameo—would be attired: "black leather California motorcycle boots, navy blue button-up long-sleeve shirt," etc.*

the poor transportation guy who just couldn't understand how to save money. He tended to spend money on vehicles that would never be seen. I felt that if you scream and scream at the guy, maybe you'd get through. I'm not so happy with some of the things I had to do. But if everybody loves me, I'm not doing my job."

The producer also had issues with the assistant directors who he felt weren't up to snuff. The soundman hadn't done a feature in many years. "So my challenge was trying to mold these people into a professional unit," Kazanjian explained. "They were not prepared for it. Part of the promise was, 'We're here to do a number of movies.' And we did have it in control nearly all the time, we never lost control for more than ten minutes." In some respects, the crew overcompensated by asking for more people, assistants, and more equipment to handle what was for them a multimillion-dollar big-budget sequel. For Kazanjian, it was one of the smaller pictures he'd worked on. "I knew that we could do it very easily. It was a matter of convincing the crew that they could do it. It was bigger than they thought they could handle."

Shooting in the city of San Francisco had its own challenges. Kazanjian faced teamster and logistic problems when production moved downtown. Weather, of course, was a factor, too. With cameras rolling, bystanders watched a low-power van come squealing around a corner, swerve across the street, plow into a row of trash cans, and smash over a prop fire hydrant. For the next shot special effects rigged the hydrant to erupt as the van's occupants stumbled out, stoned and disoriented.

"The cops close in," an eyewitness journalist wrote, "leaving the flower children precious few moments to ingest what they had previously been smoking. One young girl, bedecked in a top hat with feathers, manages to convince the police that the van was waylaid by gun-wielding thugs, and the conned police take off in hot pursuit of the imaginary desperadoes." Norton was pleased and yelled, "Cut."

The crowd, "not used to seeing much filming ever since *The Streets of San Francisco* [an early 1970s TV show] was canceled, breaks out in appreciative applause."

Candy Clark and her boyfriend in their psychedelic car, for what would be a split-screen sequence, are pulled over by a policeman played by Harrison Ford in his cameo as Bob Falfa (from *Graffiti*). Coppola was driving by and stopped to say hello. With Coppola was Melissa Mathison. Ford had met Mathison in the Philippines when he was playing a small part in *Apocalypse Now*. "That was where Harrison met Melissa and stole her heart," Kazanjian says.

Ford and Mathison would eventually marry.

PRODUCER'S GAMBIT

Production moved to the California Delta region, near the city of Stockton, for the Vietnam scenes, which required a set of period army vehicles and costumes—and two helicopters that would be made to seem like many in editorial. Kazanjian had wanted the cooperation of the Department of Defense for the combat scenes, "so we could have the weapons, the artillery, the helicopters, perhaps jets, and the guidance to do the Vietnam section correctly," he says. "They didn't turn us down until we were just about ready to shoot, so it was a mad scramble to get the aircraft, artillery, the weapons, and all of that, and at much greater expense."

"There were lots of worries over the helicopter work in the Vietnam sequences," Rodgers says.

"But Lucasfilm was a pleasure to work at, because I could call my own shots," Kazanjian adds. "There was nobody looking over my shoulder. If I wanted to spend $40,000 on a second helicopter, I made that decision. I'd say to George, 'I just spent $40,000 on top of the budget, but I'll make it up somewhere else.' And I would."

On the upside, Kazanjian had Debbie Fine and Paul Hensler on the crew, whose work was essential in making the picture. Fine was the film's researcher and had done the same for *Apocalypse Now*; Hensler had served in Vietnam and was one of the film's technical advisors. He and Fine provided necessary information to the art department and other heads of departments (HODs) so that the two helicopters and military uniforms were altered appropriately.

The Vietnam story starred Smith as Toad and costarred Bo Hopkins as Little Joe, previously of the Pharaohs, the gang of hoodlums from the first film. On October 24, 1978, Army Archerd wrote in his

RECEIPT OF SCRIPT ACKNOWLEDGEMENT

I, __HOWARD KAZANJIAN__, do hereby acknowledge receipt of one copy of the script titled STAR WARS, EPISODE FIVE, THE EMPIRE STRIKES BACK, script copy number __SW5D0279X00026__, dated __SWE 5D 2/20/79__, including revisions dated __SWE 5DR 2/28/79__.

I understand this script is solely for my own use, is not to be copied either in part or in whole, and is not to be shown to any person outside the Company. I agree to return this script to the Production Office upon completion of my work in connection with the script.

SIGNED:

NAME	DATE OUT	DATE IN
HOWARD KAZANJIAN	March 5, 1979	

CLOCKWISE FROM TOP LEFT: *At the wrap party for* More American Graffiti *are Kazanjian, writer-director Bill Norton, and casting director Fred Roos, who not only advised on* Star Wars, *but also cast* American Graffiti *and* The Godfather. • *On location in Stockton, California, for* More American Graffiti *are: executive producer George Lucas; Lucas's father, George Lucas Sr.; Kazanjian; Bill Norton (unit manager Tom Joyner is mostly hidden behind Norton).* • *While filming the Vietnam sequence, DP Caleb Deschanel, Kazanjian, and Lucas watch as a Huey helicopter skims across the water in a shot (off-camera); the trio is dressed in army fatigues in case one the helicopter cameras above should pick them up on the ground.* • *Kazanjian signed a receipt for one script draft for* The Empire Strikes Back, *dated February 20, 1979, signed and dated, March 5, 1979.*

Variety column that both actors "are back from shooting segs of the sequel *Purple Haze*—and happy to be alive. A helicopter in which they were filming a Vietnam war sequence . . . hit a tree. They were able to land with a damaged rotor blade. 'It was scary,' admits Hopkins, 'but we went up again in another chopper.' Among those viewing the not-in-the-script drama was George Lucas."

In actuality, when the helicopter was lifting off, a rotor blade had hit a small limb of a nearby oak tree. The pilot set the helicopter down, with minimal risk of life, and showed Kazanjian a thumb-size dent that might throw the rotating blades off. He sent to Los Angeles for a replacement blade at his own expense. Late the next day the helicopter was back up in the sky.

When the special effects crew rigged a napalm explosion, however, many of the cast and crew were a little too close. "I felt this wave of heat go past my body," Friedman recalls. To create plumes of black smoke, crew burnt old tires for hours.

After Norton wrapped principal photography, Kazanjian summed up the experience in a 1979 prerelease interview: "It actually turned out to be a fairly difficult picture to make, although we were very well prepared and organized. It should have been easier."

Kazanjian and Charlie Weber visited another troubled production at around this time, Spielberg's *1941*, in part to gauge the director's commitment to *Raiders*. (Filmmakers often visit each other's sets, but Spielberg had been a no-show during *Purple Haze*.) "I sat in the dressing room," Kazanjian says. "Milius, who was executive producing, was there, and I met Kathy Kennedy, who was Milius's assistant. We went on the set and watched them shooting, talked to Steven a little bit, and left. We really couldn't tell if Steven was going to commit because he had so many things going on. At one point George said he didn't know if Steven would commit because of those other projects, and we should start thinking about another director. I remember suggesting that George direct, but he declined. Steven always had several hot projects on his plate and usually decided late which one he was going to take on next."

In January 1979, also in the service of *Raiders*, Howard and Carol Kazanjian went to Egypt on a vacation/location scout. "George said, 'Take the script,' meaning, 'Read the latest draft.' So I read the script, and part of my trip was to find out, can we shoot this in Egypt?"

One of their visits was to the ancient Abu Simbel temples, carved into a hill. The entrance was flanked by four giant statues of a seated Ramesses II. At the end of a two-hundred-foot corridor flanked by larger-than-life standing statues, they found a room with four life-size figures, one of which was the pharaoh Ramesses II. According to Kazanjian the temple had been excavated from the rising Nile River, but had originally been built so that on the summer solstice the sun shot a beam of light onto the four statues inside.

Kazanjian reported his find and more to Lucas.

"As a teenager I'd seen a movie in which a treasure hunter places a glass between two twin peaks high up in a mountain," Howard says. "On a certain day the sun marked the spot in an old temple where the treasure would be. Cut to the treasure hunter breaking a small hole in the wall where the sun had marked the spot. POV inside the open cavity as the hunter puts his hand in looking for the treasure. Inside are snakes. If you take these two incidents, from my scout and the earlier movie, you have, eventually, Indy and the Staff of Ra marking the exact location of the Ark in the miniature city." (Charlton Heston starred in another ancient treasure movie, *Secrets of the Incas*, in 1954; Kazanjian once mentioned its similarities to *Raiders*, but Lucas and Spielberg said they'd never seen it. Kazanjian would also recall two other movies in which the sun played an important role: *Journey to the Center of the Earth* (1959), in which sunlight penetrates a hole between two mountain peaks to reveal an entrance; and *Mackenna's Gold* (1969), in which the rising sun behind Arizona's Canyon de Chelly indicates the entrance to a rich gold vein in the mountains; as mentioned, a young George Lucas was on the set of the latter movie.)

Kazanjian told Lucas that Egypt was the wrong place, so his boss recommended that he look at Tunisia, where he'd filmed many of the Tatooine scenes of *Star Wars*.

Empire, with Kershner at the helm, began its principal photography on location in Finse, Norway, on March 5, 1979. That film's action in the frozen wastes was designed in part to explain why Luke Skywalker's face had changed since the first film. Actor Mark Hamill had been in a terrible car accident just before the release of *Star Wars*, so Lucas had created a monster (a Wampa) in the story that attacks Skywalker and scars his face.

After a couple of weeks, production moved to Elstree Studios in England for the rest of spring into summer. Kazanjian flew over and toured the studio because Lucas wanted him to know as much as possible about the setup and its English crew before producing the third *Star Wars* picture.

"It's not like Howard's an outsider coming in," Hamill says. "He's somebody from the Lucasfilm family. It was clear that he and George had a great rapport. You ask around and people fill you in. They say, 'Oh yeah, they were frat brothers,' and all that stuff.

"By the time of *Empire*, it was like two separate movies were going on," Hamill adds, "because I went off on my own. I missed the days of running around bumping heads on the Death Star with 'Carrison' and 'Harry,' as I used to call Carrie and Harrison. I'd see them walking in the opposite direction to their soundstage as I was going to my soundstage. They went off on their own adventure and met Lando. I was pretty much in the swamps."

Back in Los Angeles, Lucasfilm corporate consisted of a relatively young and inexperienced team of executives—president Charlie Weber, vice president John Moohr, and a couple of others—whose job it was to oversee *Empire*'s financials. They were receiving Kurtz's daily production reports and, in a typical game of office politics, were trying to learn about film production without letting on that much of it was new to them. Kazanjian became frustrated: "Every time I asked, I was told the picture was on budget, but a few days behind schedule. Of course, I knew that no picture on a tight budget could be falling behind and still remain on budget. I kept telling Charlie and John it was impossible. On more than one occasion, John told me that he had the paperwork and to stay out of it. I said I knew about production and, even sitting several thousand miles away, I knew there was no way they were on schedule and on budget."

The London production office, however, confirmed to Kazanjian that the film was doing fine. What no one knew was that "Gary Kurtz had given orders to the accountant, Arthur Carroll, not to tell the home office anything, especially that they were over budget," Kazanjian adds. "And he didn't. But this is where he should have gone over his boss's head to the super boss and report his findings. He did not. [Production manager] Robert Watts most likely knew, but must have been silenced by Kurtz."

"Everybody brings a particular skill set to the table," Louis Friedman says. "Budgeting and scheduling, and the logistics of making pictures was not necessarily Gary Kurtz's forte. It was, however, Howard's. This is what he was trained to do. And the fact that George and Howard were friends meant, I guess, that George trusted Howard to see those issues more clearly."

"Then one day Gary requested through the accountant an additional five million dollars," Kazanjian says (*Empire* was budgeted at around $25 million, so the request represented something like a 20 percent overage—with no end in sight). "There was no more hiding. The London production needed more money to pay the employees." Lucas's financing through Bank of America fell apart. On July 16, the bank pulled their loan. Lucasfilm was overextended. "The bank went crazy. And it wasn't over yet."

Weber found a potential bailout in the First National Bank of Boston. A meeting was scheduled at the Egg Company. Lucas flew down to talk with the bank reps; Weber and Kazanjian were also at the table. "The bank shot bullets at George," Kazanjian recalls. "In all my time with George, I have never seen or heard anyone speak to George as did the bank: 'You have no credibility' was what they said. Although George was not getting the proper information from his people, he was the big cheese and the buck stopped with him. George said that he understood what they were saying and said, 'If this film does not break even, even if it takes me the rest of my life, I will pay you back.' One of the bank executives replied, 'That's real easy for you to say.' The bank executives were on the line, too."

211

Bank of Boston demanded a new producer, someone they could trust who would report the financial facts to them daily. "George responded, 'Rather than bring in someone from the outside, I would like you to consider Howard Kazanjian.' I'm sitting there hearing this for the first time. George continued, 'You can check him out with anybody in Hollywood.' The bank said, 'We already have, we've investigated him, and we'll accept him.'"

"I was aware that Howard stepped in at that juncture," Friedman says, "and then became the new head of production for all films."

"We had to go and completely refinance the movie halfway through with a different bank," Lucas said. "We had to switch banks in a period of something like ten days, but they were willing to go the extra $5 million."

"I think it still rankles George that *Empire* went over budget," Hamill said in 2019.

On July 24, Lucasfilm signed an agreement with the Bank of Boston and Kazanjian took over the financial side of producing *Empire*. His first job was to redo the budget and provide the bank with an accurate forecast. Fortunately, he already knew about ILM's costs, so all he had to do was add in the weeks left of filming, and a few other items. Kazanjian reported his analyses to Weber, who spoke with the bank—for the producer was going to be busy in London.

T-Man

At Elstree late that summer, Kazanjian discovered that Kurtz was blaming the DP, Peter Suschitzky, who was very good, but rather slow, for the delays. The sets were complicated and difficult to light, so Suschitzky was doing a lot of bounce lighting. Kershner was also rather slow and meticulous, while Kurtz's attitude was that the sequel would easily recoup whatever overages they incurred. When Kazanjian visited the set, Kershner was filming Luke and Yoda inside the latter's hovel. Lucas would arrive shortly thereafter and, to put things back on track, would work with his director to cut a few Yoda scenes and move things along.

212

"Everybody wrapped, and it was just me and Yoda left," Hamill says. "And it seemed to go on forever, but that's only in contrast to how quickly we made the first movie. Yoda was a sophisticated puppet, but it was constantly breaking down and being rushed to Stuart Freeborn's workshop. And the intricate choreography for that duel with Vader, which was a shot over a period of many, many weeks, was the most physically daunting job I'd ever had. It was exhausting."

Kazanjian went over the numbers again, looked in on the various departments, spoke to the HODs, and made his reports. He had multiple phones on his desk: one for the back lot; one for local calls; and one a direct line to the United States. He never told Kurtz that he was on the outs, "as it was not my position, but I think he knew."

"George might've said, 'Gary's over budget,'" Marcia recalls. "He would've played it down. Because they had history together, so that's hard for George to fire somebody."

"Gary wasn't exactly a real gregarious, outgoing sort of person," Duwayne Dunham says. "Not like Howard. Howard goes up to people, he's got a smile on his face, and he can talk to anybody about anything and make you feel very welcome. I'm not saying Gary didn't, but Gary wasn't that gregarious kind of outgoing guy, not the guy that I knew, anyway. Howard, on the other hand, made work seem like a happy adventure we were all on."

"I told the accountant, Arthur Carroll," Kazanjian adds, "that I would use him on the next picture—but I expected him always to report the facts to me and to the head office at Lucasfilm if asked. He was relieved to hear that and we got along perfectly. Arthur was a gem from then on and always kept me informed day by day."

"I put Howard on the picture, but I didn't really officially take Gary off," says Lucas. "Bob Watts and Howard Kazanjian were the ones that actually did most of the work. This was all or nothing, basically. I had to get the film made and that was all I really cared about at that point, making it as good as I can while getting it done."

"I used to tell trainees and students at universities," Kazanjian continues, "that you have to be able to tell people to go to hell in such a way that they say, 'Thank you, I will.' It's diplomacy, and some people can get away with that. I can. You don't tell them to go to hell, you have to straighten them out sometimes, but they have to understand why, what they did wrong, how we can help them, how it would be better for them. So it's diplomacy. I learned about that at home. My mother was like that."

More Is Less

Back in Northern California, Kazanjian and Lucas had another film to finish. "We'd had a great deal of trouble getting the dragsters to run while filming," Kazanjian says. "They really never ran correctly. In postproduction, with a much smaller crew, we finally got them to run."

Lucas cut the film with editor Tina Hirsch, at 321 San Anselmo Avenue. Hirsch had worked on several low-budget films for Roger Corman, so *More American Graffiti* was a step up. "You have to be the kind of person who can stand behind the director," Hirsch would say. "The ego goes away and it's all about creating his vision for him."

Dunham was also moving up, working as one of the assistant editors, a couple of whom were from Hollywood. "George loves to edit, so he played a big part in that," Dunham says. "Ben Burtt and Sprocket sound was downstairs, and we were upstairs. And Howard was the nicest guy. It was always, 'What do you need?' And the resources were always given. Questions were asked, of course, but there was a trust factor."

"The thing about George," Burtt says, "and then Gary, and then Howard, was that there was a lot of respect paid for the schedule and delivering things on time, and not getting distracted with chaotic changes. Lucasfilm was well organized and Howard fit in nicely. Sometimes you work with producers, and you feel like they're not telling you everything that you need to know. They're just telling you little bits of information about what their goal is. With Howard, it was never that case. I always felt Howard was completely open, completely frank about what was going on, willing to listen to suggestions. You want honesty, and we had that all those years."

"There was a concern that people would not be able to follow along," Friedman says of the four story lines in the sequel. "It was a

214

checkerboard story. Here's a four-minute scene from 1964, then a four-minute scene from '65, and so on to '67, then back to '64. In the story, some people had already passed away, and that was maybe too much nonlinear information for the average moviegoer to follow. *American Graffiti* cut around to four stories, but it was always in a linear progression during a single night."

"Marcia wasn't involved much with cutting," says Kazanjian, who notes that the changing aspect-ratio was another concern. Marcia recalls, "I look at a whole movie as a whole movie. When I work, I want to work on the whole movie. But I was so relieved not to be in the cutting room fourteen hours a day, seven days a week. Then George asked if I would come in and cut some split-screen scenes. I said, 'I can do that.' So I went in and spent some time, and I edited some split-screens of Candy's story."

"Every studio says, 'Show me something different,'" Friedman adds. "'Show me something new.' So, okay, here's something that hasn't been done."

"Six or eight months prior to the opening, *More American Graffiti* was the number-one wanted picture out there," Kazanjian says. "The public knew it was coming and wanted to see it. We were gung ho and excited about it and worked long hours and the cut looked good."

The final sound mix was done at Goldwyn, because Lucasfilm's sound facility, Sprocket Systems, wasn't ready yet for that stage. Sid Ganis, long active in Hollywood, had been hired to head up the marketing department. "I joined Lucasfilm—and there was Howard!" Ganis says. "I got to know him right away. He couldn't have been more personable, easy to talk to. And such a non-movie-looking guy. I got that George and all those guys went to USC together; he looked like a graduate of USC. But not a movie dude. The engineering school. Chinos. He wasn't the hippest, coolest guy to look at, but then you got to talk to him, and he was totally knowledgeable about movies, production, and was the hippest, coolest guy to work with and to learn from. Howard and I had the great experience of producing the *More American Graffiti* soundtrack, the music from the movie." The soundtrack featured songs performed by the Byrds, Simon & Garfunkel, the Supremes, Bob Dylan, Aretha Franklin, Martha

215

and the Vandellas, and others. "The music was sensational."

Lucas previewed *More American Graffiti*, as he'd done for *Star Wars*, at San Francisco's Northpoint Theatre. Kazanjian remembers, "As we were leaving at the end, George's mother came up to him and said, 'George, it's not as funny as the first one.' Ned Tanen was standing there listening, and George didn't say anything."

Things got worse a week before the wide release when Universal premiered the picture in about forty theaters. "Something unusual happened," Kazanjian says. "I went to Ned Tanen's office with his marketing people, and we were told that the theaters were only about half-full. Now, when you have a premiere or sneak preview, no matter what the movie is, the theaters are full. Why were we half-full? We never got an answer to that, so we started worrying."

More American Graffiti was released on Friday, August 3, 1979, and didn't do well. On Monday, Lucas and Kazanjian met with Tanen, and Lucas asked if he could take one day to recut the first reel in order to tell the stories, 1, 1, 2, 2, 3, 3, 4, 4, and then 1, 2, 3, 4, 1, 2, 3, 4. He thought it would better enable audiences to better grasp the film's structure. Tanen said no.

"I recall George admitting to me that he really didn't know if he had a magic touch," Kazanjian says. "This was the first and only time I've ever heard skepticism from him."

"When I saw a cut of the movie, I was disappointed in the film," Marcia says. "I think I mentioned to George once, I said, 'You cut around too much. I think it needed some restructuring.' George said, 'Why didn't you tell me?' I said, 'Are you kidding me? You almost divorced me because I wanted to restructure the first one.' I wasn't going there." (The Lucases had argued over how rigidly the original one should have to follow the four-story sequence—strictly, as 1, 2, 3, 4; 1, 2, 3, 4, or in a more organic fashion; Marcia favored the latter sequencing.)

One theory offered to explain the sequel's lackluster performance was that people were confused by the fact that the first film had been rereleased only months before, touted by a poster that exclaimed: "With additional original scenes never shown before!" Not only that, the poster featured photos of the complete cast, asking people to "Look again!"—at

216

another set of photos below the first to show how the first film's young actors had become big stars. It was possible that many people thought the sequel was the same movie as the rerelease, and stayed home. One thing that everyone agreed on was that the absence of Dreyfuss was a big factor.

"The studio also thought the word 'More' didn't work," Kazanjian says. "They scrambled and did testing of title changes. In the south they called it *American Graffiti 2*." In Europe distributors dropped the "More" and/or sometimes changed the title. In France, it was *American Graffiti—La Suite* ("the next/following"); in Italy it was *American Graffiti 2*. One foreign poster read *More American Graffiti: The Party Is Over.*

"This was my first 'produced by' picture," Kazanjian said in 2004. "Am I disappointed in the quality of the film or the production value of the film? No. Did it fail? No. Nobody lost any money on it. The reality may be that it wasn't a fun picture, but it wasn't a fun time in American culture. We were dealing with the war; we were dealing with Haight-Ashbury and the hippies; we were dealing with Ron Howard and Cindy Williams, whose characters were now married and having problems as a married couple; we were dealing with Toad going AWOL."

The reviewer in *Variety*, Dale Pollock (who would write a biography of Lucas only a few years later called *Skywalking*), bordered on the positive: "May be one of the most innovative and ambitious films of the last five years, but by no means is it one of the most successful. . . . Norton overloads the sequel with four wholly different cinematic styles . . . The aural counterpoint via period recordings . . . is again employed to excellent, if more downbeat, effect. . . . Work of cinematographer Caleb Deschanel and the optical coordinators Peter Donen and Bill Lindemann is extraordinary in meshing the four film sizes, which are beautifully handled in effortless segues. Especially noteworthy are the Vietnam sequences, filmed in Central California and almost as impressive as some of the *Apocalypse Now* footage. . . . Lucasfilm Ltd. has amassed an extraordinary cast and crew that succeeds in almost snatching victory from the jaws of defeat."

CHAPTER 11: *Out of Indiana*

T he Egg Company opened for business, after several delays, in the fall of 1979. By all accounts, its interior design was extraordinary. The luxury compound included two office buildings, a separate restaurant, and a parking lot. The restaurant floor doubled as an exercise space during lunchtime. A photo stills lab would be added later. Kazanjian, Weber, Moohr, and other staffers were provided with beautiful offices. The "Egg Company" name hid from the public the fact that it was the center of *Star Wars* activities; likewise, the door to ILM up north was labeled "Kerner Optical" (because it was on Kerner Boulevard).

"Even then, I knew that George wanted us *all* up north, eventually," says Kazanjian.

"They did such a magnificent job," Carol Kazanjian says. "It was a hit. It had Frank Lloyd Wright class. Full of antiques, absolutely gorgeous. One of the prettiest—if you had to work there, you would stay at work; you wouldn't go home."

A reporter from the *Christian Science Monitor* was so impressed that he wrote of Sid Ganis's office: "a tasteful and expensive combination of high-tech and plush, it overlooks the huge, skylight-covered courtyard that the Egg Company seems to grow out of. Lots of brick, lots of wood (oak), and plants everywhere." Sid Ganis reassured the reporter, "We're for real. Believe me, this is not an illusion."

The Egg Company was eventually honored by BOMA—Building Owners and Managers Association—as the best building of less than 25,000 square feet west of the Mississippi. "Rarely did I go out for lunch," says Kazanjian. "We had a cleaning lady who also made our lunches. I had the same chopped salad every single day. It was great,

218

because I just kept working. We had a gorgeous kitchen with a twelve-by-twelve-foot island."

"I don't know that George had an office there," Dunham says. "They were beautiful, beautifully remodeled buildings. We would go down when we had screenings. Howard was always gracious, and he was pretty much the face of the place. And very talented; he knew talent and respected talent. George had a tremendous amount of respect and trust in Howard."

Kazanjian was also learning a great deal about publicity, marketing, distribution, legal contracts, and union negotiations, as well as story concept, development, and execution. "In the beginning, everybody knew everybody," he says. "We were small enough, seventy-five people. We knew everybody by name and we knew what everybody was doing—we communicated, we talked to each other, we asked for help. 'This is happening in production, think about a book, think about merchandising.'"

At one point, however, Lucasfilm stopped paying Kazanjian. *More American Graffiti* was out, *Empire* was in trouble, and *Raiders* wasn't officially in preproduction yet, so his salary somehow fell through the cracks.

Ironically, the corporate executives had decided to give themselves expensive company cars. One exec received a BMW. Ganis was gifted a Porsche. A secretary was gifted a fancy car, which caused problems. When Lucas noticed, he was given a Mercedes-Benz. Miki Herman recalls, "They got this fleet of cars. After *Star Wars* was such a big hit and everything, they hired all these Wall Street–type guys. George kind of divorced himself from all of those corporate people, Charlie Weber and those guys."

Kazanjian already owned a white Cadillac Seville, with a red leather interior. When offered a company car, he sold the Cadillac and took the Mercedes. "All these executives were flying around in first class and staying in five-star hotels," Marcia Lucas says, "George had an executive down in Los Angeles who was driving around in a Ferrari or something. These people got very full of themselves."

"Several months later I went to Charlie," Kazanjian recalls, "and said, 'You've given me this very nice car, but I can't eat it.' Charlie said, 'What do you mean?' I said, 'I'm not being paid anything!' They had just forgotten about me, vice president of production."

219

Let's Make a Great Deal

Kershner wrapped principal photography on *Empire* in September of 1979, and Lucas began post. Kurtz stayed in London at first, while Kazanjian stayed on top of the film's financials. Its visual effects work would be remembered by most ILMers as the most difficult the facility ever worked on.

In editorial, Marcia Lucas, although not cutting herself, would occasionally look in. One day she came and saw them working on the sequence in which Darth Vader confronts Luke in the carbon freezing chamber (where Han Solo is put in hibernation). Their lightsaber duel began "on this big platform that was all red, like being in hell, with the devil," she says. "But the sword fight wasn't working for me. So I looked at some dailies and I added some cuts. And there was this wide shot they had that was so breathtaking, but it wasn't in. *Oh my god, they're editing it out?* I thought, *Why didn't they use this?* It was so visually great. Cut it in." Paul Hirsch, the film's primary editor, would eventually thank her for the assist.

Lucas was sometimes frustrated, Kazanjian realized, because Kershner had already cut scenes in camera, like Billy Wilder—as mentioned, a classic technique utilized by directors to protect themselves from meddling producers and editors in post. By cutting the scene in camera, only shooting what they needed for a specific editing style, with little to no coverage, directors made it impossible for anyone to cut the scene together except the way the director had envisioned it. Lucas had to call in Kershner to explain how some of the pieces fit together. (Lucas hadn't made it clear to his director that he wanted more coverage— master shots, two shots, close-ups, and so on.)

Hirsch recalled that "George asked Marcia to do a 'guest cut' on a romantic scene between Han and Leia, because he felt a woman's touch was needed. She happily obliged."

Kazanjian was now working primarily on early preproduction for *Raiders*, which still lacked financing. Lucas was not going to pay for the film and was looking, given his track record, for a very good studio deal. In order to give potential investors an idea of what the film's hero would look like, Lucas had asked famed comic book artist Jim Steranko to do four concept paintings: a hero pose; Indiana facing off against a cobra; Indy on horseback; and so forth. The four were reduced down to 8.5-x-11-inch reproductions and included with Kasdan's script for presentation to the studios.

The first packets were sent to Fox and Universal. At the former, Alan Ladd, who had championed *Star Wars*, was on his way out. Kazanjian and Weber met with Ladd, the former head of production, who told them if it were his decision, he would make the film. Instead, it was up to Chairman Dennis Stanfill. "Charlie and I had lunch with Stanfill and his team in Stanfill's private dining room," Kazanjian remembers. "They had all read the script and they asked a few questions. I recall Stanfill saying he knew little about the picture business. Fox passed. Fox should have said, *we don't understand this picture, but we know George. He's made tons of money for Fox; we need to put our trust in him. He's only asking $20 million to make the picture.* They did not."

At Universal, it was up to Ned Tanen, Kazanjian's old boss, who had a spotty record with Lucasfilm; Lucas owed that studio a film, however, so it would be a nice fit. Spielberg wasn't officially attached, but he was considered a great asset at Universal, where studio exec Sid Sheinberg had mentored Spielberg since the beginning of the director's career (Spielberg had started out doing episodic TV and had hit the jackpot with *Jaws*). Kazanjian asked Tanen to give them an answer the following day. Tanen asked for the weekend.

Over that weekend in late August/early September, Tanen and Sheinberg saw a sneak preview of Spielberg's *1941*. That film's budget had soared to $35 million, a huge sum. The story goes that Sheinberg got up in the middle of the picture and walked out. That same weekend, reportedly, the studio heard from Chicago that *The Blues Brothers* (1980), a John Landis film, was way over budget, too (and that its stars—John Belushi and Dan Aykroyd—were using cocaine). Landis was a good friend of Spielberg's. To the execs, the young mavericks, guilty by association, were clearly out of control.

"It didn't sound good and Ned passed," Kazanjian recalls. "There could have been other reasons, but Ned never said. Back in his office that Monday morning, as he passed on the project, Ned said, 'I have one suggestion. Tell George to take the Germans out of the script.' I froze as I tried to analyze what he'd just said to me. The look on my face must have been blank, so Ned added, 'The picture won't do well in Germany.' I turned around and left with the script and illustrations in hand. I went back to George and told him Universal had passed, which somewhat upset him, and I told him what Ned had said about taking the Germans out."

The Nazis stayed.

Kazanjian could not understand why they passed. Even if Spielberg had perhaps faltered, the producer had a proven record of bringing in pictures on time and on budget at the studio. "Director Steven Spielberg and executive producer George Lucas, he passed," Kazanjian muses. "Figure that out!"

Kazanjian met with Paramount executives on September 11 and 21, 1979, with Lucasfilm's legal rep Tom Pollock attending at least one of the meetings. Despite negative industry buzz on *1941*, Spielberg was still in play. Paramount president Michael Eisner "wanted to do it," according to Kazanjian, and convinced Paramount chairman Barry Diller that it was a good idea. A meeting with both executives at the Egg Company followed.

Variety announced the Lucasfilm-Paramount deal in November, with Spielberg attached. Lucasfilm and Paramount lawyers continued to negotiate the finer points in letters dated December 3, 7, 12, and 20. "The beginning of the deal took a week," Weber says. "Fighting over every line that they wanted to take back probably took another two or three months."

Lucas insisted on his terms. Though Lucasfilm would be using Paramount's money, his company would own the negative and "everything that goes with the film," Kazanjian said. "This way George can call the shots."

That December, *1941* opened and bombed. Prudently, Spielberg officially signed onto *Raiders* in January 1980. A profligate director in the eyes of the industry—*Jaws* and *Close Encounters* had also exceeded their scheduled days and budgets—he was out to redeem himself. "If we went over budget on *Raiders*," Lucas said, "a lot of penalties would be involved for both Steven and I. But I'd talked with

Kazanjian in his office in San Rafael, Marin County, about ten minutes' drive from Parkway, Lucasfilm HQ; behind him hang the four original concept paintings by the innovative comic book artist and illustrator Jim Steranko for Raiders of the Lost Ark *(1981).*

Steven about it, and explained that we really needed to do this like a TV show: really quick and dirty, using old-fashioned tricks. Steven said, 'Great, that's the way I want to make it.'"

There was also a carrot.

"George said that he was going to give Spielberg very generous terms," Kazanjian says, "if *Raiders* came in on budget. I also told Steven it had to come in on budget. We had $20 million to make the picture—and only $20 million. But Steven was very good. He allowed me to do two boards. Charles Maguire, who I'd worked with several times, was now the head of physical production at Paramount, and he trusted me. So I did two boards, one for an eighty-eight-day shoot, and one for seventy-three. I gave the longer schedule to Paramount and kept the other one secret, except to Steven and George."

The restaurant at the Egg Company was converted into a work space for Spielberg, Marshall, and Spielberg's assistant, Kathleen Kennedy. "Steven was barely able to do *Raiders*," Kazanjian adds, "because of an obligation to Universal and the lawsuit that was going on between George and Universal. Universal even tried to say that Steven owed them a picture and could not do *Raiders*. Steven's attorneys or agent got into that and settled it. Steven knew he owed them a picture and said he would deliver it as his next one."

Filming would take place on location in Tunisia; Hawaii; La Rochelle, France; and on the soundstages of Elstree Studios once again. Although Lucas had promised to make films locally, stages were booked abroad partially because the next sequel to *Star Wars* as well as *Raiders* would need several stages at once. "George also wanted privacy, no studio looking over his shoulder," Kazanjian says. "*Empire Strikes Back* was shot over there because props and sets from the first film were all there. The cost to move all that back to the US would have been a bit over a million dollars.

"Ultimately *Raiders* was shot there for three reasons," he explains. "The first was to keep the *Star Wars* crew busy between films. Second, we'd be close to our North African locations. Third, I recall Steven asking George why he wanted to shoot in London. George answered by saying in London, extras go home at the end of the day and keep their

224

mouths shut, while American extras call the trade and newspapers and reveal what's just been shot. I agreed with him. One of the reasons for the success of a Lucasfilm was surprise. When his movies opened, the public knew very little of the storyline or character development. The anticipation of the public was tremendous. Discussions among the movie audience of what the next picture was about, who was who, and who did what—those were things that keep the audience charged up."

DEATH

The Lucasfilm Christmas party was becoming a tradition; so was an organic turkey given to employees for Thanksgiving, both perks initiated by Marcia Lucas. The first Christmas party was held in San Francisco. After dinner, the DJ played "Rock Around the Clock"—the song performed by Bill Haley & His Comets to open *American Graffiti*—and everybody charged down to the dance floor. The family atmosphere was enhanced by Lucasfilm Christmas gifts as well. The first year Marcia and her assistant wrapped one hundred and fifty R2-D2 cookie jars (attached to the wrapping was a Christmas ornament).

A Lucasfilm organizational chart was drawn up in February 1980. Lucas was at the top, running three companies: George Lucas, Inc.; Lucasfilm, Ltd.; and Parkway Properties, which had only two members (George and Marcia). Weber was president of the other two subsidiaries. At Lucasfilm, Kazanjian was vice president of production. Its three corporate divisions consisted of ILM, Lucasfilm Licensing, and Sprocket Systems (postproduction sound and editing); under Lucasfilm were also subsidiary production companies for individual films with Kazanjian VP of each.

In early 1980, he attended mixing sessions for *Empire*; Gary Kurtz flew over to attend as well (Kurtz was not on the org chart). Kazanjian watched and, in one session, heard Yoda say, "There is another" at the end of a reel. It was an important plot point that let audiences know that Luke Skywalker was not the galaxy's only hope. Kazanjian recalls, "They're listening to it over and over, and adjusting the sound, and I said, 'It's very hard to hear what Yoda says. It sounds like 'mother' to me. Gary pushed up the volume. But I said, 'If the projectionist cuts that off on the reel change, you're not going to know there is *another*.' So they went back and made the reel change later so there was no chance the projectionist could cut off Yoda's line."

Scouting continued for *Raiders* locations. Spielberg, Kazanjian, and Frank Marshall flew to London and introduced the director to his crew at Elstree. In Paris, France, they boarded a private jet to Tunisia with Tarak Ben Ammar, a relative of the president of Tunisia. In advance of their stay, to procure their Tunisian locations, production had paid Tarak about $75,000 to smooth things over, another line item in the budget. The airline provided them with soft drinks, water, and a box of donuts. "Tarak had never seen a jelly-filled donut," Kazanjian says. "With his first bite, the jelly poured out of the small air hole at the end and ran down his white shirt. Steven, Frank, and myself couldn't help but laugh.

"We were flying over desert, which looked all the same—and the pilot asked Tarak several times where we were going. Tarak put his head between the two pilots and looked out the window for certain landmarks. After several of these moments, Tarak yells out, 'There it is!' and we landed."

They visited villages and various desert spots. Throughout the trip, Marshall carried two cases filled with audio cassettes for Spielberg's listening pleasure. The music consisted of film scores, which the director listened to on a portable Sony Walkman.

Back in the USA, actor Tom Selleck was the frontrunner to play Indiana Jones. "I didn't see him as Indiana Jones, no matter what George or Steven thought," Kazanjian says. "Just take a look at the *Magnum, P.I.* pilot and the first episode [shot early 1980]. I often wondered if either of them had ever watched the pilot episode. (Over the years, though, Tom has improved his skills and persona to become a fine actor.)"

Over two hundred actors had read for the part of Jones, according to Spielberg, filing through the Egg Company. "A lot of that [casting

226

talk] happened at the Egg Company," Ganis says. "Selleck would come in; Spielberg had an office. I thought Selleck would've been great. It seemed like absolutely a great idea. Selleck was a big star at CBS; I was looking forward to him doing it."

"We interviewed and read nearly every young male actor," Kazanjian says. "Some memorized their lines; others read from the script. Some we videotaped. Some even helped Steven in the kitchen bake cookies as they were being interviewed and put on video." At the UK casting auditions, one well-known actor apparently couldn't help himself and badmouthed Spielberg's *1941*. That actor wasn't hired.

Selleck was often paired with candidates for Indy's love interest, Marion Ravenwood. "Every evening I would come home and say we're getting nowhere with our leading man," Kazanjian says. "I told Carol, 'If only George and Steven would think of Harrison Ford.' I always wanted Harrison and kept bringing up Harrison to George and Steven. But George said he never uses the same person twice, except for a sequel. They both wanted Tom. And I can tell you Steven nearly fired me once after I'd suggested Harrison several times for the role. Steven vehemently and quietly opposed Harrison to the point where he spoke to George about dropping me from the project. But that didn't last long. The next day Steven retracted his remarks."

"Selleck was more of a star than Harrison was," Ganis adds. "Harrison was the ensemble player, with two others and Chewbacca in the background." (He'd also been part of an ensemble cast in *American Graffiti*.)

Selleck was offered the part of Indiana Jones in April 1980. Looming ahead was an "almost 100 percent" chance of an actors' strike, because negotiations between SAG and the union producers were not going well. Selleck was supposed to star in the TV series *Magnum, P.I.*, which had already been sold, but that plan was in jeopardy. "We asked Universal to give us Selleck during the strike," Kazanjian says, "and we'd give him back a star—after shooting *Raiders*." The strike wouldn't affect Lucasfilm, because it planned to hire its US actors through British Equity, not SAG, having formed an English subsidiary company to make *Raiders* (appropriately called the Raiders Company).

227

"Steven and George, my newest pals at the time," Selleck would say, "offered me the job and I said, 'Well, I've done this pilot.' And they said, 'Well, thanks for telling us, some actors wouldn't do that, but we've got cards to play.'"

Their played cards couldn't trump those of Universal and producer Glen Larson, who blocked the deal for Selleck because of the ongoing lawsuit.

That same month Alfred Hitchcock passed away. Kazanjian and Hitchcock had continued their tradition of lunching together about once a week up until the director's death. During one of their meals, Kazanjian had learned that Wasserman and Universal had canceled the director's last film. "They told Hitch, 'You can't do it. There's no way you can go out and direct this picture.' Hitch told me so in a very sad voice during one of our visits. Peggy Robertson had said, 'Bring on Howard to be Hitch's crutch,' but I was doing *Raiders* so I couldn't." Kazanjian has since maintained that the cancellation of Hitchcock's last project was, for the director, the "nail in the coffin."

"There was something special about Alfred Hitchcock and Billy Wilder," he adds. "They were from the old school; they had an experience and understanding of the filmmaking art that none of the others really have or could compare to. They thought about story more than gimmicks or explosions, because they had to. I rank those two men at the very top of my list."

THE CASE OF SOLO

"Finally, George suggested to Steven that he look at Harrison Ford," Kazanjian says. Spielberg agreed to look at Ford's last three movies: *Star Wars*; *Hanover Street* (1979), a period romance; and *The Frisco Kid* (1979), a comedy Western. A projectionist was sent over to Spielberg's home to run the movies that evening.

"The next day Steven comes into the office," Kazanjian continues, "and George was in town. Steven says '*Hanover Street. Hanover Street*? How can I make *Raiders* with this guy?' He mentioned

228

that he watched only one reel of *Star Wars*, because he knew Harrison in that film, and Han Solo wasn't the guy he saw in *Raiders*. I don't remember his comment on *The Frisco Kid*. I went home that evening and confided in my wife. Carol suggested that I invite Steven, George, and Harrison to dinner. George thought it was a good idea so I did." They ate at the Brown Derby restaurant on Vine, above Hollywood Boulevard. "George barely said anything other than hoping it would all work out. We didn't talk about the film. It was really for Steven to see Harrison and hear him, and for Steven to visualize if this is Indiana Jones.

"The next morning the three of us happened to meet outside the mail room at the Egg Company. Steven thought the dinner went well and was beginning to like Harrison. He turned to George and said, 'George, you are going to make three Indiana Jones movies and have to live with that same actor. I am going to direct only one. The leading man will be in all three. The leading woman will be in just one. You should pick Indiana Jones, and I will pick the girl."

Spielberg wanted Debra Winger, but they couldn't get her, so Karen Allen, the runner-up, was cast as Marion. Steven also wanted Danny DeVito as Sallah, Indy's sidekick for part of the film. "He wanted him bad," Kazanjian says. "Danny was doing television at the time [*Taxi*] and wanted $300,000. We only had $100,000 for Indiana. We were willing to pay Danny $50,000. So we decided that the role of Sallah would be cast out of London [the part went to John Rhys-Davies].

"And George picked Harrison Ford. I went home late that evening and Carol was waiting up for me. I told her Harrison would be Indy. All I had to do was call his agent and negotiate the deal. That's the truth. George did say to Steven at the Egg Company that he did always have Harrison in mind when he created the story. He may have. If you look at the Steranko paintings, there is a strong resemblance to Harrison."

(In the year 2000, Harrison Ford would be honored with a lifetime achievement award by the AFI at the Beverly Hilton Hotel in Beverly Hills. Lucas and Spielberg would present the award to Harrison. "George said to the audience he had Harrison in mind when he wrote the script," Kazanjian says. "Steven said Harrison was always his first choice for

Indiana Jones. I was sitting home with Carol watching this on television. We just looked at each other!")

"I totally remember where I was standing," Ganis says, "when I heard that, no, Selleck was not going to do it, that CBS wouldn't let him out of his deal. And then it was very quickly Harrison. Very quickly."

By May 1, Ford had signed on, but his addition did create one problem. Ford asked for and received $500,000, $400,000 more than budgeted for Indy, which Kazanjian had to make work financially. Lucas also planned on giving Spielberg a percentage of dollar one at the box office—otherwise known as, "first dollar." Kazanjian recalls, "When I heard what the numbers were with Steven, I said, 'That's crazy, George.' But George said, 'If it's successful, he deserves to make it. If it's a failure, he'll never see it anyway.'"

The Lucases flew down south, and stayed at the Baylor Hotel where they had a meeting with Spielberg, Ford, and Kasdan. Apparently the issue of Indy's character was open for debate now that they had cast Ford to play him. "George invited me to go into his meeting," Marcia Lucas says, "which was unusual, but he did, and they're all sitting there talking. The thing was, Harrison Ford wanted the character to be an alcoholic. That's what Harrison wanted. I said, 'I'm not sure that's a great idea, Harrison. To begin with, Jones is a college professor. Secondly, the United States of America hires you to go out and do the work of the government, to stop the Nazis from getting the Ark of the Covenant. Why in the world would any of these people put up with an alcoholic? I don't think that works.' Even in the opening scene, an alcoholic's not outrunning that ball and getting that statue and being sharp. Steven and George looked at me and went, 'Well, we don't know.' Anyway, when we left the meeting, Larry Kasdan said, 'Thank you, Marcia.'"

Kazanjian adds, "In the original story, Indy smoked and he drank; I fought and fought against that and got him to not smoke, and then eventually to not drink came about."

230

A Simple Solution

Norman Reynolds was production designer for *Raiders*. He and his art department at Elstree Studios made a large-scale model of the archaeological dig location in Tunisia, where the Nazis are looking for the Well of Souls. The miniature, on display for discussion, was landscaped with hills, towers, a miniature flying wing airplane, and spotted with plastic green toy soldiers.

"I brought Steven in, and Frank was there, too, and I said, 'This is all you're getting,'" Kazanjian recalls. "Steven asks, 'What are these, ants?' (meaning plastic army soldiers). I said, 'No, those are your Arabs.' After a minute Steven said, 'The size of the plan [table] is not big enough.' So, a couple days later, we go back and Norman has made the table bigger, and Steven looks at it, looks at it, looks at it, and says, 'We don't need this much.' He asks Norman, 'How much have we saved?' $700,000 or something. Now Steven tells George he just pulled $700,000 out of the budget. I had to explain the whole story to George."

Another budget story revolved around the flying wing, the expensive set piece for the dig location. "At another one of our production meetings at the Egg Company, in the conference room, we'd just received the flying wing model and loved it," Kazanjian continues. "But we didn't love the $1 million price tag for the life-size one. I got a message that George was pulling up at the back door. I left the meeting and met him as he was getting out of his car. He asked how things were going. As we entered the building, I told him we were discussing the flying wing and its price tag. George didn't respond.

"In the conference room George picked up the flying wing and asked what it would cost. I said, 'A million dollars.' Holding the flying wing, he broke off the two wing ends, snapping off two of the four engines. 'Now how much will it cost?' I replied, 'I think it's in the budget.' Steven was shocked, as were most of the production team." The final price tag was about $750,000.

During a following discussion about snakes and how hundreds of them could have slithered into the Well of Souls (a big set piece) and survived, Kazanjian mentioned that, based on a documentary he'd seen, snakes could conceivably eat each other and give birth to baby

231

snakes. That idea prompted Spielberg to suggest procuring hundreds of snake eggs and to photograph them hatching. A hatchery was reserved at Elstree for snake eggs and a schedule plotted. But only one or two eggs ended up hatching at a time and the idea was dropped.

Also added to the schedule was composer John Williams, whose services needed to be booked a year in advance. The recording studio and key musicians had to be lined up as well. Those dates couldn't budge. Everything was being locked into place.

Adventure on the High Seas

Kurtz supervised production of the 70mm prints of *Empire*, with a few assistants and Kazanjian's help. When Kazanjian saw the film's credits, he was surprised. He hadn't asked for a credit, but had figured he would receive one. When he didn't, Kazanjian had to assume that either Lucas had forgotten or decided against it, or it was not put in by Kurtz.

Star Wars: Episode V *The Empire Strikes Back* began its limited 70mm run on May 21, 1980, with a wide release planned for June. "George always figured if *Empire* did only 30 percent of the first picture, we would still be in the black," Kazanjian says.

The sequel did much better than that. With a cliff-hanger ending and a darker mood, however, it wouldn't reach the financial heights of the first. "I was going through some old notes," says Miki Herman of her diary, "and I found one from 1980, where George said he liked *Star Wars* better than the *Empire Strikes Back*."

The title of the next *Star Wars* film, Episode VI, was made public on May 14 (to little fanfare in those days): *Revenge of the Jedi*. "George had told me in secret months earlier that its title was *Return of the Jedi*," Kazanjian says. "I didn't like it and told him it was a weak title. It reminded me of *Return of the Pink Panther* [1975]; there were a number of 'Return' pictures in Hollywood during that period. He came back one or two days later and said, 'We're calling it *Revenge of the Jedi*' and that's what was announced."

"We pretty much started right away," Lucas said. "There was a little breather period in between films, but, you know, you've got to get

232

going." Kazanjian notes, "I think if maybe George had it to do all over again, he wouldn't have done *Star Wars*. Because once he did *Star Wars*, he tied himself up for the next ten years."

Meanwhile, prep for the filming of *Raiders* went into high gear for a June start date. "I was cast late—like two weeks before the cameras were scheduled to roll," Harrison Ford said. By May 1980, coincidentally, Ford had also verbally committed to the next *Star Wars* film, also the result of a Kazanjian campaign. "Ford's decision to return to the franchise changed the whole direction the second sequel was taking," the producer says. Lucas hadn't been sure his star would return and had consequently encased his character, Han Solo, in carbonite. "I asked George why we don't bring Harrison back for *Jedi*. He said Harrison just wouldn't do it. 'What if he said yes?' I asked. George replied, 'Ask him. If he says yes, we will unfreeze him.'"

Because Kazanjian had just negotiated Ford's deal for *Raiders* with Phil Gersh of the Gersh Agency, he called again. Gersh said he would speak with Ford. When Kazanjian followed up, Gersh was on vacation and his son, David, took the call; they negotiated Ford's deal for Episode VI. Kazanjian says, "When Phil returned to the office several weeks later, he called me and said I had taken advantage of his son in the negotiations. I had not. But agents are agents."

As mentioned, Ford's salary for *Raiders* meant its producer had to trim the budget. The script had Indy climb on top of a German submarine that's transporting the Ark, and lash himself to its periscope with his whip. "Steven joked that sharks should attack Indy," Kazanjian says. "The submarine was to enter a hollow volcanic island through a giant underwater door, but the sequence was thrown out when I reminded everyone it was exactly like the set that Disney had used for Captain Nemo's submarine at the end of *20,000 Leagues Under the Sea* [1954]." The omission of that sequence helped decrease the budget deficit.

Production united in London for the last days of prep before traveling to the La Rochelle location in France. Indiana Jones's jacket had become a last-minute decision, put together the Sunday before Monday's shooting. "Although many discussions had been held on Indy's

233

look," Kazanjian recalls, "the total costume wasn't ready until the last day in London. I had previously asked if the jacket was ready and Deborah Nadoolman, our costume designer, had said no, she was working on it. Steven had asked for Deborah because she was married to John Landis, and Steven was close to John. Weeks passed and we still had not seen it."

"The unit production manager was ruthless," Nadoolman said in 2005. "It was not pretty. I had budgeted for ten jackets and to save money I'd ordered them from the very reasonably priced Wilson's House of Suede and Leather in Los Angeles, who custom-made them for me based on a prototype I'd made at Western Costume Company. This is before any of us ever went to London to begin preproduction at EMI Elstree Studios."

"Now the Sunday before Monday's first day of shooting in France," Kazanjian continues, "George and I are walking the stages checking the sets at Elstree [for their return]. Deborah comes around the stage corner with Indy's leather jacket in her arms. George looks at it and says, 'This is nothing like I've told you, Deborah. This is wrong; it should be a bomber jacket.' He instructed Deborah to go out and buy a bomber jacket off the shelf. But every store was closed in London on Sunday, so she had to get a few of them to open. She brought back a selection for us to see early Monday morning. George approved a store-bought jacket. She aged it down a bit and it was ready."

"When the jackets arrived from Wilson's, I understood they would be unusable for the film," Nadoolman said. "As I tried to age the first one, the leather peeled away in my hands, immediately the color of the leather came off and giant holes appeared. I discussed this with Steven, George, and Harrison. And it was Harrison who became my ally and advocate. I simply could not use these low-grade jackets—it would be impossible to wear them in stunt situations and they would never look right. Finally, after much fighting about money—which was ridiculous given that the jackets were the centerpiece of the film—finally I was given the okay to design and make another set of ten at Bermans & Nathans costumiers once we arrived in London."

Although the producer's and costume designer's stories differ in the details, they do agree that the final jacket was decided on only days before cameras rolled.

234

Filming began in La Rochelle, France, on location for submarine scenes in an authentic World War II submarine pen built by the Germans. Lucas was on hand to make sure everything got off to a smooth start, though he had increasing confidence in his vice president of production. "Perhaps the jacket we first used was the store-bought one," Kazanjian says, "and then Bermans made ten of them based on that." (The brown leather jacket Ford wears in the submarine pen scenes is, in fact, slightly different from the jacket[s] he wears in the rest of the movie.)

"Howard was the voice of George," Carol Kazanjian says. "George would say something, but he was very shy. Often he and Howard would walk together, George would say something quietly and Howard would make sure it got done."

"What George wanted was between the lines," Kazanjian explains. "You had to know what George really meant." Kazanjian was also mentoring Frank Marshall. "Frank tended to deal more with the personalities and people, while I dealt more with the money and the logistics. We almost always knew what the other was doing."

One day Kazanjian received a cable from Louis Friedman, his assistant back at Lucasfilm south, informing him that Deborah Nadoolman's sketches, presumably for costumes yet to be made, were locked in the safe of her husband, John Landis. "And Landis is out of state for three more weeks," his cable noted. A solution was found, but another costume issue arose that month. ILM wired to say that Marion's long, pink silk nightgown was "the worst possible material and color" for bluescreen shots during the opening of the Ark. Its reflection "will cause problems and look terrible." The gown would be changed.

"I was the one production person who stayed back home," Friedman says. "I was coordinating shipments, logistics, film, freight. I was doing prep for the location shoot later in Hawaii, at ILM, in LA. I would get up very early in the morning and start speaking with these various areas of the world. We were using Telex, but the communication systems were basically horrible."

They shot a "submarine" on the high seas outside the port. The German U-boat was actually a barge with everything above the waterline built to period specifications. The barge could be pulled by

235

another boat, but could not move under its own power. "We were not to use it if waves were higher than eight feet," Kazanjian recalls. "One day we were out in twelve-foot swells. Many of the crew got ill, including George. Steven kept shooting—perhaps he was used to it after *Jaws*. I had to return to shore and prepare for the next day's shooting. I was lucky, but a bit wobbly."

A good deal of the behind-the-scenes action was captured on film. It had become common practice on important pictures to hire a B-roll unit, which usually shot in 16mm, to acquire footage and document a few key moments for promotional purposes and/or future home video releases. Kazanjian had hired Phil Schuman and a sound assistant to accompany production, unusually, for the complete shoot.

Pssss . . .

At Elstree in early July, writer and pressman Derek Taylor, former press secretary for the Beatles, joined the production. Taylor was writing a book on the making of the film. "George and Steven used a general-purpose table in what became known as Kazanjian's office," Taylor observed. "Howard's place tended to be a leisure room, especially since it had a very addictive electronic Asteroids game glittering and whizzing in a far corner."

Spielberg and company were on Stage 3, where the giant Well of Souls set piece had been built. "I didn't like going on the snake stage," says Kazanjian. "In fact, the line in the script that Indy says is my line—'I hate snakes!' We had big boas and small ones. After each take, crewmembers and snake handlers jumped in and picked up dozens in their arms, like spaghetti, and put them in large plastic containers."

"George, Larry, and I didn't know that snakes love fire," Spielberg said at the time. "Cold-blooded, they warm to it. So we'll have to find something else that they hate: a smell, a pesticide. This will be the most aggravating sequence in the film, because I'm aggravated already and it's my first day."

"I believe 50 percent of directing is knowing where and what to do with the camera," Kazanjian says, "and 50 percent is how you direct the

236

actors. George is great with the camera, quiet with the actors. Steven is great with both. Steven can walk into a set he has never seen before and immediately know how to shoot it. This was 180 degrees different from Sam Peckinpah, who needed an hour or two of excuses to figure out how he was to shoot a scene."

Spielberg, preparing for an overhead shot, decided that he actually needed more snakes to fill the cavernous set. Kazanjian informed his director that more snakes were already on order from Scandinavian countries. He and Watts had visited the set at the end of construction and come to the same conclusion about the number of snakes. (They had started with about two thousand rubber snakes, controlled in groups of twenty by air pressure mechanisms underneath the floor that made them twist and move in different patterns. On top of the rubber snakes, they added about two thousand live snakes.)

When shooting the cobras, Kazanjian had Watts arrange for an ambulance to stand by at the stage door. When serum from India didn't arrive on time, shooting of the cobras was delayed at least a day. Upon arrival of the serum, a gurney was on stage near the camera with a hypodermic needle already inserted into the vial of serum should it be needed quickly. The cobras turned out to be quite calm, placed in their large, rectangular glass bowl with high sides; the wrangler even had to agitate them so they would rise up and hiss.

While Kazanjian avoided the snakes as best he could, he studied *Raiders'* master DP, Douglas Slocombe, at work. "He and I would have conversations during breaks," Kazanjian recalls. "Doug was sixty-eight, but you'd have never known it. I especially enjoyed watching Slocombe light a set. Like Surtees, he was so creative in achieving the look of the picture. I once asked Doug why he never used a light meter. His response was that 'it never said what he wanted it to say.'"

Between setups Spielberg occasionally thought of his next picture or two. He still owed Universal a picture. Before leaving the States, he'd asked creature effects artist Rick Baker to work on a family of aliens for a film called *Night Skies*. Another picture the director was talking about became *Poltergeist* (1982), a comedy horror film. Kazanjian suggested putting the haunted house on top of an old graveyard. "While shooting

FOLLOWING SPREAD: *Harrison sits; George makes a bet with Steven; Kazanjian* 237 *and Marshal look on, laughing.*

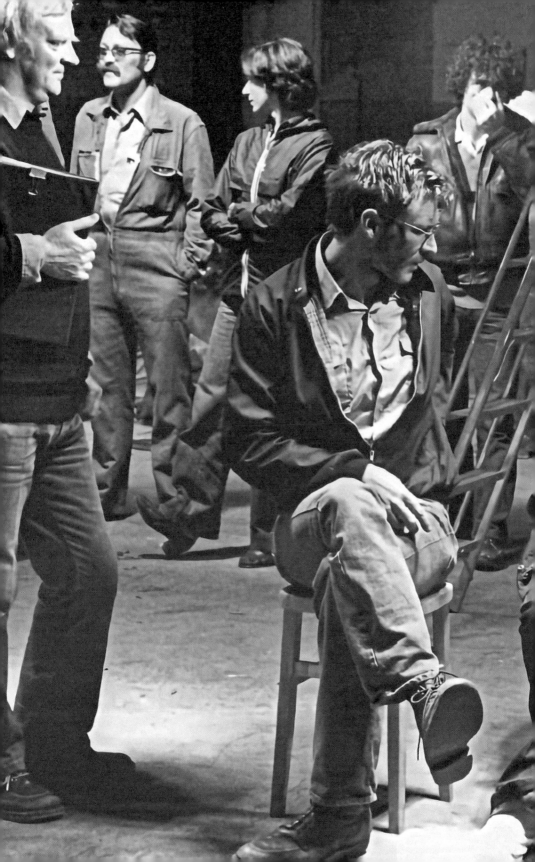

Raiders in London, Steven was also working with a writer on a musical project," Kazanjian says. "One weekend he flew to Los Angeles to meet with Sid Sheinberg and flew back in time for a Monday shoot. The studio passed on that one."

In late July, as predicted, SAG went on strike, but *Raiders* wasn't affected. Production continued with more snakes, tarantulas, and a rolling boulder that chased Indy. The rolling ball was on an arm attached to a track. When the ball was put in motion, it rolled down the track toward camera; inside was a mechanism that turned the ball to simulate rolling while it crushed stalactites and stalagmites in its path. A second ball was used on a flat tunnel floor, pushed by prop and grip personnel (the exterior of the entrance would be shot on location in Kauai, Hawaii).

"Suddenly, on a Friday, Steven said we needed a longer tunnel for Indy to run out of," Kazanjian says. "I agreed. We had a second ball standing by, but not a longer tunnel. Fortunately, Norman Reynolds always seemed to be prepared for more, so for $60,000 we built an additional fifty feet, with a bend going around a corner. That was a lot of money, but worth it. Reynolds and his crew finished it over the weekend and we didn't miss a day."

Different combinations of Spielberg, Marshall, Kennedy, and Kazanjian would drive together each day to Elstree. Food at the studio commissary was good and heavy, and there was a bar. Many of the crew members would drink during their lunch break, come back to the set and still be productive. Mandated tea-trolley breaks took place mornings and afternoons. Ford invited Spielberg, Kazanjian, and Marshall to his home one weekend and they watched TV. Spielberg once told Kazanjian that the best producer he ever had was Julia Phillips, who had produced *Close Encounters*. "Every morning when Steven sat at his desk," Kazanjian says, "on one side of his blotter were the telephone calls he was to make, and on the other side, his appointments for the day. But this is what a secretary does, not a producer. I really don't think Steven knew what a producer did back then."

Kazanjian missed a few days in early August, as Carol approached her due date. While Spielberg shot more footage of the snakes, Kazanjian

240

jetted back to California; he was by Carol's side for the birth of their first son, Peter, but had to fly to Hawaii on August 11 to work out the logistics for that location shoot. He wouldn't see Carol or his newborn son for another two months. He was back at Elstree just in time to see Indy climb the giant Jackal sculpture and ride it through a breakaway wall.

Upon his return the producer was told by the head snake wrangler that some of the smaller pythons and boas were disappearing. After a little investigation, Kazanjian discovered that the English love snakes and that many crewmembers were carrying out the smaller reptiles in their satchels and canvas bags to keep as pets.

Every so often he checked in with Paramount to tell studio executives how things were going per the schedule and budget. "Charlie Maguire said the production reports were not matching up with the board," Kazanjian says. "I didn't tell him that we had two boards. I told him we were shooting in a different order, but on budget. That was all Charlie needed to hear."

Spielberg was keeping his promise. Kazanjian even overheard the director telling Ford, "We're making a B-movie, so no one is winning an Oscar." Ganis recalls, "It was a throwback to another kind of moviemaking."

Still the director was planning each shot carefully while moving forward as rapidly as he could. "George gave me a great piece of advice," Spielberg recalls. "He just said, 'I promise you, if you're tough on yourself, and you throw out your first or second ideas 'cause they cost too much money, I bet you anything your compromises are better than your initial ideas on storyboards.' And he was right. We had a whole roller coaster chase, and it was impossible to shoot because it was too expensive. I threw it out. George really taught me the art of the compromise."

The other good news was that Lucas and his company were no longer in financial danger per *Empire*. A letter dated August 6 from an official at the Bank of Boston read: "*Empire* has done exactly what all of you at Lucasfilm said it would do."

"You know what the difference is [between Lucasfilm and the major studios]? It's so simple," Ganis told a reporter in 1980. "People at big studios are seldom focused. The other studios I worked at, it was much easier not to think because I was much too busy. The majors are too big. They have to sustain a product lineup just to clear overhead and make money . . . At Lucasfilm, we have the luxury of working on one film, more or less, at a time. All of our energies go into that one film so that when it is released, it represents the best of the talent Lucasfilm has."

SICKNESS AND SHOOTING

In late August, production made a complex logistical move to Tunisia. "Going from England to France to Tunisia," Frank Marshall said, "you have to have customs lists, and ship things days and days ahead of time. You have language barriers, vaccinations, passports, hotel reservations, the transportation of equipment and construction teams. All those things have to be considered."

On the first of September, they shot on location near Tozeur, where Reynolds and company had built the massive "Tunis Digs" archaeology set. "For a while on that first morning, Lucas, Spielberg, and Howard Kazanjian sat on the canvas seats with their names slotted over the backs," Taylor wrote. "It was not a sight we ever saw again. George and Steven and Howard were talking. Frank was on his feet and moving quickly around the first setup, which required John Rhys-Davies as Sallah to pretend to be a stupid Arab working for the bullying Nazis, one of whom is hungry and demanding food. A little scene—but they were tense, no doubt about that."

Three hundred extras were budgeted at the digs for the master shots. The following days the number was cut to one hundred and fifty. Spielberg had asked Marshall how much more it would cost to have the three hundred for another day and Marshall had given him a dollar number, "but had miscalculated," Kazanjian says, "because he didn't include additional shovels, costumes, transportation, camels, etcetera. What Frank also didn't calculate was changing US dollars into English pounds into Tunisian dinars. But visually and financially, it all worked out fine." Kazanjian coached Marshall on stuntmen's fees, because the latter didn't understand at first that when a stunt person performs a special stunt, it cost extra. Marshall had also sent the tent (in which Marion is held prisoner) in the same locker with the director's canned food stash, but had neglected to list the canned goods and oranges on the manifest. The shipment was therefore delayed at customs for days. Spielberg finally had Marion's tent shipped back to Elstree, at his own expense, to finish the scene. "Frank had the energy and stamina of someone half his age," Kazanjian adds. "And he got along well with Steven. He was a good listener and learner."

Everyday problems arose and solutions were found. After the explosion and destruction of the full-scale flying wing, production left it on location for locals to scavenge. "The Tunisians appreciated us leaving the wing behind and we saved on cleanup," Kazanjian says. "It had been known and we'd seen that if one left a broken-down car on the road with a flat tire or engine trouble, by the end of the day only the rusted frame was left as scavengers had done their job."

During down time, Lucas and Kazanjian spoke about Episode VI. "George told me the direction he would be taking with the story, many of the elements and characters. I really didn't know too much until we had a number of meetings, both formal and on the run somewhere."

By the third week in Tunisia, many of the crew were too ill to work due to poor water and food treatment, and the unrelenting heat, which once climbed to 130 degrees. One of those too sick to go on was 1st AD David Tomblin. When Spielberg was told, he looked at Kazanjian. "Howard was ready to go back to Los Angeles and see his baby," Spielberg says. "But I remembered that he'd worked with Sam Peckinpah as an AD. I thought if anybody could work with Peckinpah, they can sure work with me. So I made Howard stay three more days to AD, and he was wonderful. He's more like me. He's a vocal pusher. Howard was running around the set saying, 'Okay, we ought to be ready now. Let's go! Let's go!' It took the pressure off me those three days."

Kazanjian kept healthy by eating carefully, avoiding lettuce and locally grown fruits and vegetables, and supplementing his diet with vitamins. He ate just enough to survive, but was losing weight.

Cast and crew moved to Kairouan on September 17. On the third day of Kazanjian's AD duty, they were to shoot Indy's duel with a large, sword-wielding local (Terry Richards). Ahead of that was a setup with

243

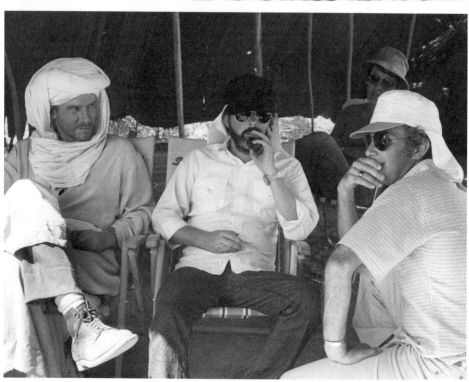

TOP TO BOTTOM: *Lunchtime on location in Tozeur, Tunisia, for* Raiders: *Kazanjian and Lucas face a tired Harrison Ford (Indiana Jones) and director Steven Spielberg over a checkered tablecloth, 1980. Ford had been cast as Indy at the eleventh hour thanks in part to Kazanjian's efforts. • Taking a break in Tozeur are: Ford, Lucas, and Kazanjian, who have their hands over their mouths because of the flies.*

244

Karen Allen as Marion. "Steven was not feeling well that day," Kazanjian recalls. "He didn't admit he was not well; we could see it in his behavior. He was talking very little to me and Douglas Slocombe. He was sitting hunched over, which was unusual for him, atop a six-foot parallel with the camera. I was looking up and talking with him. He had his Walkman earphones on, I was talking about the scene we were setting up and I was asking him questions; he could hear me, but was not answering. I'd never seen Steven like this before. I asked Doug if there was a problem with Steven, and he nodded his head 'yes,' but shrugged his shoulders to say he didn't know why. We made a take, and I asked if it was okay. Steven barely replied."

"I hate it here and I want to go home," Spielberg said at the time. "I hate this desert; I love the Tunisians, but I'm not crazy about shooting in 110 heat every day. The crew is going crazy; they'd like to get out of here as much as I would. Kairouan has been probably one of my worst location experiences. Just the number of Tunisian assistants we've had to employ to get it through the heads of the crowd simply to stand back or press forward on a certain cue—no acting, just, 'Three steps back, three steps forward.'

"I really don't want to stay here another day."

"At lunchtime," Kazanjian continues, "Steven is sitting down with his tray in front of him at the end of an eight-foot table, and I bring my tray over and sit directly opposite. We're talking very little and eating, and Steven says, 'Let's go home.' I said, 'What do you mean?' And he said, 'Let's call it a day and come back here tomorrow.' And with Steven you never say no. You show him a different direction and let him say no. I said, 'Steven, today is Friday; if we call it a day, we'll have to come back here Saturday. Saturday is our move day to another city in Tunisia. If we shoot Saturday, we need to give the crew off Sunday; I can't move the company Sunday, then move Monday, and shoot Tuesday, so we're losing a day. We need to finish today."

Robert Watts came over and Spielberg also told him he wanted to go home. Watts confirmed Kazanjian's reasons for sticking it out. Ford finished his lunch and came over to sit at the end of the table between Kazanjian and Spielberg. "I'd already done every damn useless thing in the world," Ford said. "I was into my fifth week of dysentery and I was riding in at 5:30 AM with nothing to do but submit to wild imaginings. So I stormed Steven with the idea of just dismissing this maniac. I'd never unholstered my gun in the whole movie, so I said, 'Let's just shoot the fucker.'"

"Steven gave a little laugh and said, 'Funny,'" Kazanjian says. "That was enough for him to get up and go back to work. Perhaps his lunch gave him renewed energy or he loved Harrison's suggestion. Harrison didn't make this suggestion because he knew Steven was not quite himself that day, he said it because it made sense. Harrison is very good with story and cares not just about his performance, but the story and dialogue. So, we go back from lunch and we shoot that scene where the crowd parts revealing the giant Arab dressed in black with the scimitar. Harrison pulls out his gun and shoots him dead. 'Print!'"

"That's getting character in action," Ford concludes.

They also shot the fight as originally scripted; a much more involved melee involving a butcher, comical business, and Indy using his whip. Spielberg was feeling better and wrapped the location so production could travel to the next city on schedule.

CRASH ON THE RIVER

Production was in Hawaii the first few days of October, shooting on locations around Kauai. For this last push everyone was tired. "Usually the last couple of days I have insomnia," Spielberg said, "because I'm sure I've missed the most important elements that would make the film either a hit or a miss."

"I went out shopping with Steven in Hawaii," Kazanjian recalls. "Steven always bought everything with cash, and I never could figure out where this cash was coming from. I never saw anybody bring it to him, but he'd go in and buy five, ten baseball caps. Go in and buy a bunch of tennis shoes, go in and buy a bunch of socks. Wherever we went, it was cash."

A production report noted: "Unit will travel to location by boat leaving from the Nawiliwili small boat harbor at 7.20 hours." The ride up the Huleia River took about twenty-five minutes; there, they'd shoot

On location in Kauai, Hawaii, for Raiders, *Kazanjian laughs with Lucas while Spielberg and Kathleen Kennedy stand by for the next shot.*

Indy's escape on a small plane from villain Belloq (Paul Freeman) and pursuing extras costumed as nearly nude vengeful natives. "When the local extras first showed up on the set, they were very embarrassed," says Kazanjian. "They wore towels wrapped around their waists. But after a while, during the long days, you'd find them sitting with their legs spread on a log or a rock out there."

"I was the only pilot that was flying seaplanes in Hawaii at the time," Fred Sorenson said in 2011. "I had flown Frank Marshall and Howard Kazanjian around the islands in a Beech 18, looking for places to film. We went out to the Cattleman's Steakhouse for dinner, and they asked me if I could put together the airplane project and asked if I wanted to play the pilot in the movie."

Kazanjian had found the right period plane and its owner, Hank Strauch, in Oregon. Strauch had flown his Waco UBF to Los Angeles, where it was taken apart under his supervision, shipped to Oahu, reassembled, sanctioned by the FAA, and flown to Kauai, where crew painted the red-and-white over with a silver "Air Pirates" color and added numbers on the side (the call letters on its fuselage were an in-joke—"OB-CPO"—a reference to Jedi Obi-Wan Kenobi and golden droid C-3PO in *Star Wars*). "Hank didn't care that we painted it," Kazanjian says, "but he didn't want the fabric torn, especially by the arrows the natives were shooting. I promised they wouldn't, but they did shoot one arrow into it. He was okay with that. He became enamored with Hollywood and Harrison Ford and everything."

With cameras rolling, Ford hung on to one of the plane's pontoons as it taxied down the river. "It lifted off the ground as Harrison was climbing into the front seat of the cockpit," Kazanjian says. "They headed out of sight of the cameras—and we heard a crash. All of our hearts stopped beating. I didn't want to jump in the river, as I didn't know how far down the river the plane was. I yelled to the crew, 'Get down there! Call for an ambulance!'"

The plane had crashed into the riverbank. "A camera was originally mounted on the left wing," Sorenson said, "which proved to be a problem on the first take, resulting in damage to the airplane. Over the next four days we worked to repair it."

Kazanjian remembers that it was the cockpit's open door that caused the incident: "It acted like a rudder and made the plane veer to the left and crash. The pilot later said to me that he should have known and made an adjustment. The plane was about twelve feet off the ground when it crashed; Harrison told us he was laughing the whole way down. Fortunately, we had safety boats in the water and they quickly got to the plane. There was little damage, but the plane couldn't be flown."

"Harrison has a talent for plane crashes," Miki Herman says. "I wasn't on the crew, but Howard let me come to Hawaii as a little bonus. I saw the shoot in the jungle and went water skiing on the river, and it was a lot of fun."

The takeoff reshoots were filmed by a second-unit crew on a river next to the Menehune Fishpond near Lihue.

Another last-minute location was found for the movie's opening shot in which the old Paramount logo match-dissolves into a mountain and Indy appears in silhouette to start the story. It was something Kazanjian had thought up and cleared with the studio. Months earlier in preproduction at the Egg Company, he'd suggested it to Spielberg, who had okayed it. The matching mountain location was difficult to access, however; a small crew had to be helicoptered in with doubles and two donkeys. "There was some inclement weather called for that afternoon," says Louis Friedman, who was part of that team, "and Robert Watts had to make a judgment call—do we go for it or not? He said, 'Go for it,' and he put it in motion. We picked them up, and they were boxed, and we dropped them on this cliffside. We sprayed the donkeys down because they were the wrong color."

It took about three hours to fly everybody in, but they were able to get the shot and get out before the storm hit.

It was a wrap. "*Raiders* went smooth as silk," says Duwayne Dunham. "It seemed to not have any problems. And I know there were problems, just shooting where they shot caused problems. People getting sick every day. But Howard ran that ship pretty smoothly."

249

CHAPTER 12: *A Laconic Hero*

"**M**y first assignment on Episode VI was to hire a writer," Kazanjian says. "I suggested that George write the screenplay. He said he didn't have the time. After all he was building his corporate empire out at Skywalker Ranch. I suggested that we hire Larry Kasdan. George replied that Larry was a writer and director of his own projects now and would never do it." Lucas said, "That's when I decided that trying to tell somebody what the story is, like I did on *Empire* [with Leigh Brackett], just doesn't work. The only way I can do it is to write the first draft myself and just say, 'Okay, this is how it looks and feels,' and then bring somebody in to fix it up and question it and go through it."

That fall, Kazanjian saw how Kasdan's directorial debut, *Body Heat* (1981), a sultry thriller, was shaping up. Alan Ladd's production company was financing it, and Lucas was acting as guarantor: If Ladd fired Kasdan, Lucas would have to step in and direct. Lucas was consequently required to review Kasdan's dailies, duly delivered each day to the projection room at the Egg Company, which was next to Kazanjian's office. Louis Friedman would videotape the dailies off the screen and ship the videocassette to Lucas. "Every now and then Louis would come to my office and say, 'Howard, you have to look at this,'" Kazanjian recalls. "I would watch for a few minutes. In one scene William Hurt and Kathleen Turner were standing by a window looking out of it. The edited film showed them in a medium shot from the waist up, but the wider shot showed a great deal more. That shot was never used."

250

Postproduction on *Raiders* meant Spielberg's editor Michael Kahn went to work on the director's cut, while ILM created visual effects and Ben Burtt handled sound design. "Michael was very personable," Kazanjian says. "If necessary, he would take the time to explain his cuts."

Kazanjian was on top of *Raiders'* postproduction budget and helped out in other ways: He procured footage of a period passenger plane flying through inclement weather for an insert shot of Indy's travel (from Frank Capra's *Lost Horizon*, 1937; ILM created a second passenger plane for an "over the map" shot) and footage from a 1930s Washington, DC, street scene (coincidentally from *The Hindenburg*) for another insert shot.

Spielberg went off to work on his next picture, an approved project to fulfill his obligation to Universal, at last. Its title: *E.T. the Extra-Terrestrial* (1982). *Night Skies* had morphed from a family of hostile aliens into a story featuring a single friendly extraterrestrial, written by Melissa Mathison (Spielberg parted ways with Rick Baker, and hired Carlo Rambaldi to fashion his E.T., using Baker's work as a guide). Spielberg also planned to produce *Poltergeist* (1982), the haunted house built on a graveyard movie.

Another project in post was the documentary on *Raiders*; Philip Schuman had shot thousands of feet of film. He was given a suite on the first floor of a Lucasfilm building in San Anselmo and he, too, began editing.

Kazanjian was also searching for a director to helm Episode VI. On November 4 and 5, 1980, he compiled notes on David Lynch. Susan Pile at Paramount had told him, "Lynch is a great guy with forward-looking ideas." Lynch wasn't taking any offers until he made his "Ronnie Rocket" movie, but Pile wrote in a note that Lynch was very cooperative with "the mind of an artist as well as a filmmaker. At the same time, he is very down-to-earth. Sounds like a 'hayseed character from a Capra film.'"

Lynch met with Kazanjian and (possibly) Robert Watts on November 23. A notation from the meeting read, "David also now expresses concern over the possibility that a *Star Wars* film could swallow him up. Would he, for example, have input? He would want to do more with special sound (he felt that *Star Wars* and *Empire* were walls of music)."

More director interviews were held mostly at the Egg Company, but also in Marin County and in London. Carol Titelman (maiden name Wikarska) was director of publishing and sat in on the interviews at the Egg Company to take notes. "She offered her thoughts at the end of each interview," Kazanjian adds. "She was always insightful."

North-Sizing

The month of January 1981 was a lull between principal photography on the company's major films. Lucas took the opportunity to move his people north from the Egg Company to offices in Marin County. Not all were invited. Charles Weber was let go. "It was a bunch of spoiled people," said senior vice president of finance and administration Robert Greber. "Secretaries had BMWs, company cars, things like that. Now of course I didn't say 'no' when I got one. There were also a lot of people in charge of things who didn't have the ability to do those things, but I don't think that's unusual in small, creative teams."

Kazanjian recalls, "Charlie had really been told by George, 'You're running it, you can buy and sell buildings and so on, but only in California.' One of the things that Charlie did wrong was buying a radio station on the East Coast; George found out and stopped it. And George had always really wanted us all up north," he adds. "That was the greatest reason to say, 'Let's do this carefully. Let's not announce that Charlie is being fired. Let's just say Lucasfilm is moving up north. Let's pick and choose those people who we want out of the seventy or so employees down here.' We took up exactly half."

"When everyone moved up," Dunham says, "it seemed like more of a permanent move for Howard and Carol than it had been on *More American Graffiti*, which was more of a commuter thing."

"Howard wasn't a sycophant," Lucy Wilson says, "and George was surrounded by sycophants often at the Egg Company."

Lucas finished his rough draft for *Revenge of the Jedi* on February 24, 1981.

"There were times," Kazanjian says, "when George and I would drive together to the airport to fly to Los Angeles and once to San Diego, and those were quiet moments. When we were alone, I could ask things like, 'Who is the *other*? Either George wouldn't want to answer, or he'd say, 'Who do you think?' Sometimes I'd ask him, 'Why don't we do this or that?' Dead silence. Then the next day he'd give me orders to do exactly what I'd suggested. This happened a hundred times."

With several films at different stages of production, ILM was also doing occasional pick-ups or insert shots for *Raiders*. "We had this whole set built, the tomb with the skeletons and stuff," Miki Herman says. "And then Steven came and just did an extreme close-up of Karen Allen." (Lucas had built a soundstage for ILM, constructed like an English stage, according to Kazanjian, so crew could move sets using chains hung from ceiling rafters, and pulleys that could slide across I-beams, etc.) During another pick-up shot for *Raiders*, Herman had to adjust Ford's wardrobe. "I was kneeling in front of him, fixing his boots, and he made an obscene gesture," she recalls, "and the photographer took a picture—and I just had a fit. I insisted that the photographer give me the negatives. So in one of the pictures that Harrison autographed for me, he wrote, 'Okay, Miki, you can keep the negatives.'"

Raiders was a few months from its release date when *Jedi* went into preproduction. Ralph McQuarrie, Joe Johnston, and concept artist Nilo Rodis-Jamero were churning out dozens of sketches and paintings. Stages were reserved in England and recces conducted. Friedman recalls, "We were having lunch, and Howard said, 'Louis, you and Miki are going to be our supervisors for our two US locations.' Miki had seniority, so she picked the Ewok locations, Smith River up near Crescent City, which was fine; I had no problem working in the California desert that would stand in for Jabba's barge on Tatooine."

"We had dozens of new characters and George gave them all names," Kazanjian says, "even though most were not heard in the picture. George is very good with names. Gamorrean, Yessum [or Yuzzum], Ewoks. And he comes up with them very fast. I had to create three names for the skiff guards: Yak Face, Weequay. I passed them by George, and he said okay. Phil Tippett suggested several names as well."

253

For this last film of the *Star Wars* trilogy, ILM would be making more costumes and creatures than on the first two. Kazanjian set up the enlarged departments, which were headed up by Aggie Guerard Rodgers and Phil Tippett, respectively. The main new creature was an immense sluglike villain named Jabba the Hutt (who would be designed in the States, but fabricated overseas). "There is a little band in the film made of creatures, just stupid-looking monsters who play ridiculous instruments," says Tippett. "I like the lead vocalist a lot. She looks like an egg on stilts and she has these big red lips that sing."

"George would come by every three days or so and look at these concept pictures," Kazanjian says. "He'd say, 'Yes. No. I like this one, but take the tail on this one and put it on this figure over here. What if he had a horn? Shorten the legs or lengthen the legs,' and so on."

When Lucas approved a creature, sculptors would make a clay model (a maquette), which would then be dressed. They'd explore what functionality the script required of the character, to determine if would be more of a puppet or a mask. "You might have to have a person inside," Kazanjian adds, "a mime or someone; somebody would be under a raised floor, or manipulating wires from rafters or from behind a wall to make that character work."

Kazanjian's counterpart at ILM was its manager, Tom Smith. The two negotiated the facility's budget and availability. ILM was also working on or projecting costs for *E.T.*, *Star Trek II: The Wrath of Khan* (1982), and *Poltergeist*; the facility's numbers had risen from about seventy-five employees to the hundreds. "I was wearing two hats at ILM," Smith says. "I was responsible for keeping the business afloat financially and yet we had to do the work on *Jedi* at a price the film could afford. George told me to be as fair on prices for *Jedi* as I had been when doing visual effects for Spielberg and others. For his part, Howard wanted as much as he could get for *Jedi* at the lowest price. He was like a lawyer fighting for his client. When he asked for more than I felt he was paying for, I pushed back. This led to serious bartering. But I felt I had George behind me. It was odd, since *Jedi* was George's film and he owned ILM. So he was buying from himself. But George never got into the negotiating. He'd say to Howard and me, 'You guys work it out.' Throughout it all, Howard and I remained friends. I don't think either of us lost our tempers despite the tremendous pressure of our jobs." (Kazanjian and Smith still have the occasional lunch to this day.)

HAND ON THE TILLER

The search for *Jedi*'s director intensified. Lucas happened to suggest Jack Smight. Recalling his negative experiences with Smight on *Partners in Crime* (1973), Kazanjian told Lucas that Smight was the wrong candidate, "not honest, not sincere. George said nothing and never asked again."

"It was casting," Kazanjian adds. "Casting for a director or an actor is the same. Only the director doesn't read for a part, and, in our case, the director couldn't even see a script. But they had seen *Star Wars* and knew what it was about. Agents and managers were calling once word got out that we were looking for a director for what possibly would be the blockbuster of 1983."

On February 5, Lynch's agent, Rick Nicita, had phoned to ask if they were still interested in Lynch. They were. They were also considering "fifteen or so others," a note from the conversation read. They weren't "far enough along to make a commitment." Lucas had instructed Kazanjian to call Lynch and stall by telling him they'd have a start date by the end of March or early April.

In late February Lucas, Kazanjian, and Spielberg flew over to London to hear and watch John Williams conduct the London Symphony Orchestra at Anvil Abbey Road Screen Sound studios. They'd stay through early March. It would be the first time they heard Williams' music for *Raiders*. "Steven and I were like kids in a candy shop," Lucas says.

Kazanjian remembers, "Johnny Williams is considered the Mozart of today. But after hearing Johnny's first cue, George leaned over me to Steven and said, 'It sounds like *Hogan's Heroes*'" (a reference to the opening theme of the late 1960s TV sitcom that took place in a POW camp during WWII).

After seven days of recording, the filmmakers left Williams and Lionel Newman on their own. "Lionel had been head of the music department at Fox and was Johnny's watchful eye and ears in the recording booth," Kazanjian says. Williams would take another three days to record the music for the soundtrack album. (Soundtrack albums are not, generally, exact duplications of what audiences hear in the theater. Kazanjian explains: "Johnny rerecords a lot of that stuff again, or sections of it, to make it more of a 'song.'")

While Kazanjian was doing paperwork at Elstree Studios, Gary Kurtz walked in. He had resigned as a director of the Lucasfilm company back in December of 1979, a result of the overages on *Empire*, but evidently still thought he was producing the next *Star Wars* film. "Gary came down the hall from his office on some other picture he was prepping and asked, 'What are you doing here?'" Kazanjian says. "That's when I had to tell him that he was no longer producing *Jedi*. He literally changed color. He denied knowing about it, turned around, and went back down the hall. I called George and he said, 'Oh, he knew it. I told him.' George basically said, don't worry about it. I don't think George ever wanted to embarrass Gary, so he may not have told him. Again, I had learned long ago that one has to read George between the lines. Perhaps Gary had not."

The Lucasfilm press release announcing *Revenge of the Jedi* stated that Kazanjian would produce and that Kurtz would serve as production consultant "while he prepares two outside films that he will be directing." It also stated that Kurtz was "currently coproducing *Dark Crystals* [sic] with Jim Henson in London."

When Gary left, "it was a little strained, but not much," says Jane Bay, "because it was kind of like George was moving on. Gary was so involved in the movies, but I think George was happy to have some autonomy."

Lucas and Kazanjian took advantage of their time overseas to meet with the UK HODs for *Jedi*—Reynolds, Watts, et al—and to interview a few more director candidates. British directors had a leg up on their American counterparts because Lucas had withdrawn from the DGA when the union had fined him. (In their eyes, he'd put his name, in "*Lucas*film," on *Empire* as a possessory opening credit, while the director's name, "Irvin Kershner," appeared only in the end credits. The DGA cited other violations as well. The initial fine was $250,000, but was later

256

TOP TO BOTTOM: *Kazanjian gives the A-OK sign to waiting unit manager Worsley and production designer Bumstead, who had opted out of the ride.* • *Director Jim Goldstone and Kazanjian are about to test ride the Six Flags rollercoaster as part of their location scout.*

TOP TO BOTTOM: *Hal Barwood (left) and Matthew Robbins (second from right) visited George Lucas and Howard Kazanjian on location in Stockton, California. Because production was shooting the Vietnam War segment for* More American Graffiti *(1979), Barwood and Robbins were also dressed in army fatigues should they be picked up in helicopter shots from the air.* • More American Graffiti *writer-director Bill Norton (second from left) talks to DP Caleb Deschanel (right) about next shot, with Kazanjian and Lucas listening.*

ABOVE, TOP TO BOTTOM: *On location in La Rochelle, June 1980, Karen Allen (Marion), director Steven Spielberg, Kazanjian (and Harrison Ford's leg) wait for darkness to shoot a scene for* Raiders of the Lost Ark *(1981) on the steam freighter the* Bantu Wind. *Production began work on location in France after preproduction in London.* • *Off the coast of La Rochelle, Kazanjian, in black coat, watches Lucas explain to the camera operator what he wants. Spielberg's assistant Kathleen Kennedy is looking at camera; Spielberg is lower down, out of sight, on "A" camera for a shot that would encompass the* Bantu Wind *and a Nazi submarine in distance.*

OPPOSITE: *Kazanjian (left), Lucas (center), and Spielberg aboard the* Bantu Wind. *Note that the profiles of the latter two would be used in the Japanese one-sheet poster for* Raiders *(Kazanjian wouldn't make the cut, alas, but was in original photo).*

「ジョーズ」の**スティーブン・スピルバーグ**と
『スター・ウォーズ』の**ジョージ・ルーカス**が
最高最大の冒険スペクタクル映画を作った!

ABOVE, TOP TO BOTTOM: *Lucasfilm president Bob (Robert) Greber and Kazanjian on the set of the infamous rolling boulder during* Raiders *production set at Elstree. • At Elstree Studios, Kazanjian and Lucas, seated, go over business with Kathleen Kennedy while Steven Spielberg enjoys a lighter moment at the stand-up arcade game.*

OPPOSITE: *Shooting the destruction of the Flying Wing in Tunisia. The life-size craft for* Raiders *started out as a concept model with four engines, until Lucas eliminated two of them to bring down the budget. Top photo, left to right: George Lucas (in white shirt), Kathleen Kennedy, and production designer Norman Reynolds.*

LEFT, TOP TO BOTTOM:
September 1980, Kazanjian overlooks crew setting up second location, the archaeological dig, in Tunisia. Between France and Tunisia, production had shot scenes and interiors at Elstree, back in England. • When David Tomblin fell ill, Kazanjian went back to work as a 1st AD on Raiders *as a favor to Spielberg. Here, he discusses a shot with Allen (Marion) and Spielberg in Tunisia. • Harrison Ford (Indiana Jones, center, seated) and Kazanjian have a few minutes on location between setups to swap stories.*

OPPOSITE, TOP TO BOTTOM:
On location in Kauai, Hawaii, in 1980, producer Frank Marshall (left) watches a scene unfold off-camera, as does Lucas, leaning on Arriflex; Kazanjian is wearing a Hawaiian shirt behind Lucas; Spielberg, next to camera; DP Douglas Slocombe; and 1st AD David Tomblin is back, recuperated, with bullhorn (right). • Raiders of the Lost Ark *billboard on Sunset Boulevard. • Lucasfilm marketing executive Sid Ganis, Kazanjian, and Marshall discuss* Raiders *during a panel at a science-fiction convention, 1981.*

HORROR
BEYOND IMAGINATION!

ABOVE, TOP TO BOTTOM: *Security badges with the code name "Blue Harvest" produced by Louis Friedman were worn while shooting the barge sequence for* Return of the Jedi *in Buttercup Valley, California. • The tagline for their supposed horror movie, "Blue Harvest," was "Horror Beyond Imagination!"—here scrawled across a Polaroid by Friedman of co-producer Jim Bloom, Kazanjian, co-producer Robert Watts, and unit supervisor Louis Friedman himself posed on the back of a station wagon waiting for the sun to rise in the desert.*

OPPOSITE: *The team poses for a picture on the Ewok battle location: Lucas, Ford (Han Solo), Anthony Daniels (C-3PO), Carrie Fisher (Princess Leia), Mark Hamill (Luke Skywalker), Kenny Baker (R2-D2), Peter Mayhew (Chewbacca), and Kazanjian.*

OPPOSITE: *Kazanjian, director Richard Marquand, R2-D2, and C-3PO during second-unit pick-ups for* Return of the Jedi, *shot in Death Valley, California.*

ABOVE, TOP TO BOTTOM: *Miki Herman is in the background, Kazanjian and Lucas hold shovels, as they all prepare the landscape for the second unit shoot in Death Valley.* • *In a lighter moment at Lucasfilm's San Rafael offices, Howard tries on the latest consumer products sample to arrive—a humorous "Yoda" hat, complete with green ears. Similar hats were distributed to many Lucasfilm employees.*

OPPOSITE: *Kazanjian checks the script and jokes around with Carrie Fisher on location in a redwood forest for* Jedi *not far from Crescent City, California.*

ABOVE, TOP TO BOTTOM: *Kazanjian introduces son Peter to an Ewok on the set at Elstree Studios; Peter holds on to Dad for security.* • *Carol and Howard Kazanjian with the latter's mother, Rose Kazanjian, at a stop on the rebel briefing room set during a tour of the interiors at Elstree (Peter Kazanjian is standing). The sets on large, empty soundstages could become quite cold.*

CLOCKWISE FROM TOP LEFT: *Howard Kazanjian with son Peter at his Elstree studio office (a total of four telephones are visible at his work station).* • *During a fourth of July party at Skywalker Ranch: Kazanjian, holding son Peter; Lucas's old USC roommate/director Randal Kleiser; and Lucas.* • *Lucas threw Kazanjian a birthday party at Parkway House (Lucasfilm HQ in San Anselmo, California) and presented him with a Jedi apron and a velvet-covered whip, symbolic of Kazanjian's calm but authoritative approach to producing* • *Kazanjian runs his lines for Las Floristas event with his sister Janet. Las Floristas raised funds for the Children's Clinic at Rancho Los Amigos National Rehabilitation Center; it was also referred to as the "Headdress Ball" because dozens of florists donated their time and flowers to the women of this organization, who would then don these huge flower headdresses, which weighed up to fifty pounds and were as tall as ten feet.* • *Louis Friedman, Anthony Daniels (C-3PO), and Kazanjian at the Hilton Hotel for USC's Las Floristas event.*

reduced to $25,000, which, ironically, was levied against Kershner for not reporting to the DGA that he was leaving the country for the shoot. They fined Kershner because the DGA had no legal authority over the Lucasfilm production, which was technically a British entity. Lucas paid the fine for Kershner, withdrew from the union, and withdrew from the Writers Guild of America as well as the Academy of Motion Pictures Arts and Sciences.)

"He severed all relationship with Hollywood," Kazanjian says. "I'd been sent in to arbitrate with the DGA over the possessory credit. I met with Gil Cates, then president of the DGA, their national secretary, and one other body in the DGA conference room. I explained that Lucasfilm was a self-financing studio like 20th Century Fox, Warner Bros., or any other studio. They said the name 'Lucas' in 'Lucasfilm' could not be used. I pointed out that 'Warner' in Warner Bros., and 'Goldwyn' in MGM, and 'Disney' were consequently all possessory. The DGA said those names had long been established and were not considered possessory. Nothing would budge these people. The meeting ended with me asking, 'What if George Lucas bought 20th Century Fox and changed the name to Lucasfilm?' The response was 'I wish he would, but he couldn't use Lucasfilm.'"

The upshot was that Kazanjian would have to find a director for *Jedi* who was not a member of the DGA or who was willing to resign from the DGA. "And that was a challenge," he says. "I thought at first that if they were not guild members, they were not very good directors. But that soon changed. Names came up like Richard Attenborough, Michael Anderson, John Boorman, Richard Fleischer, Jonathan Demme, John Glen, John Guillermin, Hugh Hudson. Needless to say, we went through hundreds of names and interviewed over fifty."

One possibility was Richard Marquand. Bruce Beresford, who had directed *Breaker Morant* (1980), was also considered, though that film had, per a production note, "a slow beginning." David Cronenberg was a possibility. Joe Dante made the list: "ILM says [Dante] good." Lucas and Kazanjian met with Graham Baker, who had directed *The Omen: Final Conflict* (1981), released only days before. "Well photographed, okay direction, but what is the story?" read their notes. They looked at the work of Desmond Davis, but his *Clash of Titans* (1981) had been rumored to be "not good action, dialogue," and he became a "no" after Kazanjian viewed the picture. Richard Lester, the director of two Beatles movies and the more recent *Three Musketeers* (1973), "wasn't right" and was put on the B-list by Lucas.

He and Kazanjian watched an almost finished cut of Richard Marquand's *Eye of the Needle* (1981). On March 7, Marquand wrote to Lucas thanking him for "all those good things you said about *Eye* . . ." and went on to stress his enthusiasm for the project and the mythology of *Star Wars*: "I know I am a skillful, fast, creative, and decisive director. But I am also a Celt with a deep heart, and I trace its roots far down to the Druids of Wales and the occupation of the Roman Empire. *Star Wars* touches me through my heart and viscera. That is why I would like to be your director this time." He even signed his letter to Lucas, "prospective director/*Rev. of Jedi*."

Their notes on Marquand read: "He continually told us how good he was . . . Might be difficult to work with as he is quite cocky . . . Jerk potential." On March 21, Lucas put Marquand on the "A-list." Lynch joined the A-list two days later. On March 25, Marquand went to dinner at Lucas's home with Kazanjian present. "Shows desire to direct *Jedi*," Kazanjian wrote. "I still have mixed feelings." They toured Marquand around ILM the next day, but the producer noted that the director "shows no or little humor."

His note per Lynch was equally measured: "I'm somewhat concerned because he wants to make a statement." Years before, George and Marcia Lucas had joined Stanley Kubrick to watch the Lynch film *Eraserhead* (1977) at Elstree Studios; editor Gill Smith had also been in the screening room. "I will never forget it," she says, "partly because it was such an extraordinary film and partly because Mrs. Lucas shrieked with laughter throughout!"

YES, NO, YES

Raiders was looking good. The effects wizards at ILM had cracked the Ark of the Covenant sequence—by providing an assortment of vengeful spirits, angelic-looking forms, and pyrotechnics using of a variety of tricks—and was on schedule.

Because the Egg Company offices were across the street from Universal, Kazanjian frequently ate lunch with his old colleagues, Marshall and Hilton Green; Mel Sattler, the studio's head attorney; and Bill Batliner, its casting director. They sat at their usual table in the northeast corner of the dining room. "They asked me what we were doing, and I told them it was an action-adventure picture," Kazanjian remembers. "I said, 'This one's going to be a winner. Absolutely a winner.' I never knew how big it was going to be, but it was my kind of picture. A period picture, an action picture; I grew up on this type of storytelling. I grew up on the serials."

Word got round and Philip Kaufman, who had contributed the Ark idea to Lucas, decided he wanted more than one profit point (or half-point, sources vary) on the back end (the idea of the Ark of the Covenant had actually originated with Kaufman's dentist, as the story goes, and Kaufman was, early on, the slated director, but went off to direct a Clint Eastwood picture instead). Lucas had shown Kaufman an early cut, and the latter's lawyer, according to Kazanjian, wrote a letter to Weber, saying Kaufman wanted a "story by" credit.

"George Lucas and I sat down to write a story," Kaufman said in 2000. "I had the idea of the lost Ark. George had the idea of the Indiana Jones character. We talked for about six weeks and then I got an offer to do another movie. About four years later, I got a call from George saying that he and Spielberg talked about the project on a beach in Hawaii, and would I mind if Steven did it? I said fine, and that's what happened."

"A fight started," Kazanjian says. "Once you give a person 'story by' credit on a film, they always maintain that credit on all prequels and sequels. That's the WGA agreement [Writer's Guild of America West]. Story includes characters, residual payments, and so on. I was not there in the meetings, but basically the WGA agreed that Lucas could give a 'co-story' credit to Kaufman as a gift. He would not get it again on subsequent films. George and Phil did not speak for several years."

259

Editorially, *Raiders* was almost finished. The same couldn't be said for the movie's behind-the-scenes documentary. "We were just a month or two from release when I had to fly to London on pre-*Jedi* meetings," Kazanjian says. "I told Phil [Schuman] that when I returned in a week, I wanted the documentary finished and him gone. I then instructed Duwayne Dunham to take Phil's key away by week's end. Upon my return, I asked Duwayne what happened. He said, 'Phil is gone. I didn't take the key, but I changed the locks on the door.'"

There was also trouble when costume designer Nadoolman spotted the one-sheet poster for *Raiders*. There was a problem with her credit. "We had to take an ad in *Variety* and apologize to her," Kazanjian says. "I think it was because Frank Marshall made a deal with her and said she'd get a credit on the one sheet."

Spielberg and his editor, Michael Kahn, flew up to show their cut to Lucas. By this time, Parkway House had become Lucas's home in San Anselmo, and Lucasfilm HQ was located in San Rafael at ILM. But Lucas still used his projection room at Parkway on occasion. There, Kazanjian sat next to George, with Spielberg and Kahn sitting behind them. It was understood that Lucas would do the next cut, but it was an important moment. The director's cut had a temp music track and temp sound effects. The climax was long, but the sword-wielding foe was dispatched with a single gunshot. Spielberg had elected to use the short version and had dispensed with the longer comic business during the duel.

"The lights came up, and there was silence for a few beats," Kazanjian says. "George said, 'It's good. But what happened to the fight with the big Arab?' Keep in mind that Steven is very strong, and this is their first picture together. They are both powerhouses, but they respect each other. I do believe Steven was just a bit intimidated. He replied, 'I thought this worked out better.'"

The issue was tabled.

Spielberg flew back to Los Angeles; Kahn stayed to work with Lucas on his edit, which took about two weeks. Lucas trimmed the ending and made other adjustments; and spent time putting the longer Indy vs. bad guy duel back together, adding perhaps another minute of film time.

When they reconvened in the screening room, Spielberg had added Frank Marshall and Kathleen Kennedy to his team. Marcia Lucas was also present. They ran the film again. Kazanjian recalls: "George has this wonderful ability to tighten a film, to remove certain little pieces here and there to make it more action oriented. So we look at the film, and in this version we have the extended fight. The lights come up. Steven is sitting in front of George and me. It is a bit quiet. Steven turns around and says, 'Boy, you really tightened it up.' He hesitated and said, 'I like it. But, George, I think it works best with Harrison shooting the Arab.' And George says, 'We're gonna test it with an audience. We'll test it both ways.'"

"We ran the cut," Marcia Lucas says, "the movie was great, and everything was working and I was impressed. This is working like gangbusters. At the end, they tie up Indiana with Marion on a post, they open the Ark, all the Nazis are killed off, and then they cut. Indiana's in Washington, DC, in this meeting with the bigwig Washington people, and they say, 'Thank you for taking care of it.' And then a cut, and they're nailing shut the big box, and they're wheeling it into that warehouse full of a million boxes, right?

"I said, 'Wait a minute.' There was a scene in the script where Harrison came out of that meeting in Washington and he met Marion. And Marion said, 'Come on, let's go get a drink.' And they walked off together. I said, 'What happened to that scene?' 'We didn't need it.' George said it, and Steven said it. I stopped and said, 'You guys are nuts. You don't understand how good the relationship between those two is. It's magical. They were going to go walk off and get a drink together. You need that scene. You need to put a period on that part of the Marion and Indiana relationship. Otherwise, you leave her tied up on that stick.' George said, 'I'll shoot a second unit.' And George went down to San Francisco City Hall, got Harrison, and got the actors and shot the scene where they walk down the stairs together." (Kazanjian made the arrangements and assisted Lucas for the pick-up.)

The film's teaser trailer, cut together at Lucasfilm, was also tested. It was sent to Barry Diller, Jeffrey Katzenberg, and Don Simpson, the three head honchos at Paramount, for their feedback, circa January

1981. "They didn't like it and thought it wouldn't play well," Kazanjian says. "We suggested an audience test and they arranged for it to be shown at the Chinese Theatre, because they could tack it onto a film of theirs, *Popeye*. The theater was nearly empty at noon and we didn't get much of a reaction in that big auditorium. In the lobby the three ganged up on George, and the trailer was eventually changed."

A few months later, Lucas offered the job of directing *Jedi* to David Lynch. "When George told me to call David Lynch's agent and lock him in," Kazanjian says, "he also wanted me to call Richard Marquand and tell him thank you, so he would hear from me first, and not through the rumor mill. I called David, but I did not call Richard."

Lynch accepted, but then declined. "I crawled into a phone booth and called my agent and said there's no way I can do this," Lynch recalled. "He said, 'David, David, calm down. You don't have to do this.' And so George, bless his heart—I told him that he should direct it, it's his film; he'd invented everything about it, but he doesn't really love directing. I called my lawyer and he said, 'You just lost millions of dollars!'"

"The next day David called and backed out," Kazanjian says. "David told me he didn't want to do the picture because he didn't want John Williams. I was stunned. I'd work with Johnny on any and all movies. The second reason was David had his own sound effects guy. He didn't want Ben Burtt, who was George's man. George asked if I'd called Richard. I told him I had not. The next phone call was to Richard. Followed by one to his agent." (Lynch chose to direct *Dune* as his next picture. Released in 1984, its sound design was by Alan Splet, and most of its soundtrack was composed by the rock band Toto.)

"I got a phone call from Howard Kazanjian," Marquand said in 1983. "And he said, 'Richard, I thought I ought to tell you . . .' [you're going to direct the next *Star Wars* movie]. I ran into my agent's office, but he had gone to lunch, so I grabbed the first person I could find—my agent's innocent young secretary—and said, 'We are going to drink so much champagne!'"

SURPRISE HIT

Secrecy was tantamount as *Raiders* approached its release day. When a print was loaned to the MPAA (The Motion Picture Association of America) for review, it was watched over at all times by a Lucasfilm runner; the projectionist was told he could look at only a few frames of each reel in order to focus, but could not watch or listen to the film. Spielberg asked that the same drill be observed later at DeLuxe for the color timing.

"The MPAA was going to give *Raiders* an R rating," Kazanjian says. "I negotiated with them. The picture business was doing terribly and they needed our picture to come out that summer and boost business. They had five suggestions to make *Raiders* PG. One of the suggestions was to remove the guy at the end of the picture whose head blows up. I'd already asked ILM to recomposite that shot using more flames in the foreground to hide a bit of the explosion, so that was an easy change. Number two on their list was the Mongolian in the Ravenwood bar who is shot in the head. We trimmed that slightly. One of the rating persons had brought his wife to the screening, who had screamed when Indy's sidekick fell with a dozen poison darts in his back. We were asked if we could soften that shot. We did not. After the rating board viewed the picture again, the head of the MPAA Richard Hefner called and hemmed and hawed, and asked for two more changes that we didn't make. Finally he said, 'Keep your mouth shut,' and gave us the PG rating."

Lucas, Spielberg, and Kazanjian attended a surprise preview of *Raiders* for a lucky audience at the Northpoint Theatre in San Francisco on May 9. The company had made sure that families with children were in attendance, as well as different age groups. The audience had been told they were going to see a different film so had no idea what was in store for them. Lucas had decided to show Spielberg's version of the fight at this preview, to gauge audience reaction. Lucas's version would be shown at a second preview. All the final music and sound were in.

"I'm pretty numb in the preview," Spielberg says. "I usually pace. I never sit down. I stand by the back door. And if people get up and leave, I run over to them and ask why they're leaving." Kazanjian recalls, "We're sitting in the back at the moment when Indiana draws his gun

263

and shoots the bad guy—and the audience goes wild with laughter and applause. It was the biggest laugh in the movie. It was a total surprise to the audience, and their reaction was certainly a surprise to us. As the audience filed out later, George said to Steven, 'We'll leave it this way.'"

The film was structured like a serial, with a cliff-hanger every twelve or thirteen minutes. The only exception was the exposition scene with Jones and the government men talking about the Ark. "There was some discussion on whether this scene would slow the picture down," Kazanjian adds. "But it actually captured the audience. They weren't worried, because the opening sequence with the rolling ball and golden idol had told them, *This is roller coaster ride, so hold on.* Just a year or so earlier we had viewed dozens of old cliff-hanger serials at Universal. *Raiders* was the new cliff-hanger."

Questionnaires for the preview screening asked audience members to rank their favorite scenes, from "Peruvian Temple with rolling rock" to "Opening of Ark" and to list what they liked and disliked. Reaction was positive. Press previews followed on May 13 and 22.

"We were so quiet and so secretive," said Ganis. "I took a 70mm print to New York City to show to the critics just before it opened, and I remember the critic for the *New York Times*, a man named Vincent Canby, was walking into the Loews State. I was standing in the lobby and he said, 'What is this movie? What's this all about?' He was saying something very revealing—that he, a movie critic who, of course, knew what was happening in the business, really and truly hadn't been aware of *Raiders of the Lost Ark*. I said, 'Go ahead. I'll see you later.' In he went. When he came out, he said, '*Wow!*' Then I knew we had something special. I couldn't wait to tell George. I ran to a telephone and called him."

Raiders opened on June 12, 1981. "No one knew about *Raiders*," Kazanjian says. "There was very little promotion and what there was came late to theaters and newspapers and magazines."

Word of mouth spread. The film didn't open huge, but it gathered speed and soon surpassed all competitors that summer. A November 25 telegram to Kazanjian from Paramount executives on the film's superlative box-office reports read: "We don't need a Thanksgiving turkey—we've got you, Steven Spielberg, and *Raiders*."

264

The Making of Raiders of the Lost Ark documentary was broadcast and nominated for and won an Emmy (against noted filmmaker David Wolper's *Hollywood: The Gift of Laughter*). Both Kazanjian and Ganis were presented with statuettes.

Even as late as 1999, eighteen years after its release, with theater tickets having risen from $3 to $7 or more, *Raiders* was listed by *Variety* at #15 on the list of all-time box-office hits. It would spawn sequels, comic books, novels, toys, and a very large and loyal following that continues to this day.

In 1982, producer Kazanjian and executive producer Sid Ganis were presented by actor Robert Stack and actress Donna Mills with the Outstanding Informational Special Emmy for Making of Raiders of the Lost Ark *(1981).*

CHAPTER 13: *Soul of the Jedi*

K azanjian again asked Lucas about Lawrence Kasdan: "What if I can get him?"

Lucas replied that it was okay to try and recruit Kasdan to help revise the *Jedi* script. "I went out and got him." Richard Marquand, Kasdan, Lucas, and Kazanjian then got together for a five-day-long story conference that July.

In August Louis Friedman led Kazanjian, Marquand, Lucas, art director Jim Schoppe, and production designer Norman Reynolds on a location scout in the desert of Buttercup Valley, in the southeast corner of California. Here, a large crew would labor on Jabba the Hutt's gigantic sail barge. "It was definitely hot," Friedman says. "It was like being on a lunar landscape. Even at the time, I thought that there were other ways you could portray the barge rather than building it full-size on location, but that's what George wanted to do."

It would take the crew eight months in the desert to build the set and prepare the location. It was considered at the time to be the largest set ever constructed in California. The first shipment of thirty-foot beams cost $100,000; the first shipment of nails weighed 11,000 pounds.

They also scouted the redwood forest that Miki Herman had found near Crescent City, California. "We took George up to see and approve the location on a private plane," Kazanjian recalls. "That was the worst plane ride I have ever taken. I know what white knuckles are because George and I both had them. We were in a hailstorm and I thought we were going to die. We couldn't see a thing out the window and I was hoping the pilot didn't land on top of a two-thousand-year-old redwood

266

tree. I was thinking I was going to kill George Lucas. We were blaming Miki, who had arranged the flight. After we landed, I gave her a hug!"

The actual Ewok village would be filmed on an Elstree soundstage, but the Ewok battles and other related exteriors would be shot on location. Paths were cleared, roots and rocks removed, grounds leveled, and over sixteen thousand ferns planted along the paths where the Imperial bunker set would be built. "Kathy Kennedy was also looking for a forest, for *E.T.*," Kazanjian adds. "I suggested the one we'd found near Crescent City and *E.T.* was actually shot in that general area before the *Jedi* crew moved in."

The producer was also traveling back and forth to London, and often carried with him Betamax video footage of the Ewok costumes as they progressed under Stuart Freeborn's supervision. Lucas would comment on what he was shown or call Kazanjian to say if the suit looked like a rug or had too many wrinkles in the back, or to adjust color, fur, eyes, and so on. "At this time, I had to go to George and tell him the picture was going to cost more than I'd originally thought," Kazanjian says. "It's his money; I better show him the set models.

"When I was in Marin, it was fun to watch George build Skywalker Ranch," he adds. "Marcia would come in and color coordinate the carpets, tiles in the bathrooms, the towel racks, leaded windows, everything. George and I would have lunch almost every day and things were moving. One of the ongoing challenges people had working for George is they didn't listen to what he was saying and sometimes he didn't articulate what he wanted. You still had to read between the lines. A lot of people said that George never or rarely said thank you. Well, he didn't say it, but there were times where he looked you in the eye or he followed through on your suggestion, or it was a handshake. Hitchcock used to be that way, too, especially when we were walking, he would kind of silently thank you."

"It was like pulling teeth to get George to go to anything, any dinner, any award thing, any anything," Marcia Lucas says. "He was basically very uncomfortable being around people he didn't know and making conversation. I know he felt it was a waste of time to say, 'Did you have a nice day and isn't the weather nice.' Whereas, if you wanted to talk to

267

him about Vietnam or something he cared about, maybe he would speak. He could be talkative and he was funny. He had a great sense of humor."

One thing Lucas asked Kazanjian to do was rather sensitive. He wanted his producer to talk to actor Billy Dee Williams, who had been cast as Lando Calrissian in *Empire* and was due to return for *Jedi*. "I called to arrange a dinner meeting at a restaurant," Kazanjian says. "Billy was scared or something, so he asked if he could bring his agent. I said yes, because it actually made it a lot easier for me to say, 'You cannot have drugs, we don't believe in that, and you certainly can't get stuck going through customs.' He said, 'I would never,' and we got along great."

Kasdan delivered his *Jedi* draft, based on Lucas's first-draft screenplay, in September. The two of them next worked together toward a revised second draft. Lucas told his producer, on one of their trips to the airport, that he was changing the movie's title back to *Return of the Jedi*. Kazanjian recalls, "His reason: Jedi Knights don't take revenge."

As principal photography approached, the Kazanjians set up a third residence at 48 Hyde Park Garden Mews, London. "By this time we had homes in LA, Marin, and the UK," he says. "Each was completely furnished with all the baby stuff one needs: strollers, beds, changing table, high chairs, etc. Crazy." The Lucases were also preparing their home-away-from-home. They had recently adopted a baby girl and named her Amanda. "I had our daughter, Amanda, at home," Marcia says. "So I was running around from designing the ranch to home to prepare dinner."

Kazanjian took his toddler son, Peter, to see the Ewoks while the actors were learning to walk in their furry suits: "Six or seven of them gathered around my kid in his stroller, and he's now wailing, he's crying, he's scared out of his mind. Then I take him to see Jabba. He screamed again!"

Ben Burtt also flew over for two weeks to check on production recording methods on set and to gather audio effects for his sound design in post. "One of the nice things was Howard invited me to come," Burtt says, "to be there to hire the local British sound people who were going to record the film. That was a privilege. I was there to work with the

268

TOP TO BOTTOM: *On the* Millennium Falcon Tatooine *set, co-producer Robert Watts and Kazanjian talk with Hamill during the first day of principal photography,* Return of the Jedi, *Elstree Studios, 1982.* • *Kazanjian consults with Lucas on the cold stage; a Y-wing starfighter stands behind them on the set for a scene that wouldn't make the final cut.*

FOLLOWING SPREAD: *Director Richard Marquand (back to camera), Lucas, and Kazanjian listen to Carrie Fisher in her slave Leia outfit (conceptualized by Marquand and honed by concept artist Nilo Rodis-Jamero and Lucas).*

Ewoks, too [to work on their language]. George's policy was always that we develop the sound as we go along. We had a thousand recording projects on *Jedi* once I went through the script. The library that we built for *Jedi* became the core of Lucasfilm's sound library, and Howard accommodated all that."

Tom Holman, who developed the THX audio system, also wanted *Jedi* to be the ultimate sound experience. Holman chose the stock and magnetic tape supply. "Usually, if a show is shooting in London, you purchase your sound stock in London," Kazanjian explains. "We shipped ours from the US and had it transferred in London for dailies. The negative film also came from the US, not from London."

Marquand usually arrived late during preproduction. Kazanjian says, "He rarely showed up at the studio before noon. That was my challenge, because I was making the decisions that he should be making. Whether it came to construction or this wall or that wall or stuff like that, which was not my responsibility. I called George, who was coming for the first two weeks of shooting and I told him, 'Pack for longer.'"

SUPPORTIVE COUPLES

Principal photography commenced on *Jedi* with Marquand at the helm on January 11, 1982. As noted, secrecy was essential, scripts were numbered, key dialogue was changed for David Prowse, the actor playing Darth Vader, for he had tendency to give away plot points to the press; dialogue was given to Mark Hamill or Carrie Fisher often the morning before a scene. Only three scripts were complete with all the actual dialogue and action: one for Lucas, Marquand, and Kazanjian.

"On *Jedi* we were all back together again, Carrie, Harrison, and I," Hamill says. "You become like a family, and you react to the fact that Gary's no longer there. Just like in real-life divorces, nobody will talk about it. You don't want to make an uncomfortable moment for George or anybody else. So it had the elements of a broken family, and that's where Howard came in and was a soothing presence, because he knows his stuff backwards and forwards. He's well prepared, he's smart, and just what you need to avoid succumbing to the chaos. Of course, we were well aware that he had done *Raiders of the Lost Ark* and was highly experienced. I would say Gary and Howard both have unassuming personalities. They're not loud and they don't yell, they don't curse. That's somewhat atypical [for producers]. Howard projects a calm that is something very desirable in an industry that is chaotic by definition."

The first sequence they filmed was a sandstorm on the desert planet with a full-scale *Millennium Falcon*, "a day I want to forget," Kazanjian says. "We had sand and wind blowing everywhere. Sand got through our protective clothing and the cast didn't like it much either. The sand got in our eyes and hair and we shot the scene as quickly as possible. After we finished, the *Falcon* and stage had to be cleaned. The soundproof walls of the stage needed vacuuming as did the rafters in the ceiling."

"In trying to get somebody who could handle something that big, basically, I was pretty naive about it," Lucas said. "There just weren't very many people that had any experience doing it . . . As it turned out, because this film was even more complicated than the last one, I had to be there every day on the set, working very closely with Richard [Marquand]. But I was thankful to have Richard there because I did get to spend time with my daughter, Amanda; I did get to go home."

"Richard didn't have as strong a working knowledge of the Jedi mythology and its characters as George hoped he might," adds Kazanjian, who knew that Lucas was also counting on their director to record the film he needed in editorial. "I know for a fact that George told Marquand, 'You get me coverage, so I can make this movie in the editing room.' He didn't want to be in the situation he'd been in for *Empire*. We told the camera crew, too, and I made sure that they let the camera run, that they wouldn't cut in the camera."

"A couple times Marcia and I would go hang out on days off and go to the city and just fool around," Carol Kazanjian says. "I got a babysitter once a week, but Marcia might call at seven in the morning: 'I can't go, Carol; George wants me to work.' She was very smart, and he relied on her continually for many things."

"I had Amanda there," Marcia says, "and we had kind of a penthouse in this hotel. I'd walk Amanda around London in her stroller for hours and hours every day. And Howard and Carol were there to support us both. We had dinners with them. I would have dinner, lunch with the girls. Carol's very close with Marilou Hamill, Mark's wife."

"We both have babies," Carol Kazanjian says. "Marcia has a baby; I have a baby. I'm doing Amanda's wash every Saturday. On the way to work, George leaves the wash at our place, they go to work, I have an American washing machine and dryer. We had an American-style kitchen, all AC-DC appliances—refrigerator, stove, you name it. Marcia didn't want to give her baby's clothes to the hotel—they were at the Saint James's—to get washed with all the old men's clothes."

"George said to me once that my primary job was to 'keep Mark Hamill alive,'" Kazanjian recalls. "That's a quote. I figured he must be referring to his car accident just before *Star Wars* came out. George was also referring to the role of Luke Skywalker—because it was a very challenging role and Mark had to stay strong. And Mark was very good at work. He was on time, he did his job, he didn't do a lot of fraternizing with people. Carol talked to Marilou, his wife, all the time. We went to dinner once at a very fancy restaurant in London, the four of us, and Mark didn't say one word. He just sat there at dinner. Mark was exhausted from the week's physical work."

Hamill had to rehearse the lightsaber duel for hours several times a week with stunt coordinator Peter Diamond.

"They would give me pages and have me memorize them, and then shred them," Hamill says. "It was like being in the Nixon administration. One time, my three-year-old son was on set and he's saying, 'Daddy, you go with Darth Vader.' Howard says, 'This kid's a security risk.'"

"There were simmering tensions as George puppeteered the 'director' with concealed strings, once again masterminding the whole thing himself," says Anthony Daniels (C-3PO) of Marquand. "Somehow, in his gentle, polite manner, Howard managed to keep the unfortunate situation under control. But there were stresses."

Kazanjian would send out the "word of the week," which he considered his "trade secrets." "The first word is usually 'communication,'" he says. "The next word is 'honesty,' followed by efficiency, coordination, dependability, tact, sincerity, etc. There're fifteen words I send out. It's my message to everybody, how I run things.

274

The big thing is communication." As Kazanjian sent the word out each week, more people asked to be included on the list.

"During my time at Lucasfilm," says Mark Marshall, a production assistant, "Howard sent out a 'word of the week' that he felt would serve us well during our time in the industry. The word I remember above all the others was 'anticipate.'"

VADER'S TRIUMPH

In February, a telegram arrived from ILM to Kazanjian: "Congratulations on the eight Academy nominations for *Raiders of the Lost Ark*. We have just congratulated George and told him we will be toasting the film at ILM today at 5 PM with beer and crackers. Yes, Howard, it is part of our budget, and you'll be paying for it in the hourly rate. Again, congratulations for a job well done.—The Crew at Industrial Light and Magic." Four of the nominations were: Best Picture (Frank Marshall); Best Director (Steven Spielberg); Best Cinematography (Douglas Slocombe); and Best Score (John Williams). A month later *Raiders* lost in those categories, but won for: Best Art Direction/Set Decoration (Norman Reynolds, Leslie Dilley, and Michael Ford); Best Film Editing (Michael Kahn); Best Sound (Bill Varney, Steve Maslow, Gregg Landaker, and Roy Charman); Best Effects/Visual Effects (Richard Edlund, Kit West, Bruce Nicholson, and Joe Johnston)—and a Special Achievement Award for Sound Effects Editing, which went to Ben Burtt and Richard L. Anderson.

A month earlier, when the nominations were announced, Paramount chief Barry Diller had met with Charlie Weber and Kazanjian at the Egg Company. During their discussion Diller had said that *Raiders of the Lost Ark* could not win Best Picture. "The reason was Fox and Warner Bros. had financed *Chariots of Fire*," Kazanjian says. "Fox would distribute foreign, Warner Bros. domestic. Both studios would be voting for *Chariots*. Paramount had *Raiders*, *Reds*, and *Atlantic City*. Paramount would be splitting their votes on all three movies."

In England, Academy Award–winner Alec Guinness showed up that month to reprise his role as Obi-Wan Kenobi. "Sir Alec was a gentleman," Kazanjian says. "Unfortunately, he had a terrible cold and

ABOVE, TOP TO BOTTOM: *Kazanjian visits property master Peter Hancock in the props department at Elstree Studios.* • *Kazanjian shakes hand with a Yessum who has just arrived in the shop, shipped from ILM. Left to right are: Jeanne Lauren, Dave Carson, and Tim Rose, from ILM's creature crew.*

OPPOSITE, TOP TO BOTTOM: *David Prowse (Darth Vader) clowns around with Kazanjian on the docking bay.* • *A small second unit crew prepares to shoot Darth Vader's death scene, with the unmasked Sith Lord played by Sebastian Shaw. Behind Shaw (in light jacket) is Brian Archer, who built the "reveal" helmet costume prop; at right is Peter Robb-King who applied the makeup on Shaw.*

therefore had difficulty remembering lines. He was not happy about that, as he was a most sincere and professional actor."

The day before shooting a scene in which the spirits of Obi-Wan and Yoda appear to Luke in the Ewok village, Kazanjian suggested to Lucas that Luke see the Force ghost of Darth Vader, too. "George didn't answer; he just looked at me," Kazanjian says. "The next day George told me to prepare to shoot Vader with Yoda and Ben. Later that day I had second thoughts about what I had suggested. After all, two good guys were standing next to a very bad guy." According to Kazanjian, Lucas turned to him and said, "Isn't that what your religion is all about?"

"He was right," Kazanjian says. "In the end, there was redemption on Vader's part, and forgiveness on Luke's. It worked."

"Shooting out of the country is challenging," he adds. "All told, I spent eleven months in London over a two-year period. You shoot five or six days a week, prepare on Saturdays, and sleep on Sunday. At one time we had seven hundred and fifty people working for us for more than a three-month period. In total, we had just over fifteen hundred different employees on payroll. Every day I was on the phone with California."

Throughout production Kazanjian was relieved and pleased that Billy Dee Williams was true to his word. "I can say on the set, Billy Dee was the most relaxed and fun to be around," the exec producer recalls. "I love the *Jedi* creatures," Billy Dee Williams said. "I think they are funny and an extension of something very real. George has a perverse way of looking at things. Here's this little, quiet guy with all these 'things' going on in his head—and they have lots of humor. He's like Picasso, in a way. I liken George to Picasso only because I think that he's also created something quite monumental."

In dailies, they reviewed takes of Darth Vader watching the Emperor electrocute his son until he takes action to stop it. "I said, 'George, we don't have a closer shot of Darth Vader making that decision, *I'm going to save my son and kill the Emperor*,'" Kazanjian recalls. "Again, George didn't say anything. That evening he said, 'Let's get a unit together and get Darth Vader on the set tomorrow.' So we went out with a very small crew and shot these close-ups as pick-ups (and I felt great having made the suggestion)."

280

FOREST ANTICS

Cast and crew then made the big move to the United States, descending on the small town of Yuma, Arizona. They started with scenes on and around the immense barge set in the desert on April 12. "We were staying in a terrific hotel," Marquand said of their lodgings on the Arizona/California border, in 1983. "The great thing was we were moving into this new area, where we have a mixed crew of English and Americans working together, which happens very rarely. Unions hate that kind of cooperation. Our guys loved it. Because all film people talk the same language and all crews are pretty outrageous, extroverted kinds of characters. They ride in like cowboys, whether they are Cockneys or their guys from wherever."

By that spring, *Raiders of the Lost Ark* had become the fourth-highest-grossing picture in the history of cinema, behind *Star Wars*, *Jaws*, and *The Empire Strikes Back*, but Kazanjian was focused on their present location's bad weather. "A sandstorm roared into town," Friedman says. "After months and months and months of prepping down there, everybody came in from England, everybody showed up. We had all of the trucks, and production had invested a lot of money—and there was virtually nothing you could shoot, because it was a brown-out."

The terrific winds meant they had to lower the barge's giant sails in a hurry to save the set from becoming a desert shipwreck. Each morning a crew of laborers had to replace the sand that had blown off of the platform during the night. Lucas realized that his enormous investment wasn't paying off. "I can tell you now that there is only one shot in the picture of the full barge," Kazanjian said not long afterward. "All other full shots of the barge were created by ILM. Fortunately, the balance of our shoot had great weather."

Shooting went more smoothly in the redwood forest near Crescent City that month—with a few hiccups. "Howard is really straight, and Harrison, he is kind of looped all the time, so you can't really tell the difference," says Miki Herman. "Harrison is the functioning stoner. We had another situation where one of the crew members had some drugs shipped to him and he got busted. We had to keep this a secret from George and Howard. We had to raise bail money among ourselves."

PREVIOUS SPREAD: *Kazanjian watches a rehearsal of the scene in which the Emperor exits an Imperial shuttle on the docking bay set.*

The next day Marquand, Lucas, and company were filming Ewoks and this time Kenny Baker couldn't be found. Baker played R2-D2 and had also been cast as one of the main forest denizens. "So now I'm worried about Kenny," Kazanjian says. "Where is he? Did he get kidnapped? Did he get lost in the redwoods? Get run over? We sent a few people out looking for him and they found him stone drunk on the edge of a lake. He couldn't work. It was lucky he didn't drown. My team dragged him back to the hotel room, and George happens to be there. One of my guys is explaining this, and George is in hearing distance, and he says, 'We'll put in Warwick.'"

It was a big break for Warwick Davis, a youngster prodigy, whose performance on the soundstage as an Ewok had already caught Lucas's eye.

"I remember Howard wrangling all these Ewok actors," Hamill says, "who were running around with their heads off and doing the kind of things that you'd expect up in the forest. And like I say, Howard never lost his cool. That's what engenders the loyalty, treating people well. They'll reciprocate in kind."

Production wrapped *Jedi* on May 8. Now hundreds of visual effects shots had to be completed at ILM, including close-ups of the actors on the speeder bikes, along with the usual postproduction chores.

THE SWERVE

Kazanjian had already witnessed dozens of innovations at Industrial Light & Magic, in animatronics to go-motion to the creation of the computer division, before they started on *Jedi*. "It was a fun work place," he says. "Everyone was very creative. This was the beginning of the digital age. Once we brought Johnny Williams into a big empty room [to discuss music for the Ewoks] and all of a sudden George explained how a whole symphony or orchestra soundtrack would go through a keyboard. Once I said, 'We really need to build a vault for the negative.' And George said, 'No, no, no. Someday we're going to record a whole film on a disc that you can send in the mail.'"

"But we were just finishing three big pictures," visual effects supervisor Richard Edlund said. "Dennis [Muren] had *E.T.*, Ken

[Ralston] had *Star Trek II*, and I had shot *Poltergeist*, but the pictures had backed up on one another and nobody had time for much of a breather between them."

And Lucas didn't seem to be his old self. "I had to drag George through the new 'C' building and other parts of ILM," Kazanjian says. "I told him, 'George, your employees need to see that you exist.'"

The owner and creator of the company was busy. On May 30, he handed in his treatment for their next film: *Indiana Jones and the Temple of Death*, which Kazanjian would not be producing. "Kathleen Kennedy and Frank Marshall had followed Steven around [during *Raiders*]," says Tom Smith, general manager of ILM, "and sort of elbowed Howard out of a relationship with Spielberg."

Kazanjian says, "My personal producing contract with Lucasfilm was short and did not include prequels, sequels, and so on. Because I was part of the family, the idea was I'd be taken care of, 'everything would be okay.' I was doing *Jedi*, so I couldn't have done *Temple of Doom* anyway. But after that, I was left out. Producers are always entitled to sequels, but now you're dealing with a new administration. I don't know if they really talked to George, and I didn't pick up the phone and call George to say, 'George, I'm being left out.'"

As for *Jedi*, Lucas finally rolled up his sleeves and took a long, hard look at the film and the effects shots he'd need in editorial. November 22 became known as "Black Friday," for it was the day Lucas finished restructuring the visual effects sequences. "So we're in a kind of upheaval at the moment," said visual effects supervisor Ken Ralston at the time. "George wants a real feeling of grandeur and awe, and is trying to get a much bigger sense to the size of these things."

Counts differ as to the exact number, but up to one hundred effects shots and many script pages of action were changed, added to, or deleted. "Ken Ralston just threw his hands up and was like, 'What's going on here?!'" optical supervisor Bruce Nicholson said. "A lot of the stuff cut was work that he'd supervised, that they had worked months on producing. It was called 'Black Friday' because it was the equivalent of the stock market crash."

"On Black Friday I was in my cutting room late at night, at Sprockets," says Duwayne Dunham, now the effects editor working with

ABOVE, TOP TO BOTTOM: *Kazanjian explains a shot to editor Sean Barton on the Jabba the Hutt set. It would seem that Kazanjian is explaining something to R2-D2 as well on the same set.*

OPPPOSITE: *Kazanjian holds an umbrella over actor Billy Dee Williams (Lando Calrissian) while the camera crew prepares for a shot in the Sarlacc Pit, on location in Buttercup Valley, California.*

284

Lucas in "C" building, or Sprockets. "ILM was right across the parking lot, and Howard rushed in my room carrying a plastic yellow spool of 35-millimeter film, a bunch of film rolled up, maybe fifty feet. Howard was out of breath, completely beside himself. He held this film spool up, and he's shaking it and showing it to me, he can hardly talk. And he finally gets it out, he says, 'This is $250,000 worth of film right here— you can't just cut it out of the movie!' I said, 'I didn't do it, Howard. But maybe you can use it in the next one.' He looked at me and turned around and walked away. There's no yelling, no anything. When you say, 'We don't need this,' and you've already invested a quarter of a million dollars in it—that's big."

"Well, I don't ever remember shaking and being hardly able to speak," Kazanjian says. "That's not like me even in panic mode. Things do happen and scenes are removed from the final version that do cost thousands of dollars . . ."

THE EMPRESS OF LIFE

Lucas, Marquand, and Kazanjian supervised ADR, Automated Dialog Replacement, at Goldwyn Studios, with a couple of breaks, from December 6 to 22. At this point the real dialogue for Darth Vader was given to actor James Earl Jones, for his voice-over. "In ADR, Billy Dee Williams was like lightning," Kazanjian recalls. "He would hit the word on ADR like nobody. I asked him, 'How do you do that?' He said, 'I do a lot of voice-overs. I do so much; I just know how to do it.'"

On one trip south, Lucas, Kazanjian, and Sid Ganis were touring a USC construction site for a building being built with the Lucases' money. They wore hard hats and were accompanied by: Frank Price, head of Universal Television; Sid Sheinberg, president of Universal; Spielberg; and two or three others. Lucas wanted to show the Universal folks the enormity of the task being undertaken, so they might also pitch in. After the tour, they boarded a tram for a restaurant and Kazanjian heard Sheinberg say to Lucas: "George, isn't it a shame that we're fighting each other over *Battlestar Galactica*? Let's just end it. Let's settle the suit."

Lucas replied, "Great."

TOP TO BOTTOM: *Kazanjian and Lucas hear what Ford has to say on location for* Return of the Jedi's *Ewok forest near Crescent City, California, 1982. • Kazanjian, Lucas, and Ford in front of the bunker doors on location, waiting for the next setup to be ready. (The VistaVision effects camera can be seen in background.)*

Sheinberg said happily, "I'll tell the lawyers it's over."

"No, it's not over," Lucas corrected. "We're settling—when you pay off."

"It was a funny moment to hear these guys [laughs] misunderstanding each other," Kazanjian says, "with George having the last word. I wish I could have filmed it."

(The suit would finally be settled on November 18, 1983. An "Agreement for Settlement of Lawsuit and Release" followed on March 5, 1984: a $225,000 settlement paid to 20th Century-Fox.)

Back at ILM, things weren't going much better. Edlund and a small crew had built a Quad Optical Printer, but it wasn't performing to expectations. "The current tally on the whole picture, I think, is more than five hundred shots," Edlund said at the time. "I don't know how we're going to do it. The Quad printer that I'd sort of designed for *Empire* has been split into two separate printers. I fought the idea at first, but when we actually looked at the situation, it was a better deal to have two printers than one super 'trick' printer."

"The Quad Printer just didn't work," Kazanjian says. "It was designed for four pieces of film to go in at one time, but it didn't work. Tom Smith ran ILM, but I was the one that had to come down to the projection room and say, 'You guys are going too slow.' I was going in every single day to see dailies with George. He would leave and I'd stand in front of the screen and say, 'You guys are not going to meet the deadline, and if you don't meet the deadline, all of us are out of a job and you've ruined the name of ILM.' I said that a couple times."

The solution was to go into "negative cutting" in order to have prints of the film ready to ship on time: an expensive process whereby ILM's effects shots were spliced into already negative cut reels, which meant an additional $40,000 of negative cutting over the original budget. Kazanjian allowed ILM to improve their shots despite the added cost.

In editorial, despite having the coverage he required, Lucas was having problems, too. "George struggled in editing," Kazanjian says. "I said, 'Let's bring on Marcia to help, as we usually do.' George said, 'You're going to have to ask her.' So I did. Marcia is a brilliant storyteller.

288

She knew how to cut a picture and to tell the story. She concentrated on the actor's performance. She didn't care if in one shot the actor's hand was up, in the second shot the actor's hand was down."

Kazanjian, however, thought it a little odd that Lucas was asking him to ask Marcia. The Kazanjians and Lucases had been having dinners at restaurants or at the latters' home, but that had stopped. George and Howard still had lunch almost every day, but when Kazanjian asked when Marcia would start, Lucas would only reply that she was busy. Marcia wasn't playing softball with the company either. "I found out later they were going to therapy," Kazanjian says. "George would say, 'I have to leave early tonight,' and he had terrible headaches, terrible backaches. I'd ask what was wrong and he'd say it was just pressure and nerves. I said, 'Have you been to a masseuse? Do you think you need a chiropractor?'"

Finally Marcia Lucas began helping out in editorial. "Marcia had really good ideas and she wanted to focus on story and character," Herman says, "whereas George, he focused on action. Faster, faster, and so she put in a lot of things that wouldn't be there otherwise."

"George liked to give me heavy dramatic scenes," says Marcia. "And that's why George pulled me in to do *Jedi*, because the English director and editor didn't fully understand the Jedi philosophy. What Marquand did when he was directing is he had Luke being angry a lot. George said, 'A Jedi isn't angry. I need you to come in and look at these scenes, and find out what you can do to soften this.' I looked at the cut, and when Obi-Wan Kenobi appears in his ghostly form and Luke is saying, 'Why didn't you tell me?' about Vader—Luke was very angry and upset. So I had to recut that scene. I had to find Mark's softest performance, which was there. Sometimes I even had to print an outtake that wasn't printed because I was looking for a reading on one line, 'Why didn't you tell me?' (softly) Not, '*Why didn't you tell me*?!' Luke was also very angry in the scene where Yoda dies—'*Is Darth Vader really my father?*'"

Marcia noted that when Vader threw the Emperor down the "chasm" in the first cuts—"he just would fall and plop down, and he's dead and let's get on with the scene," she says. "I said, 'This is not going to work. You cannot kill the most powerful man in the galaxy, who can shoot electric bolts out of his hands, and have nothing happen. We need ILM and Ben Burtt to make a cacophony of noise and sound and an atomic reaction. So I recut all the death scenes. I used to enter the editing room and say, 'The queen of death is here.'"

Lucas said to Dunham about Marcia: "Always save a person whose opinion you trust for the very end."

"I spent hours in the editing rooms every day," Kazanjian says, "with our three editors coordinating what sequences they were editing with what ILM was doing. George spent many, many hours in editing, polishing, changing, tightening, and so on. Obviously as a producer you have comments and suggestions. We all made suggestions. At one time Marcia and George and everyone discussed what worked and what did not."

"I love film editing," Marcia told a reporter at the time. "I have an innate ability to take good material and make it better, and to take bad material and make it fair. I think I'm even an editor in life."

Confused Farewells

While Kazanjian was overseeing the credits and the crawl, he urged Lucas to take a cowriting credit with Kasdan, in addition to a story credit. "For a long time, George refused," he says. "It was only when I was doing the titles after the picture was shot, that he said okay. Because he certainly wrote 50 percent of the script, but he never liked taking a lot of credits."

The producer sent Louis Friedman to retrieve the pretitle intro that had started the two previous *Star Wars* films. "I came across the original," Friedman says. "'A long time ago, in a galaxy far, far away,' right? The original wording, which I could see had been covered up, was, 'A long time ago, in a galaxy far, far away, *a great adventure began.*'" (Production may have shot a new title card for *Jedi*, whereas *Star Wars* and *Empire* had used the same edited one.)

As the impending release date approached, Kazanjian took a chance with Tom Holman, who had developed a new higher quality film process than Technicolor's for the magnetic sound striping on 70mm prints ("striping" is the laying down of the magnetic tape on film in a

290

semiliquid form; the sound is recorded onto that magnetic tape). "I chose a new company that had very little expertise in this process," Kazanjian says. "George let me make that decision, but frowned at it. And at first the process was sloppy and covered part of the image. At times the machinery would not cover all the edges and left spaces. But Fox worked closely with me, and all destroyed film was financially covered by DeLuxe and the studio. The end result was a superior quality magnetic strip."

One day the producer had to find a place for the full-size chicken walker, a walking Imperial canon, which had been used on location. Lucas said, "We'll put it out at the ranch." Kazanjian had told Jim Schoppe to take the walker apart before shipping it, but crew at the ranch informed him that the location gang had simply cut it up; the walker couldn't be reassembled.

"Bury it," Lucas said.

"So it's buried at the ranch," Kazanjian explains. "Only the guys who buried it know where it is."

The preview showing for *Return of the Jedi* took place, once again, at the Northpoint Theatre, in April. The audience had been told they were going to see an animated film, *Twice Upon a Time*. "I went up and I apologized to them," Kazanjian recalls. "I said, 'Today we're not able to show you the John Korty film—then I paused—but instead we're going to bring you the third *Star Wars* picture.' The audience goes crazy."

"I was relieved that we finally got the thing done," Lucas said decades later. "When you're working on something like that for ten years, just reaching the finish line is a huge relief. And I thought it worked well. There were issues. I was never quite happy with the music at the end of the movie. It fell short in a few places where I had wanted more—but all in all, I was happy."

The preview was a success.

Jedi was slated for a 70mm release, the biggest in Fox's history: 210 prints. Each print cost thousands of dollars; each fifty-pound set of film reels had to be checked and stored in a small warehouse before being shipped. That job fell to Kazanjian, Friedman, and Herman. Their job

291

would continue even after the release, for, during a theater run, one or more reels would usually have to be replaced, having been chopped up in a projector or some other mishap, which required more checking and shipping. By the end of a theatrical run, the reels were useless. Fortunately, Lucasfilm's TAP, Theater Alignment Program, helped theater projectionists throughout the United States with torn or missing reels, aperture problems, focus or even reels threaded upside down.

On top of this, Carol Kazanjian was expecting their second child. "Fortunately, I was in Los Angeles, working in the labs nearly twenty-four hours a day, getting the prints ready," her husband says. "Just a week before *Jedi* was released, Noah was born, and I was home."

Rushing from his house back to the labs, Kazanjian supervised the shipment of "wet prints" to the theaters; production was so late—the effects shots and final reels just under the wire—that film reels weren't completely dry. Fox shipped film first to those theaters the farthest away; they shipped backup 35mm prints to those theaters they thought might receive the 70mm prints late. But only one theater had to show it in 35mm before the 70mm print arrived.

Kazanjian arranged two screenings at the Edwards Theatre for a local church to raise money for a pastor's house (it was enough). As he went from theater to theater to check on things, he saw kids lined up outside in advance and news teams interviewing them. "They're sitting there at night in tents, and a lot of them are dressed up, and they're waving their laser swords at night." He was also interviewed by a reporter. "There are thousands and thousands of fans out there that live and breathe *Star Wars* twenty-four hours a day," Kazanjian said. "Certainly they have their jobs. They have their real lives, too. But if you're ever to the tour the country like I have and meet these people, why, they *are* Luke Skywalker."

On May 25, 1983, Kazanjian was at the Egyptian movie house to introduce the film before its first midnight showing. "They filed in," he says, "half of them are dressed in costume, and they're yelling and screaming, and they're excited. The audience was screaming and it was 11:30. They're going crazy; they're standing up and it's noisy. There are kids with lightsabers and the theater is absolutely packed. You can

292

hardly hear, it's so noisy—and when the lights start to dim, they go absolutely crazy."

Sid Ganis remembered, "I had that incredible experience, the countdown by a packed house at midnight, which worked perfectly. It was an audience that started at '. . . 15, 14, 13,' but when they got to '. . . 3, 2, 1'—the projectionist was smack on the button!"

"I started it at one minute to midnight," Kazanjian says, "because I wanted the Egyptian to be the first of all the theaters. When the Lucasfilm logo came up, they sat down, but they were still noisy. But as soon as the intro ended, you could hear a mouse walk in the theater. And they loved it. I was smiling in the back. I didn't stay for the whole movie. I went to another theater."

Overall, fan response was enthusiastic, though reviews were mixed as usual. Because Lucas wasn't feeling good and generally disliked doing interviews, Kazanjian met with the dozens of journalists who needed copy for their stories.

Financially, *Jedi* was a success. The week of May 25, the film raked in $45,311,000, $30 million over the weekend, soaring past the old record of $25 million set by *E.T.* "Howard gave out some nice little gifts," Burtt says, "these Lucite plastic blocks that had a frame from the movie, your credit in the roll up, in 70 millimeter. And this little key chain that went with it said, 'Thanks.' And then embossed, 'Howard.' It was a one-of-a-kind thing a producer did. And even today it's a souvenir of so much of what's pleasant about Howard."

Jedi was released in the UK where it made over $10 million during its first eight weeks. In the US, *Jedi* earned over $70 million in twelve days and dominated the box office. "We didn't in our wildest dreams anticipate this kind of reception," Ganis said.

Kazanjian, Marquand, Hamill, and Anthony Daniels (C-3PO) flew to Japan for a week of publicity in advance of *Jedi*'s opening in that country. Advance ticket sales, with no advertising, turned out to be "astronomical," according to Ganis, with more than 123,000 purchased; *Jedi* would accumulate over $7 million its first three weeks.

"It's one of those things where there's great relief that you're finally coming to the end of this massive project," Hamill says, "and yet there's a tinge of sadness, because it's like graduating from school: I've been with these people for so long, had so many shared experiences, and now we'll probably never see each other again. You say you will, but it never really happens the way you want it to."

"George sent me to Japan to promote the movie," Kazanjian says. "He tried to call me at home before I left for the airport, but I'd already left. George tried to get me again at the airport. Finally when I arrive at the hotel in Japan, Sid Ganis calls. I hadn't even opened up my suitcase yet and he says, 'Are you sitting down?' I said, 'No, should I?' He says, 'George and Marcia are getting a divorce.' Suddenly it went *click, click, click, click*. Everything leading up to that moment now made sense. George had made Sid and the department heads come in and made the announcement with Marcia sitting there."

"They gathered us in a room and they told us," says Ganis, who at the time was working to get George the cover of *Time* magazine. "But I wasn't thinking about the company. I was thinking, *Oh my God, these two*. They'd been through so much together. They'd started from scratch."

"Marcia had always been a delight to be with and helped to create the masterpiece of *A New Hope*," says Anthony Daniels. "It seemed George had devoted his life to the sequels, especially this final episode. The strains had taken a toll on their marriage. I liked them both enough to care and be touched by the thought of them not being a couple anymore."

Dunham had found out earlier: "George had walked into the cutting room one day, he sat down and said, 'Look, here's the deal.' We were still finishing up *Jedi*. He told me what was going on—I'd had no idea—he and Marcia were getting divorced and about the company. George said he was not going to make movies for a while and was going to take some time to figure it all out. He said, 'If you want to stay on, I'm happy to have you stay on.' I told him that I was going to go out and get a job and get some more experience, and maybe someday, we'd get back together.' I assume that he probably said the same thing to Howard and to others."

"I felt badly when they broke up," Miki Herman says. "George wouldn't let Marcia have a cleaning lady, but it's a personal question. Why does anybody leave anybody?"

294

"Marcia was the world to George," Carol Kazanjian says. "She would say to us, 'I want to go to the Oscars. Can I go with you guys? George won't go.' So she was our third person."

"Marcia wanted to invite people over, but George would say he was too tired," Howard says. "The same thing if she wanted to go out to see a movie. George wanted her there. She was very smart, and she could talk to him. Marcia worked very hard with George. Sometimes that meant twenty-four hours a day. It was very hard for all of us to see them in such a sad situation."

Lucas would cite the fact that Marcia had fallen in love with Tom Rodrigues, a craftsperson working on the ranch, as the main reason for their divorce, but Marcia would say it was because they couldn't agree on their future. "I thought we needed a break," she says. "I was interested in raising my daughter, and not having my daughter raised by a nanny. I wanted to be a stay-at-home mom. My mother was a working mother. All my aunties were stay-at-home moms. And I wanted to be a stay-at-home mom. I wanted to participate in my child's development on a day-to-day hands-on way. I thought to myself, *How many Oscars do I want to line up on my mantle, or do I want to love my children and be there for my children and have relationships with my children?* That's what I wanted."

CHAPTER 14: *Alias: "Dirty Harry"*

D espite the sad news, Kazanjian continued to travel the world promoting *Jedi*. His next stop was Rome, Italy, but all he saw was the interior of a recording studio and his hotel room. He had no time for tourism. Between trips, Kazanjian followed closely the film's release patterns in foreign territories and supervised translations and dubbing. In the end, he spent a little over three years on the film, six to seven days a week, fourteen- to twenty-hour days. "You go home at night, exhausted," he says. "You have no time to take your family anywhere, because if you do, somebody is going to need you. Somebody is going to need an answer. You are living with that film. The science-fiction conventions were fun and I did enjoy them, but flying all over the country was quite exhausting. I believe Richard Marquand only attended one, because he was preparing another picture."

One perk occurred when President Ronald Reagan asked to see the film. The Kazanjians flew to Washington, DC, to screen *Jedi* with the president and his personal staff. At its conclusion, Michael Deaver, White House deputy chief of staff, asked them if they'd like to remain and see the second film, John Badham's *War Games* (1983). Audience reaction to the subject matter, a young man (Matthew Broderick) who manages to hack into Pentagon computers, was not sympathetic.

When Howard was finally back in Marin County and able to talk one-on-one with Lucas, it was a bittersweet meeting. Their film had earned its money back and then some, but Lucasfilm was in hiatus. "Months after we released the film, George told me he wasn't happy, he wasn't

296

coming in every day," Kazanjian says. "He told me he's not going to do pictures for a long while. That's one meeting."

"Let me tell you, George was very sad at this point in his life," Carol says. "Marcia was his life."

"George said, 'Wrap it up. Close the production department,'" Howard continues. "I said, 'The only ones in production right now are myself, Miki, and Louis.' Louis was paying the last of the bills and checking them against the budget (and finding a lot of errors from people billing us). When George said to close it up, my first thought was that he meant, 'I'm not doing anything for ten years.' I'm out of a job.

"So I prepared to come back to Hollywood. And then weeks later when George heard I was physically leaving, he came to me and said, 'I didn't mean you. You're welcome to stay, even though we're not doing anything.' That's almost a word-for-word quote. But we had just had our second child. I'm buying a new house down south. All of these things were happening at the same time, and George is saying he's not going to do anything for ten years. George had always said with the completion of *Jedi* there would be no more episodes for a number of years. I told him that when he does the next group of *Star Wars* movies, he should shoot them back-to-back. I can assure you there were no plot discussions for episodes ten, eleven, and twelve."

"As early as the first couple of weeks when we're out in the desert in Tunisia," Hamill recalls, "I was saying to George, 'Why are we starting in the middle?' And he said, 'Well, this trilogy is more commercial. The first trilogy is more setting it all up.' At one point he said to me, 'Hey, kid, you think you'd come back and do a cameo in the last trilogy?' I asked, 'When would that be?' Mind you, this is 1976. He says, 'Oh, I don't know, like 2011.' I thought, *Oh my God, I'll be in my fifties!* Later he told me he was just kidding. I thought that by the time they'd do the sequel trilogy, they'd use new characters. Then there reached a point where George told me flat out: 'We're not doing seven, eight, nine; I don't want to be doing these things when I'm in my seventies.'"

"It was bittersweet," says Louis Friedman, who stayed on for the *Indiana Jones* sequel. "The word was that George was going through a divorce, so he was disbanding Lucasfilm. We all prepared to move back to LA, though he said when it comes back together, you'll all have an opportunity to re-up. I always refer to the period of time I was at Lucasfilm, between 1978 and 1983, as the Periclean age, the Golden Age: We did the sequel to *American Graffiti*, *The Empire Strikes Back*, *Return of the Jedi*, *Raiders of the Lost Ark*, and *Temple of Doom*. The hits just kept on coming. I thought, *This is how it always is*. You work for a company, and every picture you work on is huge."

"It was like everybody was going through this huge transition," says Jane Bay, who stayed on as Lucas's executive assistant. "I mean really gigantic and huge, and we didn't have time to think so much about the comings and goings."

"We were just like family," Carol Kazanjian says. "They were our family for ten years."

Kazanjian adds, "George had taken *Empire* and *Jedi* out of the San Francisco area, and the *Indiana Jones* movies out of the city. So we never built that film group. And once you start to train those guys and do one or two pictures with them, what happens? They go to Hollywood for work. We never kept that promise of doing a number of movies in the Bay Area."

Many of the Lucasfilm "family" departed, never to return, though many others, mostly at ILM and Sprockets, stayed on, working on non-Lucasfilm movies. The picnics and Christmas gifts and parties continued, too, but without Marcia Lucas. "I was persona non grata," she says. "Didn't exist."

MASTER OF NONE

Over that first Christmas, *Jedi* was back on 850 screens, for a rerelease in some areas. An internal Lucasfilm memo noted, joyfully, that *Jedi* was expected to generate $200 million as of the New Year— substantially above the estimated $150 million that had been used in the company's planning projections. The film dominated the 11th annual Academy of Science Fiction, Fantasy, and Horror films (aka the Saturn Awards), held in March 1984, with victories in five categories: Best Science Fiction Film (Kazanjian), Best Actor (Mark

298

Hamill), Best Costume (Aggie Guerard Rodgers and Nilo Rodis-Jamero), Best Makeup (Phil Tippett and Stuart Freeborn), and Best Special Effects (Richard Edlund, Dennis Muren, and Ken Ralston).

Jedi lost in several categories at the Oscars—Art Direction, Sound, and Music. But Edlund, Muren, Ralston, and Tippett were honored by the Academy of Motion Picture Arts and Sciences with a special achievement award for visual effects. After saying their individual thank-yous—which included Joe Johnston, Bruce Nicholson, Mike McAlister, Rose Duignan, Tom Smith, and others—they all shouted, "Thanks, George!"

The person responsible at the company that had succeeded in the innovative magnetic sound striping, Barry Stultz, of the Film Processing Corporation, won a technical achievement award from the Academy of Arts and Sciences. Shortly thereafter, Technicolor adopted the formula Holman had created.

Lucas agreed to let Kazanjian have an office at the Egg Company in LA and to be a consultant for Lucasfilm. Kazanjian, who wanted to make his family's permanent home in the Pasadena/San Marino area, explains, "At the time, Marin County up north had the five most negative things in the nation: the most drugs, the most divorces, the worst schools, the most suicides, and so on."

When the divorce was finalized, Marcia Lucas received the Egg Company buildings. Kazanjian tried to interest her in directing pictures, but she declined. Other Lucasfilmers, cast adrift, were having frustrating experiences. "When I came to LA, it was a real shock for me," says Duwayne Dunham. "The way the business worked, and the way people conducted their business. Howard had actually spoiled me, because he's so fair and he's so honest, and he treats people very well, with great respect. He lived it every day. And, sadly, it was something lacking in that world."

"I was received very well, because of the credits I had," Kazanjian says. "I had been complimented by many of people on the look of the pictures, the quality of the pictures, the budget, delivery, and so on, but I was now returning to corporations and a lot had changed. A lot of the executives, the Marvin Davises, were going; Jack Warner had gone—all of those people had gone. It was really a corporation world. The stock market was running the studios, and the studios wanted control. They wanted to know everything. I was dealing with corporate Hollywood and I was trying to raise financing and convince studios to do my pictures, and they all expected me to bring in a *Star Wars*-style, big-budget movie for just pennies. I was also offered an Elia Kazan movie, a movie at MGM, a movie at Fox, but the major reason I said no was, I didn't want to make that long drive. When you have kids, your life changes."

To some extent, Kazanjian's Lucasfilm pedigree kept him down at first, an odd situation. He was typecast as a big-budget film producer. There may also have been some latent jealousy because Lucas and his colleagues had been perceived as being able to do whatever they wanted—without Hollywood. Upon his return to the area, there was a feeling akin to: "Now you're one of us again, and we're going to give you a hard time."

"I can see that; I'm sure there was a lot of resentment that George was able to just do it his way," Hamill says. "And people, they admire mavericks, but they also resent them. So I can imagine the challenges Howard faced coming back."

Kazanjian formed a production company. He went to Mattel toys to pitch them a movie on their billion-dollar action-figure line Masters of the Universe. "On the heels of *Jedi* and Lucasfilm, they wanted me to make the film," he says.

Producer Ed Pressman was brought in by Mattel, and, after a year in development, with a writer and director in place, Cannon Films announced the movie on July 23, 1985. However, Kazanjian had a "falling out" with Pressman. "It was a very bad experience," he says. Ultimately, he had nothing to do with the 1987 film.

NO GOING BACK

While Gary Kurtz was producing Walter Murch's *Return to Oz* (1985), Lucas again acted as guarantor to the studio (the Walt Disney Company). "Walter Murch was not getting along with Gary, so Gary was being replaced," Kazanjian recalls. "George asked me if I wanted to do the film. I said, 'I can't replace Gary Kurtz two times.' I turned it down. Plus, the film was in so much trouble, I didn't want to go to London for months to work it out."

Lucas ended up having to do much of the rescuing himself.

Kazanjian pitched more projects to studios. "But they all still expected a *Star Wars/Raiders* from me, but with a small budget. It was tough out there. Bottom line: hard times."

He was again tempted to return to Lucasfilm, when Lucas backed his friends and occasional writing partners Gloria Katz and Willard Huyck in their efforts to make a film based on the Marvel comic book character Howard the Duck. When that movie also had problems, Kazanjian was called in. He flew up to find the production in turmoil. "It's a noon call or thereabouts for a night shoot," he says. "And Gloria is on the phone, she's eating and screaming at people. Willard was being bombarded by questions from the crew. The crew's running around. Nobody's communicating with anybody. I said, 'I don't want anything to do with this.' I jumped in my rental car, drove back to the airport, and came home." (*Howard the Duck* was released and flopped in 1986.)

The pattern continued when Lucas himself wanted to make a TV show about a young Indiana Jones. Kazanjian had a third child on the way in 1986, but he returned to Marin County and they had a talk. "George asked me if I would do it, and I said, 'It has to be shot like episodic television, where you just keep going.'"

Lucas told him, "It's going to be shot in Europe over a year's time."

"George said that we'd be headquartered out of London, but we'd go to other countries. I told George that my kids didn't need to go to Europe and go into schools and move about. I said, 'You need to have a European producer.'"

Lucas hired Rick McCallum, an American producer working in London who had been recommended by Robert Watts. McCallum eventually traveled thousands of miles, almost never stopping, for a couple of years while making *The Young Indiana Jones Chronicles* (1992–93). "I don't regret not doing it," Kazanjian says. "It was wrong for me at the time. I would turn down not only George, but other location pictures, because I wanted to be home with my kids."

301

Producer Edward Pressman, director Gary Goddard, and producer Kazanjian discuss a conceptual design for Masters of the Universe *(1987), a film that the latter eventually left. (On the walls are concept designs by Ralph McQuarrie.)*

A brighter moment was when Charlton Heston visited the Egg Company offices (for reasons now forgotten). "I met with him, and I asked for something I rarely do," Kazanjian recalls. "I said, 'If I bring in a poster, would you sign it?' When I was a little boy, when *The Ten Commandments* was playing, they had lobby cards they put in the window of stores. I had one from my barber shop. Charlton Heston said yes, so I brought that in with the one-sheet poster—and he signed both."

STAND AND DELIVER!

In the late 1980s, Kazanjian, on the lookout for writers, received a sample script by Boaz Yakin. Yakin already had a film in development, *The Punisher* (1989), a vehicle for martial arts star Dolph Lundgren. The sample script was called *The Rookie*, a story about a young cop paired with a veteran cop, and Kazanjian liked it. "I asked who was making the film. His agent said, 'Nobody.' He told me the script had been everywhere and had been turned down. I said I couldn't believe that and asked if I could run with it. He said yes."

A manager friend of Kazanjian's, Steven Siebert, said he could get the script to Charlie Sheen. Sheen was hot at the time, having starred in *Wall Street* (1987) and *Young Guns* (1988). "Charlie loved the script," Kazanjian says. "So first I went to Paramount with the project. They loved it and we began negotiations. I immediately got a telephone call from Warner Bros., who said they were also interested in it. Billy Gerber, the executive, asked to see the script. I told him we were in negotiations with Paramount. He still wanted to see it. I said, 'You already turned it down.' 'I want to see it.' So I got it over to him and we had a bidding war."

Kazanjian favored Paramount, because his old Lucasfilm colleague and friend, Sid Ganis, was now that studio's head of production and Ganis wanted *The Rookie*. Gerber, on the other hand, wanted to give the script to Clint Eastwood. "I didn't want to give it to Clint," Kazanjian explains, "because he would bring in his production company, Malpaso, and I would have little control of the story. And if Clint came aboard, I knew there would be rewrites strengthening the Clint Eastwood older

303

veteran cop role. I didn't see that in the script. And I wanted more say, because I knew Clint didn't use big name actors (he did after this period). I had meetings with him about that. I also knew it would become a Clint Eastwood–directed picture, which I didn't want. But Charlie Sheen kept saying he wanted to work with Clint. We gave in to Charlie and signed with Warner Bros."

Things became more complicated when Kazanjian received a call from Peter Guber. Guber insisted that his company, Guber-Peters Entertainment Company (formed with Jon Peters), originally had the script and had given it to Warner Bros., who had passed. His company no longer had the rights, but they were 800-pound gorillas on the lot. Guber had produced *The Color Purple* (1985), *Rain Man* (1988), *Batman* (1989), and other successes. Kazanjian recalls, "Now I'm in heavy discussions with my attorney who is in discussions with the attorney of powerhouse producer Peter Guber, who wants to be a part of the picture. Guber wants to be the producer and shove me into the executive producer category, but I'm negotiating for a 'Howard Kazanjian Production' credit. We're fighting that out, but I must say, as gentlemen, with no support from Charlie because it doesn't affect him.

"The time came when I needed to personally call Peter and tell him how I felt. I planned carefully every word I would say and dialed his number. I was going to suggest we share the production credit. I called Peter and he immediately said okay. I hung up and I thought, *Something is not right here.*"

A few weeks later, fall 1989, Kazanjian discovered why Guber had given in so easily: It was announced in trade papers that Guber had convinced the Sony Corporation to purchase the old MGM lot. He was to be the head honcho but was in negotiations with Warner Bros. to extricate himself from his contract with that studio. Lawsuits followed, but the deal was concluded that November, a day after Sony acquired Columbia Pictures Entertainment, which made Peter Guber and Jon Peters cochairmen of Columbia Pictures Entertainment (now Sony Pictures Entertainment).

Michael Schulhof, vice chairman of Sony Corp. of America, said in a statement: "The acquisition of a major film studio extends Sony's

A publicity shot of actor Charlie Sheen and actor-director-producer Clint Eastwood for The Rookie, *a 1990 Warner Bros. picture. Kazanjian produced.*

long-term strategy of building a total entertainment business around the synergy of audio and video hardware and software."

"Once Guber knew the Columbia/MGM/WB deal was closing," Kazanjian says, "he was no longer interested in *The Rookie*. To his credit, Guber launched Sony and Columbia to be the strong company it is today."

HANGING ON

Guber and Peters were out. Eastwood was still in. "Clint is so powerful at the studio, he can get his way on most anything," Kazanjian says. "So Warner Bros. calls me and says we know we've negotiated your 'Howard Kazanjian Production,' but now that Clint is going to direct, it is going to be a 'Malpaso Production.' We had already signed contracts, but I was forced to give up the production credit up front." The consolation prize would be an end credit with wording like "In association with Howard Kazanjian and Steven Siebert."

"And then the script needed work," Kazanjian continues. "By now Clint had had the original rewritten to the point where it should have been retitled 'The Mentor.' But the script still needed work." Kazanjian spoke with screenwriter Steven E. de Souza, who, having written *Commando* (1985) and *Die Hard* (1988), was a "staple" at Warner Bros. Souza told him, "It's not up to me."

Kazanjian went to Eastwood, who told him, "Don't worry about the script. We'll fix it on the set." "But you don't fix it on the set," Kazanjian says, "you fix it now, not when you're shooting. But Clint was so into Warner Bros., they didn't even do a budget on the picture. No budget." When Kazanjian asked about the budget, an exec told him, "Clint doesn't have to do one, except to conform to a ballpark figure we come up with for the total picture." They did tell Kazanjian how much Eastwood was earning: $2 million to direct, $7 million to act. Eastwood's last picture, *Bird*, a 1988 biopic about jazz legend Charlie Parker, had lost money, but overall he had been a huge moneymaker for the studio.

"There was no budget to follow, which did in fact make it easy for me," Kazanjian adds. "And my back-end participation was tied to Clint's;

I wasn't getting dollar one, but I was getting adjusted gross, because I was tied to Clint's definition for adjusted gross; I was adjusted, he was gross."

With Eastwood at the helm, *The Rookie* started filming on various California locations circa April 16, 1990. As rewritten, the film told the story of police detective Nick Pulovski (Eastwood), who is unhappy about being partnered with rookie David Ackerman (Sheen). Ackerman is worried because many of Pulovski's partners have ended up dead. Together they have to take down a car-thief ring whose bosses (Raúl Juliá and Sônia Braga) are responsible for the death of Pulovski's last partner.

In an early interview, Eastwood said, "I have a project for this spring that will be full of action. It's another cop picture . . . It has its own character and if it's done well, it can turn out to be something good."

"I liked Clint," Kazanjian says. "He's tough. He usually never takes on other people. He told me I was very lucky that he was allowing me to stay with the picture. Usually a producer comes in, takes his money, and disappears."

Eastwood had bodybuilding equipment in one of his office suites. Just before shooting his first scenes, Kazanjian suggested that they tone down the gray in Eastwood's hair a little bit. "Absolutely not. I am what I am," the actor-director replied. A couple of days later, Kazanjian was talking to Eastwood in the makeup chair, and the makeup artist was toning down the gray.

Once cameras rolled, Sheen had problems focusing. He didn't look his best. Kazanjian tried to help. "I thought it was drinking, but it was drugs," Kazanjian says. "One night we were shooting and I sat with him in his trailer. He looked tired and wasn't all there. Part of Charlie's problem were a few of his close friends. Peer pressure and them egging him on."

Eastwood turned sixty on May 31. "Word went out that nobody but nobody should say, 'Happy birthday,'" Kazanjian recalls. "We had just finished eating lunch, a lot of people had disappeared already back to the set, but Tony the caterer, the only one who hadn't been told, comes out with this sheet cake, singing "Happy Birthday." The rest of us scattered."

307

An Unhappy Ending

Eastwood filmed a lot of coverage for his longtime editor, Joel Cox, to assemble into their movie. "Clint shot everything every which way," Kazanjian says. "If you were walking out of a room, we'd do a close-up, a medium shot, a wide shot; then over another character's back, close, medium; follow them out, zoom in on you, etc."

One of the film's draws was going to be a series of expensive, spectacular stunts and car chases. At the end of production, Kazanjian was told, "We came right in on budget." Depending on the source, however, the film cost anywhere from $10 to $17 million.

The Rookie opened in theaters nationwide on December 7, 1990, and grossed a reported $21,633,874. Most critics were disparaging. "Overlong, sadistic, and stale even by the conventions of the buddy pic genre," read the *Variety* review. "Clint Eastwood's *The Rookie* is actually *Dirty Harry 5½* since Eastwood's tough-as-nails cop Nick Pulovski could just as easily be named Harry Callahan, and his penchant for breaking in partners (and getting them killed) is a holdover from Harry's first three patrols . . . Eastwood the actor seems rightfully bored with the material, while Sheen continues to hammer away at his own tough-guy rep with only marginal success."

Critics also thought it strange that Puerto Rican Raúl Juliá and Brazilian Sonia Braga had been cast as Germans. A scene in which Eastwood's character was raped by Braga's character generated controversy as well. The one highlight was the stunts.

CHAPTER 15: *Development Hell & Heaven*

K azanjian had read Peter Lenkov's script for what would become *Demolition Man* (1993) and had optioned it back in 1989. He had lunch with Lenkov and gave him notes for a rewrite; he made the studio rounds and pitched the project. Eventually, he met with Carolco and its founders, producers Mario Kassar and Andrew Vajna. They liked the script because it fit into their preferred genre: over-the-top action/violence, as featured in *First Blood* (1982), *The Terminator* (1984), *Red Heat* (1988), and *Total Recall* (1990).

Kazanjian's development of the property became more difficult from this point on. "Lawsuits proliferated long before the cameras rolled," he says. "Extremely fast-forward to several months passing whereby two 'producers who had never produced' claimed they had the rights to the script. Also, an earlier employer of screenwriter Peter Lenkov claimed she owned the script because it was typed on her typewriter. Carolco dropped the project until I could settle the impending lawsuit. After months of delay and lawyers fighting lawyers, Peter's agent suggested we take the script to Warner Bros. and producer Joel Silver, and have Warners fight it out. So we did. The months that passed were another 'Welcome Back to Hollywood' for me. Joel Silver was 'the king of popcorn films.' Joel made it into a bigger action picture than I had planned to do."

At one point Kazanjian was going to make the film in Australia where it would have starred Mel Gibson, while Silver was going to do *Beverly Hills Cop III* (1994). But Silver was fired from that production and came back to *Demolition Man*. When action-film star Steven Segal came aboard, Silver left the project because the two "didn't get along," says

309

Kazanjian, who oversaw two or three rewrites with Lenkov, some based on notes provided by Segal, over a ten-month period in 1990.

Then Segal bowed out and Silver jumped back in. Arnold Schwarzenegger, Jean-Claude Van Damme, and Jackie Chan were attached at one time or another as either hero or villain. Box-office champ Sylvester Stallone, also attached to the film before, came back. He wanted to play good guy John Spartan, a cop unfrozen in the future to combat a villain (also unfrozen) who's on a rampage in a world no longer equipped to handle violence. Wesley Snipes signed on as Simon Phoenix, the villain.

"Three years later, after about thirteen rewrites by approximately six writers, we were ready to go," Kazanjian says. "Stallone was paid a million to write the script per his contract. However, the WGA never allowed him to receive credit. He rewrote the endings. The story had a huge finale that would have cost a million or more to shoot, and he eliminated that. Also when Stallone writes, he writes the script as he is and how he speaks. When you read the script you know it's Stallone." (A script dated February 1993 was credited as: story by Peter Lenkov, Daniel Waters; screenplay by Daniel Waters and Jonathan Lemkin.)

It would be the directorial debut for Marco Brambilla, a veteran of TV commercials. Silver and Brambilla had been working on a different film, *Richie Rich* (1994), to star Macaulay Culkin. "At the last minute we weren't able to get him for the budget," Brambilla said. "David Fincher suggested me as a director for *Demolition Man*, and it came together really quickly. I met with Stallone a few days after getting attached. I started . . . rewriting the script with Dan Waters immediately, and we went into production six to eight months after." (Donald Petrie would direct *Richie Rich* with Culkin.)

"I was a visitor on my own set," Kazanjian says (somewhat like his experience on *The Rookie*). "I never saw a budget or schedule. It was a Joel Silver picture. In the end, millions of dollars over budget, it was Joel and his director who wrecked the movie. Brambilla couldn't handle the immense production and the questions that were continually asked of him. Besides, Stallone usually had a say and heavily influenced the direction."

The film was released in October 1993 and was profitable worldwide. It was also the first starring role for a young actress named Sandra Bullock. "I'm on the [licensed] pinball machine [of the film]," Bullock said decades later. "All the men in the film got one and I'm the only one that didn't get one."

"I do give Joel Silver credit for making it all happen," Kazanjian adds. "He and Warner Bros. saved the day by settling the lawsuits. The original script, however, and the first rewrite that Lenkov did are far better than the finished picture."

A ZIG AND A JAG

Kazanjian had to move out of the Egg Company building when it was seized by the government in a case of eminent domain. Metro Rail was expanding. In 1994 the beautifully restored edifice was razed for a parking lot for buses; Marcia Lucas organized a wake for the building the day before. "They were going to give me a penny on the dollar," she says, "so I had to get a lawyer. It was a nice building and I'd worked hard on it."

"It was sad," Carol Kazanjian says. "The officials told me they'd never realized how beautiful the building was until they walked inside. 'We would have made other choices,' that's what they said."

"I stayed in the Egg Company until they took the building and leveled it," Kazanjian says. "It really was a sad day."

Shortly after completing *Demolition Man*, Kazanjian received a telephone call from the agent of Don Bellisario, a TV writer-producer who had worked on *Quantum Leap* (1989–1993) and, ironically, *Magnum, P.I.* (1980–1988), among other shows. He was invited to meet Bellisario and declined. "I didn't want to do TV," Kazanjian says. "After a third telephone call, I agreed to meet Don because I respected him as a fine producer of series television, but I said, 'Please tell him in advance the answer is no.'"

They met at the producer's Paramount offices. Bellisario was looking for a motion-picture producer who could do a two-hour pilot that looked like a feature, but on a television budget. "I was that guy," Kazanjian says.

311

"Don proceeded to tell me a little about the project. When I left his office with the pilot screenplay in hand, I was ready to sign on. After reading the script, I gave Don just a couple of notes. It was one of the few scripts I'd ever read that was a polished screenplay ready to go before the cameras."

The plot concerned Commander Harmon Rabb Jr. and Lieutenant Colonel Sarah MacKenzie, JAG lawyers ("Judge Advocate General's Corps," the legal branch of the U.S. Air Force, Army, Coast Guard, and Navy), who investigate and litigate crimes committed by military personnel.

It was already late October and *JAG* was scheduled for a quick shoot of a few months beginning in January. Negotiations with the studio were the fastest and simplest Kazanjian had experienced in many years; the contract was written on single sheet of paper. He organized a crew and traveled to Texas to scout a mothballed aircraft carrier, the USS *Lexington*, which was currently a museum. The Navy did not want to cooperate with the production because in the screenplay pilot, someone on an aircraft carrier at sea is thrown overboard. The Navy didn't want that shown. "So they didn't want us shooting on this museum ship they still owned," Kazanjian says. "The museum could have easily lost their license to operate by allowing us to shoot there. I had to go and make peace."

He succeeded and permission was granted. Kazanjian also consulted on the casting and championed actor David James Elliott. After the actor's audition readings, he submitted positive notes and told Bellisario, "He's the guy." Bellisario and the network agreed, and Elliott was cast as Commander Harmon Rabb.

JOIN THE NAVY

Bellisario, who would direct the pilot, traveled with Kazanjian, cast, and crew to Texas. They filmed for only about a week on the *Lexington*, but those scenes were key in establishing the show's realism. Jets were placed strategically on deck for the camera, and fake bombs and missiles were loaded under the wings of F-14s. To keep everything on track, Kazanjian brought back an old friend to be coordinating producer: Louis Friedman. "I had gone off and started my own career in LA," Friedman says, "so

While shooting TV pilot movie JAG *(1995), Kazanjian talks to leading man David James Elliott (Commander Rabb) on the aircraft carrier USS* Lexington *docked in Corpus Christi, Texas.*

I met with Bellisario. I met with the head of production at Paramount Television, and so I did the pilot."

They delivered an edited picture on schedule, April 27, and the pilot sold to NBC immediately. Kazanjian was told by Paramount to begin preparing the series. "But I had only agreed to do the pilot, I hadn't signed on for the series," he says.

Paramount informed him that anyone who produces the pilot always does at least the first year of the series. "I could have fought and asked for more money," Kazanjian says, "but I really liked the cast, the pilot, and especially working with Bellisario. I'd been warned long before I took on the pilot and the series that Don was very difficult. But Don was one of the best people I've ever worked with."

On September 22, 1995, *Variety* reviewed their TV movie: "*JAG* borrows from recent features *Crimson Tide* and *Apollo 13* in being jargon-heavy to help generate atmosphere, but as Rabb's character is allowed to develop, *JAG* could become one of the season's highlights." The two-hour "hardware-heavy" movie acted as an introduction to the sixty-minute episodic series, which was scheduled to begin its regular 8 PM Saturday night run on September 30. In order to produce the first season, Kazanjian would need help. Friedman stayed, and Duwayne Dunham signed on.

"I directed a couple of episodes over there," Dunham says. "And I'm sure I wouldn't have worked on *JAG* if it wasn't for Howard. He brought me in. It was the same old Howard. He has his way and that whole office was run like Howard. It's just like walking into his living room. You're welcomed and treated fairly, and 'What do you need?' and 'Let's do this' and 'How are we going to do that?' And somehow you get through it. TV is such a different animal, but they spent a lot of money per episode. You're there for about three weeks: You have a week of prep, a week to shoot it, and about a week to sit in the cutting room. So it goes by pretty quick." (Dunham directed "War Cries" and "Rendezvous.")

"I did ten episodes," Friedman recalls. "Of all the different types and mediums and formats for filmmaking, the one-hour drama is the most difficult by far. *By far*. It's eighteen hours a day, five or six days a week. When you're in the middle of a season, there's always a show that's almost ready, which needs additional footage; one that you're shooting; and one that's prepping. It's a conveyor belt that never slows down, it only speeds up. But Howard and I always got along. I loved working with Howard, because we saw the world very similarly. We're both very exacting and very precise, and really try to dot all of our *j*'s and *i*'s, and cross all of our *t*'s. Howard trusted me and gave me a lot of responsibility, which I enjoyed."

The Navy came to appreciate the show's popularity and, moreover, its value as a recruitment vehicle. They started supporting the series around episode 10. Kazanjian was able to secure a Lockheed C-130 Hercules, a large transport plane, at Marine Corps Air Station El Toro, near Irvine, California. The Navy gave *JAG* full cooperation for the second season and beyond. Kazanjian left after the first series, but *JAG* endured for nine years. It was even picked up by CBS after being dropped by NBC, and spawned a spin-off, *NCIS*, in 2003 (Naval Criminal Investigative Service), a series that continues to this day.

CHAPTER 16: *Reunions*

K azanjian kept up his Lucasfilm ties. He was invited to the opening of the Temple of the Forbidden Eye, a Disneyland attraction based on the Indiana Jones film franchise. In Anaheim he joined celebrity guests George Lucas, Michael Eisner (now Disney CEO), Dan Aykroyd, Arnold Schwarzenegger, Carrie Fisher, and other VIPs for the opening on March 3, 1995. "I always thought *Raiders* would be like a Disneyland ride, but I never thought Disneyland would have a *Raiders* ride," Kazanjian says. Later rechristened Indiana Jones Adventure, the ride went on to be one of Disneyland's biggest attractions.

Kazanjian also visited Lucas at Leavesden Studios, not too far from London, in August of 1997. The writer-director was filming the first part of his prequel trilogy: *Star Wars*: Episode I *The Phantom Menace* (1999). "George knew exactly what he wanted and how he would edit the film," Kazanjian says. "It basically was bring the actor in, find your place and we'll shoot." Once again he appreciated Lucas's groundbreaking efforts on behalf of digital, aided by producer Rick McCallum and ILM. The fact that Lucas had chosen to tell the story of how a nice little boy evolves into the greedy and evil Darth Vader—instead of how the mature Sith Lord decimated the ranks of the Jedi (what audiences anticipated)—revealed once more his friend's iconoclastic side. Lucas was still the independent maverick.

"George is, in his heart and soul, a good guy and a talented filmmaker," Marcia Lucas says. "I wish he would've kept directing [other kinds of] movies. But when I went to see Episode I—I had a friend who worked at ILM, who took me as a guest to a preview—I remember going out to the parking lot, sitting in my car and crying. I cried. I cried because

316

I didn't think it was very good. And I thought he had such a rich vein to mine, a rich palette to tell stories with. He had all those characters. And I thought it was weird that the story was about this little boy who looked like he was six years old, but then later on he's supposed to get with this princess who looked like she was twenty years old. There were things I didn't like about the casting, and things I didn't like about the story, and things I didn't like—it was a lot of eye candy. CG."

"I was impressed that the prequels had their own identity," Hamill says. "They were criticized because they were exposition-heavy and more cerebral and probably, like he said back in 1976, they weren't as commercial. It's a darker story. But in the age of social media, people's voices are amplified and I'm shocked at how brutal they can be, not just in the case of the *Star Wars* films, but across the board."

Kazanjian recalls, "George said to me after Episode I, 'I didn't even get a nomination for costumes or sets.' And if you look at that picture, whether you like the costumes or not, it was a costume picture, and it was a huge set picture. Hollywood had dumped on George."

EAST OF HOLLYWOOD

In 1995, Kazanjian had executive produced a TV movie called *Rattled*, which told the story of a family terrorized by a horde of rattlesnakes. A year or so later, he began a partnership with Craig Darian. He and Darian had met during the early days, before Lucasfilm had set up Sprocket Systems; Darian, an executive at Ryder Sound, had lobbied to do sound mixes for the company. They kept in touch and eventually teamed up to make several independently produced projects during the late 1990s and early aughts. One was *The Amati Girls* (2001). In 1999, Kazanjian read the script by Anne DeSalvo, who would also direct and "called the shots." Kazanjian helped negotiate deals with a number of talented actors, including three Oscar winners: Mercedes Ruehl, Lee Grant, and Cloris Leachman. Sean Young, of *Blade Runner* fame (1982), starred in what was a small picture concerning four sisters who disagree about everything, except helping their mother after the death of their father.

317

An executive producer brought in the financing for the film, which was budgeted at around $5 million. The exec producer then decided he wanted to be the actual hands-on producer and maneuvered Kazanjian and Darian into executive producer roles. "But he didn't have the necessary experience," Kazanjian says. "When the picture got into trouble, I had to come in and try to contain the director while Craig contained the unions. In all, there were thirteen producer types, six of whom I never met, and I was on set every day. Later I found out that they had put money into the project and were promised associate producer credits."

In post the director was fired. "I'm not happy or proud to say that, but it needed to be done," Kazanjian says.

The producer's company got into more trouble because of the way money had been raised. The business plan had been written by an ex-Securities Exchange Commission (SEC) attorney, but only about $2.5 of the $5 million raised had actually gone into the picture. Kazanjian realized that he would be the first target of a federal investigation because his was the highest-profile name attached to the picture. "Craig and I immediately went to a tax attorney friend and explained what was happening," he recalls. "He said the best thing to do was to go to the government. It cost me $34,000 in legal fees, but at the second SEC meeting, they said, 'Thank you very much for coming in. You did the right thing. We hold nothing against you.' It taught me a lesson about how to raise money, and I don't raise money. I'll anchor money—meaning, I'll take the film and deliver a finished picture—but I'm not going out to find the money. Anyway, the feds came in and some of the raisers went to jail; one of them died in jail from a heart attack."

The movie was not a success at the box office or with critics.

During their partnership years, Kazanjian and Darian tried to make a movie with the former's old classmate Randal Kleiser, who had directed the box-office smash musical *Grease* (1978) and other films since their days at USC. "The three of us tried to launch a movie called, *The Laughing Man*," Kleiser says, "based on Victor Hugo's novel, *L'Homme qui rit*. We took that around to studios for many years. Never was able

318

to raise the financing. It was like Hugo's *Hunchback of Notre Dame*, and it was kind of expensive. Nobody got it, and they didn't know how we were going to shoot this disfigured character. I did a CGI test showing how the mouth would work, how he could look handsome but when he smiled, it would look grotesque. That was a project we were all obsessed with. It was our dream project, we really thought it would work. It was eventually made in France by a French director [Jean-Pierre Améris, in 2012], and it didn't do well."

A project that did work out for Kazanjian and Darian was a foreign distribution deal made under their banner, Tricor Entertainment. A Taiwanese-backed financial group VisionNet Intl., which owned EVA Air and the largest container company, came to the two producers and asked if they were interested in building movie theaters in Vietnam. "At that time, the majority of the Vietnamese population was under twenty-five years old," Kazanjian says, "because the older adults had mostly been killed off in the war, and the younger generation wanted American movies. EVA, our partner, built the first theater. We wanted a multiplex, but they said the Vietnamese don't want multiplexes."

Variety reported in 1999: "The company, San Marino–based Tricor Entertainment, headed by former Lucasfilm veep Howard Kazanjian and showbiz veteran Craig Darian, has inked a deal with London-based United Intl. Pictures for exclusive Vietnamese theatrical distribution rights to as many as twenty pics annually from Paramount, Universal, DreamWorks and MGM." Darian added: "In the post-war era, Vietnam's population of more than seventy-five million has been largely untapped by Hollywood, in part because of rampant piracy. But since last year's signing of the Bilateral Copyright Agreement, the country has begun to crack down on intellectual property violations."

Indeed, Kazanjian and Darian were instrumental in persuading the Vietnamese government to sign the Berne Convention for the Protection of Literary and Artistic Works, an international agreement governing copyright (aka "the Berne Convention" because it was first accepted in Berne, Switzerland, in the nineteenth century). "The Vietnamese would say, 'We're stealing American films, because you won't give them to us,'" Kazanjian recalls. "So we started distributing them."

Tricor would send over three prints of each film, usually big-budget films from that era and before, more than fifty films in all over the years. Among the first were three from 1998: Paramount's *The Truman Show*, DreamWorks' *Deep Impact*, and Universal's *Mercury Rising*.

"But then the Koreans and the Chinese came in with a lot of money," Kazanjian sighs, "and they started building multiplexes. They were paying four or five times what we were to distribute the films, losing money—they didn't make money for years—but they killed us that way."

| The Producer's Role

| Kazanjian says, "Normally, a producer oversees all of film production. The role of the producer can vary, however, and often be confused with the role of an executive producer, or the two roles may overlap. A producer can either be employed by a studio/ production entity or can work independently. A producer plans and coordinates various aspects of film production, such as selecting the script, novel, or idea; coordinating the writing, directing, and editing; and arranging financing if needed.

"The producer's first primary role is to find the material. If it is based on an existing script, then he is ready to take the next step in finding a home for the project. Finding a home can mean a studio, network, or independent financier. If the idea is from a novel, or even a life story or a personal tale with an interesting subject, then the producer must hire a screenwriter. In the past, studios were quite open to a producer pitching an idea, treatment, synopsis, or novel. Today it is expected for a proven producer to bring in a package; the package may have one or more of the following: writer, director, talent.

"The producer also supervises the preproduction, production, and postproduction stages. One of the

320

In his USC Cinema hat, Kazanjian takes a moment from watching crew set up the next shot on location in Buttercup Valley, California, for Return of the Jedi *(1983).*

ABOVE, TOP TO BOTTOM: *Kazanjian, at Seattle's Norwescon, circa March 1983, to promote* Return of the Jedi, *points to the next person with a question.* • *At the White House, Deputy Chief of Staff Michael Deaver chats with Carol and Howard Kazanjian after a screening of* Return of the Jedi *for President Reagan and his guests.*

ABOVE (CLOCKWISE FROM TOP): *Kazanjian discusses the next shot with actor Anthony Daniels (C-3PO).* • *Silhouette of Kazanjian in the blazing hot desert sun.* • *Kazanjian, director Richard Marquand, George Lucas on location, ready for the next take.*

ABOVE, TOP TO BOTTOM: *On location for pick-up shots for* Return of the Jedi *in Death Valley, California, Kazanjian shakes the hand of Daniels/C-3PO.* • *Kazanjian and Louis Friedman wait for R2-D2 to be ready for the next shot.*

OPPOSITE, TOP TO BOTTOM: *Kazanjian and Lucas keep Sir Alec Guinness (Obi-Wan Kenobi) company on the Elstree stage as crew make ready the next shot; the veteran actor had a cold while filming his part.* • *In the California desert for* Return of the Jedi, *Lucasfilm marketing executive Sid Ganis visits Kazanjian on the barge set location and poses for a photo.*

ABOVE, TOP TO BOTTOM: *Kazanjian stands on the roof of the Endor bunker set on location while being interviewed for a promotional film (an AT-ST is in background).* • *Co-producer Robert Watts, Lucas, Kazanjian, and production designer Norman Reynolds on a frigid soundstage with a full-scale X-wing fighter behind them on the Tatooine sandstorm set.*

OPPOSITE, TOP TO BOTTOM: *Kazanjian and Lucas checking on things in ILM's Creature Shop, located in San Rafael's industrial zone, circa 1981. Both were concerned with making progress on the sixty creatures required for populating sets being constructed in England.* • *At Elstree, Kazanjian stands beneath the Emperor's shuttle while crew finish building the set.*

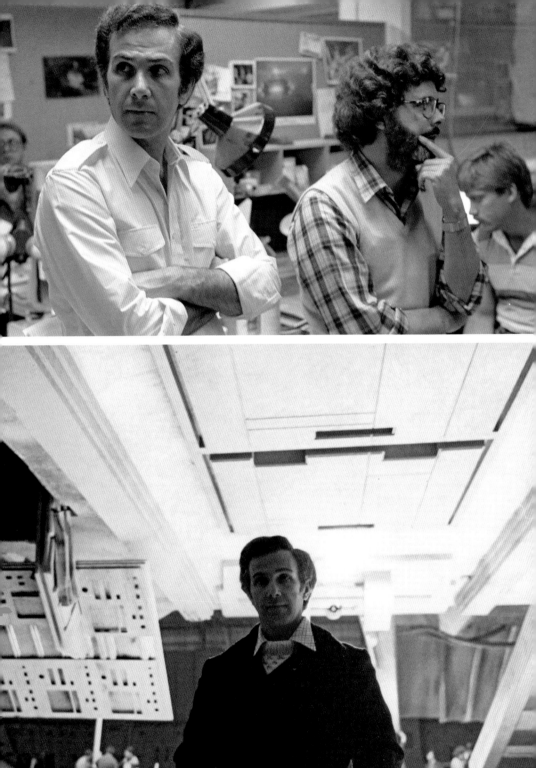

Kazanjian with Darth Vader (David Prowse) on the Imperial docking bay set at Elstree.

TOP TO BOTTOM: *Kazanjian adjusts a miniature speeder bike trooper on ILM's bluescreen stage.* •
*Kazanjian poses for a photo by the complete Imperial Star Destroyer model and a detailed model of
a ship's bridge area on ILM's bluescreen stage (note the destroyed deflector shield dome; an X-wing
hangs in the background).*

TOP TO BOTTOM: *In Italy, promotional efforts included roadside posters advertising* Return of the Jedi. • *On the promotional tour for* Jedi, *Anthony Daniels (C-3PO), Kazanjian, and director Richard Marquand spent several days in Japan in 1983.*

May 16, 1983

Mr. Howard Kazanjian

Dear Howard:

Writing a letter to you seems strange since we talk so
freely together, however, I thought it would be
appropriate to document my real feelings about your
terrific performance as Producer on RETURN OF THE JEDI.

The film is a triumph, particulary from your vantage
point. Anyone, and I try to include myself, who knows
anything about filmmaking has to be impressed with the
scope and magnitude of this project. It is to your
credit that this picture was produced so smoothly and
in such an orderly planned fashion. You obviously
don't need my kudos as I am sure that the rest of the
public seeing this film will feel as I do.

We have worked together for nearly four years now and I
just want it to go on the record at least once in
telling you how much I appreciate, admire, and respect
your work.

Best regards,

Robert M. Greber
President
Chief Executive Officer

RMG:ml

P. O. Box 2009, San Rafael, California 94912   Telephone (415) 457-5282
Telex: 330499 LFL SRFL

Mr. Howard Kazanjian

P. O. Box 2009, San Rafael, California 94912

OPPOSITE: *Letter and envelope from Lucasfilm President Robert Greber addressed to Kazanjian, after the former saw a sneak preview of* Return of the Jedi, *dated May 16, 1983. The letter commends Kazanjian for his work on the blockbuster and for having assured its smooth and "orderly" creation. (Greber was president after Weber.)*

ABOVE: *Kazanjian supervises production on location for* Jedi *in Buttercup Valley.*

CLOCKWISE FROM TOP: *Kazanjian aboard the aircraft carrier USS* Lexington *in Corpus Christi, Texas, shooting the television pilot for* JAG, *circa 1995.* • *Former National Security Council staffer Oliver North, Bellisario, and Kazanjian take a break for lunch while shooting an episode of* JAG *in the California desert. The controversial North appeared as "Ollie" on three episodes over the years.* • *Kazanjian meets with actress Andrea Parker (Lt. Caitlin "Kate" Pike) and director/executive producer Don Bellisario on the aircraft carrier USS* Lexington.

TOP TO BOTTOM *Who some humorously called the "Big Four"—Marquand, Lucas, Kazanjian, and Watts—walk a narrow alley between the towering soundstages at Elstree.* • *At ILM's unofficial fortieth anniversary event, in San Rafael, standing outside the soundstage, are: Kazanjian, former ILM art director Joe Johnston, now film director (*The Rocketeer, *1991;* Captain America: The First Avenger, *2011); and Academy Award–winning sound designer-editor-director Ben Burtt.*

TOP & BOTTOM: *The Kazanjians at the grand opening of Galaxy's Edge at Disneyland, California, and press conference on May 30, 2019. The new "neighborhood" at the legendary amusement park included a* Millennium Falcon.

next most important tasks is to hire a director and other key crew. Whereas the director makes the creative decisions during production, the producer typically manages the logistics and business operations, though some directors also produce their own films. The producer must see that the film is delivered on time and within budget to the distributor/studio entity. Most producers have final say on all creative decisions, with the exception of a very strong director-producer. Studios also can override producers and directors on the final cut.

"There are times when the producer will hire a line producer to do the day-to-day work on the sets. Oftentimes, the role between the executive producer and producer are reversed. I worked on two films where the inexperienced producer who financed the film wanted to produce and wanted the producer credit and moved me into the executive producer position. But I still did the work.

"Once the movie is in the can, the financing duties aren't over. Distribution of the final product also needs to be sorted out, and that's squarely in the remit of the producer."

THE NEGOTIATORS

Another disappointment for Kazanjian was *The Bridge of San Luis Rey* (2004), directed by Mary McGuckian and with another great cast: F. Murray Abraham, Kathy Bates, Gabriel Byrne, Geraldine Chaplin, Harvey Keitel, and Robert De Niro. Based on a book by Thornton Wilder, it told the story of five people killed when a high rope bridge collapses in Lima, Peru, during the eighteenth century. A priest tries to understand what brought these five people from different walks of life to their mutual demise and whether it was divine intervention. The film would be shot mostly on locations in Spain, France, and the UK.

Kazanjian and Darian were asked to join at the development stage because the production was having difficulties obtaining the desired cast for the desired price. Darian was able to lock in De Niro for a fee based on a fixed number of working days. Consequently, Darian and Kazanjian came on as executive producers. "We gave our notes, which were added in the script," Kazanjian says. "Off to Europe the director went. As it was a European/Canadian production, only a few US citizens could be on set. Overseas, the script was altered without our knowledge and the picture made. Months later, we saw a one-sheet at the American Film Market that excluded us as executive producers. We went into arbitration with our attorneys. To make a long, difficult story short, we were eventually given our due credit. No sides enjoy this kind of arbitration."

The Bridge of San Luis Rey was a box-office disaster: Costing a reported $24 million, its domestic gross was less than $50,000.

The year the film came out, the Kazanjians—Carol, Howard, and their boys—were invited by Lucas to his sixtieth birthday party, circa May 15. Lucas was in the middle of wrapping up the third film of his *Star Wars* Prequel Trilogy, whose episodic title finally made use of the word "revenge": *Revenge of the Sith* (bad guys *can* seek "revenge"). What had been Lucasfilm HQ was now part of a discrete complex of Lucas-owned homes and additions in San Anselmo. At these kind of reunions Kazanjian would sometimes run into Kleiser. "We would hang out," Kleiser says. "All of George's major birthdays. His fortieth, his fiftieth, his sixtieth. He'd invite everybody to different places. I think his fiftieth was at a restaurant in San Francisco. I went to all of those and saw all the usual suspects there. All the people from the *Star Wars* movies and *Indiana Jones* movies, directors and the former students, classmates, we'd all convene."

"George had built a gorgeous stone bridge across a street and owned the whole hill," Kazanjian recalls. "Behind his house we walked up two football-field lengths to two tennis courts on top of the hill. They're next to a gorgeous cabana with a giant fireplace. They put grass mats down to cover the courts and took off the nets for the party. Katie, his younger daughter, was there and Carol asked, 'This is beautiful, how often do you play tennis?' And she said, 'I've never been here before.'"

QUEEN FOR A NIGHT

In 2003, Kazanjian produced his first animated show, *Danger Rangers* (2003–2006). He was introduced to the creative and financial folks through his friend Ilie Agopian, who was executive producing the series for PBS. Their production needed someone on the West Coast to organize the animation crew, hire a director, and so on. Kazanjian signed up and spearheaded work on the first season.

The half-hour shows were designed to educate children on how to be safe. In each episode the Danger Rangers—a seven-member action-adventure team of animal characters—faced an "archnemesis" who was not playing by the rules. The voice of Danger Ranger Burt, a green turtle safety expert, was performed by an old friend, Mark Hamill. "Howard and I don't play golf together or have a weekly poker game, but our wives hit it off," Hamill says. "Carol and Marilou have always got along great. So it wasn't a constant connection, but it was one that all of a sudden—there they are again. We became friends."

The show aired its sixteen episodes over one hundred PBS stations. Season two was underway with commitments from another hundred-plus stations when the executive producers/owners of *Danger Rangers* were unable to continue financing the production. Five partially finished episodes could not be completed, and the company closed down.

More Lucasfilm alumni reunions, large and small, were held. In 2007, Lucas was asked to be the Grand Marshal of the annual Rose Parade. By coincidence, Kazanjian was one of the three judges for the Tournament of Roses. The *Star Wars* float was not among the more spectacular but did win in its category. In 2011, the Academy of Motion Picture Arts and Sciences celebrated the thirtieth anniversary of *Raiders of the Lost Ark* with a digital screening at the Academy's Samuel Goldwyn Theater in Beverly Hills. An onstage discussion included key members of the crew: optical supervisor Bruce Nicholson; sound editors and designers Gregg Landaker, Steve Maslow, Richard L. Anderson, and Ben Burtt; as well as Frank Marshall. An audience member asked Marshall, "How did you know how to produce if you'd never produced before?" Marshall answered in two words: "Howard Kazanjian."

In 2012, Lucas sold his company to Disney, which included the *Star Wars* and *Indy* franchises (he kept Skywalker Ranch and its associate archives). "I was surprised by the sale, but it was understandable," Kleiser says. "Trying to keep that franchise going and not be attacked by the fans every time, it looked like it was not fun anymore for him. Who needs that kind of angst? Getting a gigantic paycheck and relaxing, what a good idea."

Lucas had appointed producer Kathleen Kennedy, Spielberg's assistant decades before, to head up Lucasfilm before the sale, and she stayed on. "George likes women around him," Kazanjian says, "and I don't mean that in any weird way. He just likes women around him. So I wasn't surprised when he picked Kathleen; she also has the stellar record. She's picked a lot of winners story-wise. She ran her own company [Kennedy/Marshall, a production entity]. Steven loved her. Maybe Steven was influential in George's choice."

In 2015 the old ILM soundstage was reserved for a nonofficial celebration of the facility's fortieth anniversary (Lucas had moved ILM to San Francisco, minus the model shop; its former premises had been occupied by a series of VFX companies). Dozens of present and former ILMers showed up, including Dunham, Kurtz, Edlund, Herman, Muren, and the Kazanjians. George Lucas elected not to go, so the special guest turned out to be Marcia Lucas. "Marcia got a lot of credit," Miki Herman says. "She had a lot of laughs and she looked very happy."

"It was Marcia's night," says Carol Kazanjian. "Those were her people. They couldn't kiss her, hug her, or love her enough that night. It was the biggest testimony to her. They'd been waiting to see her for over thirty years. Out of the blue everyone said, 'This is Marcia's night.'"

In the old days "Marcia Lucas had been 'the wife of,'" Ganis says. "Yes, she was an editor, but she was the unsung person in that group. She was Mrs. Lucas. Since then she's become a personal friend, and now she's sung. And rightfully sung. She's getting her recognition. I didn't know her as the incredible force in the look and feel of *Star Wars*, which she was; I didn't know her that way. Totally. George is an editor, too; he's told me many times over the years that his love was editing. But I did not know that Marcia was such a powerful person in the way *Star Wars* finally appeared. It took years, but I started hearing it."

"I was queen for a day," Marcia says. "I was thrilled to go to the fortieth reunion. I thought it would be fun and I enjoyed it." Marcia has heard many times that George was the head and she was the heart of *Star Wars*, but she says that's not accurate: "I wouldn't think so. I definitely made scenes work. I made the end battle work. I definitely had a lot to do with making it work, but I wasn't the writer and I wasn't the director, and I didn't come up with the creative names, Darth Vader, Luke Skywalker. All those names are classics. George came up with all of it using his amazing imagination."

TOYS OF THE JEDI

"I said to Howard, 'I keep getting these offers to be hosting UFO mysteries TV shows,'" Mark Hamill recalls. "They're always space-related; I said, 'It just seems too on the nose.' Howard said, 'We should do something together.' I said, 'Well, if we can think of anything that would be appealing to us both, I'd love to work with you.' We were sitting in my room, and if you look around my room, it looks like a nostalgia toy store. There's Aurora monster model kits and puppets and board games and action figures and Beatles memorabilia. So he said, 'This should be the show.' I said, 'What? What?' He says, 'Just all of this. Why do you like all this stuff? Why do you collect all this stuff?' It worked out perfectly."

"We came back," Kazanjian says. "I mean, we never went anywhere, but we came back together strong with *Mark Hamill's Pop Culture Quest* [2016–2017]. Carol and Marilou [Hamill] have always been close, doing things together. They see each other often. So when we came up with the *Pop Culture Quest* idea, it was Carol who said, 'Think about Mark Hamill' as host. I've always thought about Mark Hamill and I'd tried to get Mark on other projects. But this was perfect. Mark is a huge collector of pop culture, starting from long before *Star Wars*, though he also has a huge *Star Wars* collection. He has a gardener's cottage loaded with boxes of all kinds of toys and memorabilia. He has a warehouse in Malibu. Wonderful things to look at. He's been careful how to collect it. People may not realize it, but Mark is a very articulate and thoughtful narrator on subjects close to him. His remarks are noteworthy."

"I bought my first collection when I was in college, from a girl who needed quick cash," Hamill said in 2016. "I gave her $126 for fourteen or fifteen pieces of Beatles memorabilia, with the bobblehead dolls, lunch boxes, etc. That was the first time I went, 'Wow, I just bought a collection!'"

Kazanjian and Hamill pitched the show to studio executives at Lionsgate. Hamill impressed them by talking about the artwork on their walls, about the artists and the context. Lionsgate bought the show. After Hamill returned from shooting *Star Wars: The Last Jedi* (2017), he and Kazanjian recorded a first season of ten episodes, each from twelve to twenty-two minutes long. They were broadcast on the Comic-Con HQ channel, a new subscription video-on-demand service. "I've been a collector all my life," Hamill told *Variety*. "This show is a natural outgrowth of that passion. Now I have an opportunity to collect other people's collections! I can't wait to see what's out there and share it with the world."

The shows were a success and immediately garnered a following. "It was basically a way to fulfill a desire I have to be a collector," Hamill adds, "that obsessive-compulsive nature of mine, by creating this show where I go and visit other people's collections. I had a great time, though it was much more work than I ever had imagined, and Howard did a great job. Howard would be miles ahead of me in terms of suggested topics and so forth. Sometimes they say never do business with family or friends. With Howard, I couldn't have done it without him. He's always open. I said, 'It's weird not having somebody to talk to.' He let me hire Dan Milano, who did the bunny named Pop."

"When we aired maybe episode four or five, because we were very popular, Lionsgate should have immediately picked us up again," Kazanjian says. "But they didn't renew us. They wanted us, but they didn't say, 'Start.' And the whole thing died for us. Disney Studios considered the project for over a year, but we couldn't agree on content."

326

"They decided not to renew," Hamill says, "which was disappointing but a relief, because it was one of those things where you had to figure out what other kind of collections you were going to do."

Hamill was honored with a star on Hollywood's Walk of Fame on March 8, 2018. A large crowd gathered on that Thursday to honor the actor in front of the El Capitan Theatre in Los Angeles. The Kazanjians, George Lucas, and Harrison Ford were on hand, as was Billie Lourd, Kelly Marie Tran, and R2-D2. Carrie Fisher had passed away in December 2016. Ford said, "When thinking about today, I was really sorry that we don't have the other member of our trio here to celebrate with us. But I feel her presence."

Lucas said a few words during the star ceremony: "Mark Hamill is a character that can't be written. He is extremely enthusiastic about everything that he does, and that's exactly what I was looking for when I was looking for Luke Skywalker."

"These will be brief remarks because words truly fail me," Hamill said. "It's hard to convey my gratitude, my joy, the exhilaration of being recognized this way."

Afterward he, Lucas, and others strolled over to the Roosevelt Hotel for lunch. Howard and Carol Kazanjian walked with Ford, then sat with Lucas and Marilou Hamill. Kathleen Kennedy took a seat with them. Lucas had stated several times publicly that Kennedy and execs at Disney had pushed him out and discarded his ideas for the *Star Wars* sequels, but he and Kennedy talked for some time. "He was trapped," Kazanjian says. "He sat down on a long bench and Marilou sat next to him, and I sat on the other side."

"We were very nice friends with George and Marcia, very nice friends," Carol reflects. "I don't think there was anybody closer in the early days. We knew their family, their parents. Howard will tell you how he misses Lucasfilm."

CHAPTER 17: *Saga's End*

W ith more than fifty years in the business, Kazanjian has seen the industry change. He's seen his job title of "producer" morph into something that is often meaningless. "Today on some movies, one can find a dozen producers or more, even if only one is really doing the work," he says. "Up until about 2001, most writers insisted they get a producer credit. When a writer asked me for a producing credit, I would ask them if they would share a writing credit with me for my creative guidance in rewrites. This usually stopped them. Now the WGA prevents this from being a negotiated instrument unless the writer is actually the producer."

Directors also want a producer credit because if the picture wins the Best Picture Academy Award, it is the producers who take home Oscars. "The Producers Guild of America has now become very strong in setting guidelines," Kazanjian adds. "There is now a limit of three producers who can receive the Oscar for Best Picture. The PGA will carefully examine each submitting producer and their functions from the very first idea, to screenplay, and production through delivery."

"The producer, by definition, with the director, is really supposed to provide a cohesive vision," Friedman says. "Because most of the people on the set are like horses with blinders. They only see a very small spectrum of the picture. There's less than a handful of people who really see a picture from twenty weeks before you start shooting, the twelve or fifteen weeks you shoot, to the other weeks in post to bring it together."

However, if the executive producer does most of the work, the Academy will not recognize that. "There is no justice yet with the PGA in this area," Kazanjian says. "I recall *The Sting*, a wonderful picture that Richard Zanuck and David Brown executive produced

328

in 1973. They certainly did most of the work making the picture. The producers were not that experienced, but they collected the Oscars while the real filmmakers sat in their seats. Zanuck and Brown said they would only take producer credit on films in the future, and they won for *Driving Miss Daisy* [1989]."

Kazanjian has seen the economics change. Most studios today are part of multinational conglomerates, yet money often comes from outside, from as far afield as China. At home, the number of studios is dwindling. "Everything is so different now," Kleiser says. "It's streaming systems, rather than studio systems. Everything has completely changed. Back then, it was nice to have a structure and somebody that was at the top who could say yes to a project, based on their instincts, rather than marketing research. It was structured, but it was looser in a way. If you got a yes, you could go ahead and make a movie. You got a green light as opposed to a 'maybe' that has to go through all these hoops with various executives and marketing people, stock-holders, and all that."

"I was at Fox pitching a picture about two years ago, and the guy said, 'We're doomed here,'" Kazanjian recalls. The Fox executive already knew that Disney was looking to buy the studio. Disney had purchased Lucasfilm, Pixar, and Marvel. The executive continued, "Disney is also Buena Vista [its movie distribution company] and they have the amusement parks, cruise liners, they're huge. What do we have? They're rolling over everybody."

The era of studios run by more independent moguls has been over for decades. Kazanjian misses those days and feels and believes that the studio system was a better way to make quality movies: "When Jack Warner produced, if we had a prima donna actor who gave us trouble, Jack would fire them. If an agent caused havoc, Jack threw them off the lot. He was the boss and people respected that. Today, eight-hundred-pound actor-gorillas throw their weight around causing havoc and costing money. Hollywood is colder and calculated. This affects the filmmaker.

"Many of those creative department heads, the writers, the actors, who worked at the studios during the golden age are legends today. These men and women didn't have cell phones, the Internet, computers, or even fax machines. They worked with heavy cameras, large cranes, for

329

which it took hours to set dolly track, and they only had heavy arc lights and complicated sound and editing equipment. But they made hundreds of classic movies."

Development today at the studios, because they often lack a creative chief, is usually accomplished by committee. After Kazanjian signed a studio contract for one project, the script received thirty-four pages of notes. He recalls: "One note said the story was too dark with no humor, and another said they enjoyed the subtle humor. We later found out seven executives had read the script, and their notes were simply thrown into one document. Many of the notes conflicted with others. More time went by and we got more notes written by a writing team they'd hired without our knowledge. Naturally, the writing team wanted enough changes to get WGA credit. The project died."

"The business is full of professional bullshit artists," Louis Friedman says. "But Howard's a straight shooter; Howard is gonna tell you what he thinks, and what you see is what you get, and that is atypical in my experience."

"I would run into Howard every so often years after that," Ben Burtt says, "and Howard was always developing a script, or something. He talked to me once or twice about getting involved in something that never got made. And so our relationship was never tested again."

"There's the guy sitting there for DVD foreign who will say it's not going to sell," Kazanjian explains. "And then the guy sitting there for DVD domestic says we can do okay with the exception of Canada. And then a marketing guy says something, but if you mention the shadows in *Casablanca*, they stare at you. They haven't seen it. Some of the great films, they don't know. They don't know their names of some of the great actors or actresses, so you can't go in and reference the such and such of *Citizen Kane* . . ."

| Western Publishing

| Kazanjian has taken a slightly different direction for more than a decade, in addition to his filmmaking life. He has been cowriting books with Chris Enss, mostly on the

early West. The author of more than forty books, Enss is a *New York Times* bestseller. "We choose stories that have not been told before," Kazanjian says, "or told from a different perspective that one day can be movies for the theater or networks."

Their first book, about Roy Rogers and Dale Evans, was *The Cowboy and the Senorita* (2005), now optioned for a motion picture. It was followed by a coffee-table book *Happy Trails: A Pictorial Celebration of the Life and Times of Roy Rogers and Dale Evans.* They then requested and received permission to write a book on John Wayne from his birth to the making of *The Alamo* in 1960 called *The Young Duke.* The next was *Thunder over the Prairie*, now a screenplay by writer-director Walter Hill (Kazanjian's fellow DGA trainee). *None Wounded, None Missing, All Dead* is the story of Libby Custer. *Sam Sixkiller* was followed by *The Death Row All Stars*, also currently being developed into a movie. *Mochi's War* and the story of *Ma Barker* followed. *The Trials of Annie Oakley* came out in 2017. Kazanjian has two more books currently in manuscript form as of this writing.

Cowboys, Creatures, and Classics: The Story of Republic Pictures was published in 2018, won the Will Rogers Medallion Award Gold—and brought Kazanjian full circle, back to the physical studio where he started his career as a DGA trainee in 1965.

THE FORCE NEVER SLEEPS

When Kazanjian is not producing movies or TV shows or books, he's at home gardening. "I sometimes plant flowers with Carol. My rest is part of my recreation; I don't golf. I like antiques. And reading."

Kazanjian never did direct a film. He didn't like the films that were offered to him and wasn't able to launch his own. "I have several projects I'd very much like to make. But I learned late in life that it's not what I like that will get made. But Carol has reminded me of the time we were standing in line to see *The Godfather* and I said it's very lucky if a filmmaker has just one blockbuster in his career. I was fortunate enough to be part of two and a half really big successes, meaning *Empire, Jedi,* and *Raiders*. That's not bad."

Meanwhile Disney and Kathleen Kennedy were making a series of new *Star Wars* movies, some of which continued the story of the Skywalker family—*The Force Awakens* (2015), directed by J.J. Abrams; *The Last Jedi* (2017); and *The Rise of Skywalker* (2019)—and stand-alones such as *Rogue One: A Star Wars Story* (2016) and *Solo: A Star Wars Story* (2018). The new era began when Lucas had meetings with many parties, over several months, including a clandestine get-together with Carrie Fisher and Mark Hamill. "We were getting ready to go over and Marilou said, 'What if George wants to do another trilogy?' and I just laughed," Hamill recalls. "So when George said, 'I'm turning over Lucasfilm to Kathy [Kennedy], and they want to do another trilogy,' I kept a poker face, but inside I was floored. Carrie slapped the table and went, 'I'm in!' Later I said to her, 'Carrie, poker face. Your agent would want you to at least play hard to get.' And, of course, she cut right to the chase and said, 'Mark, what kind of parts are there for women over fifty in Hollywood?' As usual, she was miles ahead of me.

"But it took me weeks and weeks. Marilou said, 'Shouldn't you call George and at least tell him that you're thinking about it?' I was frightened; I was afraid. We had a perfect big beginning, middle, and an end. What if we come back and ruin everything? I said, 'The one thing I can rely on is that Harrison's not going to do them.' He has such a solid resume, and I know at times it's rankled him that he was ever associated with the *Star Wars* movies. I thought, *If he doesn't do them, it'll give me an out in case I don't want to do them.* So when I read in the press that Harrison was doing it, I thought, *Oh God, I've been drafted.* Because if I'm the only person who doesn't do it, I'll be the most hated man in fandom. But I was also so excited about the chance of working with Carrie and Harrison again. I said, 'Well, if he's in, I'm in.' And here we are."

The films have generated big box office. "I love Kathleen and what she's doing, I think, is terrific," says Kleiser. "She's keeping it alive. It's hard to keep that fresh and new. Everyone compares it to the originals, and is it better? Is it as good? All that. I don't really study them, the new ones. I've seen one or two, and they seem like normal blockbuster-type movies. All of them look alike now, all these big summer movies feel like a fire hose of visual effects shooting in your face."

"Generally speaking, I think that the filmmakers on *The Force Awakens* and *The Last Jedi* didn't understand the story," Kazanjian says, "they didn't understand what a Jedi Knight was all about. That's the simplest way to put it. Skywalker's the story, and I think that's what they failed at. I'm not talking about just Mark Hamill as Skywalker. It's the overall psychological story of Skywalker, and of course, the Jedi Knights. The ardent fans know more about the storyline than the filmmakers."

"I can't wait for Episode IX," says Sid Ganis, who sees Kazanjian from time to time for lunch. "Part of it is because it was such a big part of my life. I like the fact that it's concluding the trilogy. I can't imagine that George is not interested in nine. He's really busy now, but he's still the father of it, isn't he? And always will be."

"Look at the budgets," Hamill adds. "Oh my God. And corporate from top to bottom in terms of promotion and tie-ins. It was a mom-and-pop operation originally. And now it's a state-of-the art corporate entity. We were like a garage band. Now it's like a full symphony orchestra, and I'm not complaining, I'm just saying it's much different."

"I like Kathleen. I always liked her," says Marcia Lucas. "She was full of beans. She was really smart and really bright. Really wonderful woman. And I liked her husband, Frank. I liked them a lot. Now that she's running Lucasfilm and making movies, it seems to me that Kathy Kennedy and J.J. Abrams don't have a clue about *Star Wars*. They don't get it. And J.J. Abrams is writing these stories—when I saw that movie where they kill Han Solo, I was furious. I was furious when they killed Han Solo. Absolutely, positively there was no rhyme or reason to it. I thought, *You don't get the Jedi story. You don't get the magic of* Star Wars. *You're getting rid of Han Solo?* And then at the end of this last one, *The Last Jedi*, they have Luke disintegrate. They killed Han Solo. They killed Luke Skywalker. And they don't have Princess Leia anymore. And they're spitting out movies every year. And they think it's important to appeal to a woman's audience, so now their main character is this female, who's supposed to have Jedi powers, but we don't know how she got Jedi powers, or who she is. It sucks. The storylines are terrible. Just terrible. Awful.

"You can quote me—'J.J. Abrams, Kathy Kennedy—talk to me.'"

| Secrets of the Trade

| Over the years, Kazanjian has been asked to speak at many universities and gatherings, has taught seminars and has mentored dozens of people in the industry. His Lucasfilm colleague Sid Ganis eventually became president of the Motion Picture Group at Paramount, then vice chairman of Columbia Pictures. Ganis says, "Howard is such a 'steady-as-he-goes' guy; he knows this business. I like a filmmaker who knows how to talk about cameras and technology, and who also knows how to talk to actors."

Based on his experiences, Kazanjian has some words on how to succeed in moviemaking, applicable to gophers, assistant directors, producers, and any other crew:

"I have met hundreds of students and young people who want to get into our industry, mostly as directors, writers, and producers, as development executives, attorneys, or who simply want to run a studio. When I do, I look for bright, learned people. One must start with an education. I usually meet with film students, rarely a young person without a film education. Education is a must.

"But remember that the educational aspect is not the true industry film experience. One is not proficient in film until one has been trained and has truly participated in several 'Hollywood' productions. Find work on a set, get a job in the business. Now the real learning begins. Experience is gold. I cannot stress enough how important

334

this is. I've worked with young filmmakers who believe they know more than longtime professionals. They may succeed once or twice, but fail in the long run. A film student with four years of film training is not a professional. If you think you can get to the top without climbing the ladder step by step, you are going to miss crucial steps in the learning process. You won't know the full process of filmmaking. You won't know what your crew or department contribute. The bottom step is education and knowledge. The highest step is creativity and success.

"Film has its own language. Know what each on-set and behind-the-scenes job entails, from director and producer to line producer to gaffer to art director to each crewmember regardless of your actual job. Understand what each and every industry job includes, from administration, legal, and development to production.

"Have a dream and goals. Follow through with your dream. Before you can attain your goals, you must have a dream. Before that you must have what I call 'cinema experience.' You won't succeed until you understand the industry. Then your dream can come true and you can move on.

"Be prepared to work long and hard hours. The job is not nine to five, but five to nine. If your crew call is 6 AM, be there, ready, at 5:50 AM. And don't be the first out the door at the end of the day. One must have determination, stamina, and the discipline to survive in our industry. Your whole mind and body will need physical strength, but don't be afraid of any job. You may be asked to do jobs that are difficult and challenging. The answer is always 'yes.'

"Learn the rules of our industry, its laws and regulations. Every day making decisions, you'll need to understand your guild or union bylaws and be familiar with those rules of other unions, guilds, teamsters, and so on. If you don't understand these laws, you will make costly mistakes. This is especially true if you begin as an assistant director. And while we're on the subject of assistant directors, here are few quick rules to keep in mind:

- If you don't have an answer to a question, get one, including for extras.
- Extras are not just bodies, they need to know the situation/story (of the film).
- An assistant director never sits (unless in a meeting), even if given a chair with his name on it.
- An AD never puts his hands in his pockets, no matter how cold it may be.
- Learn how to tell people to go to hell in a way that has them reply, 'Thank you, I will.'
- Read between the lines. Your colleagues may not be clear or not want to tell you the full story.
- Learn to read body language.
- Anticipate.
- Smile and don't let the challenges of the day show on your face.
- Never show fatigue.
- Run an absolutely quiet set at all times.
- Never, ever be late. If traffic or a situation delays you, call ahead even if delayed five minutes.
- Don't always say 'yes.' Say 'no' on occasion even if the answer is yes.
- If someone complains about any subject from food to parking, if you don't have an answer, ask them how they would fix the problem.
- Run or walk swiftly, don't walk.
- Dress one step ahead, be ready for next promotion.
- Remember my 'words of the week,' among them: communication, anticipation, sincerity, efficiency, coordination, dependability, tact, honesty.

"To reiterate: as a 2nd AD, working for 1st AD Hank Moonjean on *Cool Hand Luke*, I learned to never sit, stay

336

next to the camera—and anticipate. Always be there. Be ready. Hank would begin a sentence and I would finish it. I'd often leave him to execute the job before his full order was given. I was in his head. As a 1st AD, I had that rapport with my assistant Gary Daigler, and later with Robert Brown. Get into that mode! This is true with all your superiors throughout the industry. I also rarely shouted or screamed. I spoke softly but firmly, which made people listen. Even on a shooting set. Once I did, others did as well. (Bob Greber, president of Lucasfilm at the time, gave me an Indiana Jones whip sheathed in soft red velvet to illustrate how I conducted myself with authority, yet quietly. I still have that whip in my office.)

"As an executive or producer, you are not just making a film. You should be involved in story, casting, locations, and budget, from scheduling to marketing and distribution, color timing, merchandising, CDs and DVDs, and perhaps even foreign language dubs. Remember also that you are an ambassador of good will to the entire crew.

"The future: I entered the industry when moguls such as Jack Warner still ran the studios. Today corporations and stockholders run them. In those days when a 'normal' picture was greenlit, it would be in the theater a year later. Today a greenlit picture, especially one with a large budget, may keep you busy for three years. I was there when the industry moved from the bulky Mitchell camera to Panavision and into the digital age. Heavy arc lights were pushed through sand and difficult terrain, while today smaller, lighter lights can do the job. Film went from 200 ASA to 25 ASA. Magnetic two-inch tape shrank to quarter inch and then to digital. What I'm saying is: Keep an eye on the future. There will always be change and innovation.

"Know all these things and your magic begins. The future of filmmaking belongs to you."

OF THE MUSE

The tension, as mentioned, between Lucas, Kennedy, and Disney CEO Bob Iger is of public record. Iger wrote in his memoirs, *The Ride of a Lifetime*, published in 2019, that he wishes he'd handled Lucas's involvement in the new films better, while Lucas has said that his original ideas were basically ignored and discarded. Instead he's been focused on the building and establishment of the Lucas Museum of Narrative Art, which is scheduled to open in 2021. Lucas remarried, tying the knot with Mellody Hobson in 2013, and they have a daughter named Everest. Marcia Lucas married the Skywalker Ranch craftsman Tom Rodrigues. They had a daughter and eventually divorced.

"George, at first, was shy, and introverted in a way, very quiet," says Kleiser. "Now he's got so much confidence. He's not shy anymore. And he's kind of become a curmudgeon about the world, his philosophy of where we're heading. He has a bleak view of the future, but hopes that we can change it. He's living his retirement in a way where I guess he can do anything he wants, and he's living a wonderful lifestyle and has a new baby. He's living life, rather than making movies."

Kazanjian remains proud of his work with George Lucas and Lucasfilm: "It was a family. It was one of the greatest experiences in my life. Every minute was remarkable with great and sometimes private memories. George hired incredible loyal and talented people to make his films. They should never be forgotten. George and Steven were at the top. Look at their credits. I've been asked many times why and how do Steven and George make popular, blockbuster films. My answer is twofold: They know how to pick what the audience wants to see, and the creative part of their films is made by one or two people, not committees. These people have a small group of producers and writers around them, but they know that teamwork makes the actual movies, writers, actors, and technicians. It is very difficult to be successful with one of these talents missing. I've also said you can give the same script to George Lucas, Steven Spielberg, and Francis Coppola and get three good pictures, though different."

"We [his USC classmates] were amazed at what George was achieving for all those years," Kleiser says. "To create the first digital editing system, EditDroid, which became Avid. THX sound went through all those iterations. ILM, which did all the special effects. George is a genius. It's so crazy, because when I was a kid, I had a map of Disneyland over my bed, and Walt Disney was my idol and hero, but I never thought that I would be rooming with the next Walt Disney. Years later, to see him become the new Walt Disney, it was very, very surreal."

"We at Lucasfilm may not have realized it," Kazanjian says, "but we were breaking ground, changing the way pictures would be made in the future. George created ILM and owned it outright. It became the finest and still is the finest visual effects house in the world. George was one of the first to use Dolby sound. He created TAP (Theater Alignment Program) and THX sound for all the theaters in the United States. George created the tools for his movies and for those of others. George Lucas pioneered digital moviemaking in all of its forms, from effects to sound to cameras to projection."

"When digital came along, I said, 'This is a godsend for women,'" Marcia Lucas recalls. "Because all those films I worked on, the studios wanted them yesterday. I worked twelve, fourteen hours a day; I went in on Saturdays and Sundays. I worked long hours. I was really a workaholic. I could never leave a scene until a scene was as good as it could be. I had to go back and keep reworking the scene, until I knew it was working and it was good, and the director liked it, because I worked for the director. I don't work for a studio. Digital made editing so much easier in relation to all that."

"I still receive countless mail from fans or they come up to me to express their thoughts to this day," Kazanjian adds. "George created an American fairy tale. It's still alive and exciting after four decades. He is without doubt the most innovative filmmaker of the twentieth and twenty-first centuries. His characters are everlasting. When I'm with Mark Hamill, he's chased for a signature, a hello, or they just watch him pass by. Mark and Harrison are remembered by cheering fans wherever they travel. *Star Wars* is also intergenerational: Grandfather, father and son, brothers and sisters, all love *Star Wars*. It was out-of-the-box filmmaking and story, story, story, with great characters. *Star Wars* generated the Force. It wasn't based on a TV series, a book, or children's nursery rhymes. It caught people off guard and immediately captured their imagination. Fans became loyal supporters for each character. Consequently, George Lucas shall be remembered as the man who changed the direction of filmmaking.

"He created fast editing, less dialogue, quicker scenes, again, with story, story, story backed up by great music. He dreamed up creatures of every size and shape, spacecraft, planets, and characters, heroes and heroines. And a lot of this was happening while he was building Skywalker Ranch. His fingerprints are on everything, from construction and film production to one-sheets and distribution. George also gives back. He has put millions into the USC Cinema School and now he's building a museum for American artwork."

On Wednesday, May 29, 2019, Kazanjian had the pleasure of escorting Carol to the grand opening presentation of Galaxy's Edge at Disneyland, a kind of *Star Wars*–land. Chairman and CEO Robert Iger delivered the opening remarks followed by George Lucas, Harrison Ford, Billy Dee Williams, and Mark Hamill. Over eight hundred journalists from around the world attended. "The *Wall Street Journal* wrote three full pages," Kazanjian says. "All that, the impact created by one man; it's the American dream."

"I know they drag George out to the opening screenings," Marcia says, "and he shows up and puts on a pleasant face."

"I must give great credit to Marcia Lucas, who was a heavy influence on George," Kazanjian says. "At that time she was his editor, confidante, love of his life, and always commented on his scripts. Marcia was a brilliant editor and an Oscar winner, and understood story.

"May their work endure . . ."

Who's Who

Jane Bay, EXECUTIVE ASSISTANT TO GEORGE LUCAS

Edward Carrere, PRODUCTION DESIGNER

Francis Ford Coppola, WRITER/DIRECTOR/PRODUCER

Caleb Deschanel, CINEMATOGRAPHER

Duwayne Dunham, ASSISTANT EDITOR/DIRECTOR

Joel Freeman, PRODUCER

Louis Friedman, PRODUCTION ASSISTANT/PRODUCER

Hilton Green, PRODUCTION MANAGER, UNIVERSAL STUDIOS (FORMER ASSISTANT DIRECTOR)

Marshall Green, HEAD OF PRODUCTION, UNIVERSAL STUDIOS (FORMER ASSISTANT DIRECTOR)

Miki Herman, PRODUCTION ASSISTANT/PRODUCTION MANAGER

Alfred Hitchcock, DIRECTOR/PRODUCER

Willard (Bill) Huyck, WRITER/DIRECTOR

Lawrence Kasdan, WRITER/DIRECTOR

Gloria Katz, WRITER/DIRECTOR

Carol Kazanjian, WIFE OF HOWARD KAZANJIAN

Howard Kazanjian, ASSISTANT DIRECTOR/PRODUCER

Kathleen Kennedy, PRODUCTION ASSISTANT/PRODUCER

Randal Kleiser, DIRECTOR

Akira Kurosawa, DIRECTOR

Gary Kurtz, PRODUCER

Charles Lippincott, MARKETING EXECUTIVE/PRODUCER

George Lucas, WRITER/DIRECTOR/PRODUCER

Marcia Lucas, EDITOR

Richard Marquand, DIRECTOR

Charlie Maguire, PRODUCER/STUDIO EXECUTIVE

Frank Marshall, PRODUCER

John Milius, WRITER/DIRECTOR

Hank Moonjean, FIRST ASSISTANT DIRECTOR

Walter Murch, SOUND DESIGNER/EDITOR

Sam Peckinpah, DIRECTOR

Steven Spielberg, DIRECTOR

Jack Warner, PRODUCER/COFOUNDER WARNER BROS. STUDIO

John "Johnny" Williams, COMPOSER

Lee Wilson, GAFFER

Lucy Wilson, ASSISTANT TO GEORGE LUCAS/ACCOUNTANT/PUBLISHING DIRECTOR

Robert Wise, DIRECTOR

HOWARD KAZANJIAN: *Complete Credits*

Television

As assistant director trainee:

Burke's Law (Season 3: "The Prisoners of Mr. Sin," October 27, 1965; "Watch the Man Die," broadcast as "Peace, It's a Gasser," November 3, 1965; "The Man's Men," December 8, 1965; "A Very Important Russian Is Missing," December 29, 1965; "Deadly Music, Parts 1 & 2," broadcast as "Terror in a Tiny Town: Parts 1 and 2," January 5 & 12, 1966)

The Big Valley ("The Murdered Party," November 17, 1965; "Night of the Wolf," December 1, 1965; "The Guilt of Matt Bentell," December 8, 1965; "Into the Widow's Web," March 23, 1966; "Beware, Married Women," broadcast as "The Fallen Hawk," March 2, 1966)

The Smothers Brothers Show ("It Don't Mean a Dang If It Ain't Got That Twang," November 19, 1965; "Boys Will Be Playboys," November 26, 1965; "Happiness Is a Guy Named Happy," December 24, 1965; "The Ghost Is Clear," February 18, 1966)

Honey West ("Rockabye the Hard Way," December 24, 1965)

Ace of the Mounties ("The Call of the Mild," pilot, 1966)

The Sea Wolves (pilot, broadcast as "Pursue and Destroy," August 14, 1966)

High Noon: The Clock Strikes Noon Again (pilot, 1966)

Mister Roberts ("A Turn for the Nurse," March 4, 1966)

The House of Wax ("The Hook," pilot; later released as a feature film, *Chamber of Horrors*, 1966)

The F.B.I. ("The Defector, Part I," March 27, 1966)

As 1st or 2nd assistant director:

Secrets of the Pirates' Inn (TV movie, 1969)

Smoke (TV movie, 1970)

Menace on the Mountain (TV movie, 1970)

Decisions! Decisions! (TV movie, 1971)

Cool Million (three TV movies, 1972)

Partners in Crime (TV movie, pilot, 1973)

Griff (pilot, 1973)

Scent (broadcast as *Trapped*, TV movie, 1973)

A Case of Rape (prep only, 1974)

The Rockford Files (TV movie, pilot, 1974)

As producer:

JAG (TV movie, pilot; and Season 1, 1995–1996)

Rattled (TV movie, 1996)

Danger Rangers (Season 1, 2003–2006)

Mark Hamill's Pop Culture Quest (Season 1, 2016–2017)

Feature Films

As assistant director trainee:

Not With My Wife, You Don't! (1966)

An American Dream (released as *See You in Hell, Darling*, 1966)

The Cool Ones (1967)

As 2nd assistant director (sometimes acting as 1st assistant director):

Cool Hand Luke (1967)

Camelot (1967)

Chubasco (1968)

Finian's Rainbow (1968)

I Love You, Alice B. Toklas! (1968)

The Wild Bunch (1969)

Once You Kiss a Stranger (1969)

The Great Bank Robbery (1969)

The Arrangement (1969)

As 1st assistant director:

The Christine Jorgensen Story (1970)

The Fifth of July (unproduced)

Now You See Him, Now You Don't (1972)

The Girl From Petrovka (1974)

The Front Page (1974)

The Hindenburg (1975)

Family Plot (1976)

As producer:

Rollercoaster (associate producer; 1977)

More American Graffiti (1979)

Star Wars: Episode V—The Empire Strikes Back (uncredited, 1980)

Raiders of the Lost Ark (executive producer; 1981)

Star Wars: Episode VI—Return of the Jedi (1983)

The Rookie (1990)

Demolition Man (1993)

One Dozen (1997)

The Sky Is Falling (1999)

Carlo's Wake (1999)

The Amati Girls (2000)

Extreme Days (2001)

The Homecoming of Jimmy Whitecloud (2001)

Shortcut to Happiness (2003)

The Bridge of San Luis Rey (2004)

Redline (2007)

Documentaries

As producer:

The Making of Star Wars (1977)

The Making of More American Graffiti (1979)

The Making of Raiders of the Lost Ark (1981)

Theme Parks

The Mouse Factory (1971)

Disney World attraction (1975)

Awards and Nominations

César Award, Académie des Arts et Techniques du Cinéma, 1982: *Raiders of the Lost Ark*

Hugo Award, Best Dramatic Presentation, presented at Chicon IV, 1982: *Raiders of the Lost Ark*

Saturn Award, Academy of Science Fiction, Fantasy and Horror Films, 1982: *Raiders of the Lost Ark*

The People's Choice Award, Favorite Motion Picture, 1982: *Raiders of the Lost Ark*

Home Video Citation, 500,000 units sold, 1984: *Raiders of the Lost Ark*

The Inkpot Award for Outstanding Achievement Cinematic Arts, San Diego Comic-Con International, 1982

Primetime Emmy, Outstanding Informational Special, 1982: *The Making of Raiders of the Lost Ark*; shared with Sidney Ganis (executive producer)

Certificate of Nomination, NAACP Image Award, 1983: *Return of the Jedi*

Hugo Award, Best Dramatic Presentation, presented at LA Con II, 1984: *Return of the Jedi*

Saturn Award, Academy of Science Fiction, Fantasy and Horror Films, 1984: *Return of the Jedi*

The People's Choice Award, Favorite Motion Picture, 1984: *Return of the Jedi*

Golden Reel Award, Motion Picture Sound Editors, 1993: *Demolition Man*

Golden Reel Award, Motion Picture Sound Editors, 1996: *JAG* ("Smoked")

Audience Award, Best Feature Drama, Marco Island Film Festival, 2000: *The Amati Girls*; shared with Craig Darian (executive producer), James Alex (producer), Steven Johnson (line producer/producer)

Award of Excellence, Heartland Film Festival, 2000: *The Amati Girls*

Saturn Award, Best DVD Collection, Academy of Science Fiction, Fantasy and Horror Films, 2005: *Star Wars Trilogy*

CINE Golden Eagle, Telecast, Professional Nonfiction Division, Children's Programs, 2006: *Danger Rangers* ("The Great Race"); shared with Mike D. Moore (executive producer), Larry Huber (executive producer), Ilie Agopian (executive producer)

Telly Award, 2006: *Danger Rangers* ("Where the Fun Never Stops")

The Robert A. Briner Impact Award, Life Achievement for Excellence in Media presented to Howard Kazanjian, 2009

The Oklahoma Historical Society, Outstanding work on Oklahoma History presented to Howard Kazanjian, coauthor of *Sam Sixkiller: Cherokee Frontier Lawman*, 2013

Pan Pacific Awards, Stellae Lifetime Achievement Award presented to Howard Kazanjian in Recognition to Your Contribution to the Entertainment Industry, 2015

William Rogers Medallion Award for *Mochi's War*, 2016

William Rogers Medallion Award for *The Trials of Annie Oakley*, 2019

Memberships (Past and Present)

The Academy of Motion Pictures Arts and Sciences

The Academy of Television Arts & Science

Assistant Directors Training Committee, Board of Trustees

California Film Commission, appointed by Governor George Deukmejian

California Film Commission, appointed by Governor Pete Wilson

Trustee at Azusa Pacific University

Honor Membership USC Associates

USC Cinema-Circulus

USC Universal Studios-Cinema Program

USC School of Cinema-Television, USC/Universal Summer Cinema Program

BIBLIOGRAPHY

Interviews by J. W. Rinzler (2018–19)
Jane Bay
Ben Burtt
Duwayne Dunham
Louis Friedman
Sid Ganis
Miki Herman
Carol Kazanjian
Randal Kleiser
Howard Kazanjian (several times, with many follow-up emails)
Marcia Lucas
Aggie Guerard Rodgers (email)
Tom Smith (email)
Lucy Autrey Wilson (email)

Interviews by Brandon Alinger
Anthony Daniels (email)
Mark Hamill (phone and archival interviews)
Mark Marshall (email)

Books
Goldman, Michael. *Reality Ends Here: 80 Years of USC Cinematic Arts*. San Rafael: Insight Editions, 2009.
Hearn, Marcus. *The Cinema of George Lucas*. New York: Abrams Books, 2005.
Hirsch, Paul. *A Long Time Ago in a Cutting Room Far, Far Away: My Fifty Years Editing Hollywood Hits—Star Wars, Carrie, Ferris Bueller's Day Off, Mission: Impossible, and More*. Chicago Review Press, 2019.
Kapsis, Robert E., and Kathie Coblentz. *Clint Eastwood: Interviews*. Jackson: University Press of Mississippi, 1999.
Kurosawa, Akira (trans. Bock, Audie E.), *Something Like an Autobiography*. Translated by Audie E. Bock. New York: Vintage Books, 1983.
Rinzler, J. W. *The Complete Making of Indiana Jones*. New York: Random House, 2008.
———. *The Making of Return of the Jedi*. New York: Random House, 2013.
———. *The Making of Star Wars*. New York: Random House, 2007.
———. *The Making of The Empire Strikes Back*. New York: Random House, 2010.
Sellers, Robert. *Hellraisers: The Life and Inebriated Times of Richard Burton, Richard Harris, Peter O'Toole, and Oliver Reed*. New York: Thomas Dunne Books, St Martin's Press, 2009.

Stubbs, Jonathan. *Hollywood and the Invention of England: Projecting the English Past in American Cinema, 1930–2017*. New York: Bloomsbury Academic, 2019.

Taylor, John Russell. *Hitch: The Life and Times of Alfred Hitchcock*. New York: Pantheon, 1978.

Vaz, Mark Cotta, and Craig Barron. *The Invisible Art: The Legends of Movie Matte Painting*. San Francisco: Chronicle Books, 2002.

Newspapers and Magazines

Block, Alex Ben. "*Jedi* sets new highs at box office." *Los Angeles Herald Examiner*, June 1, 1983.

Bock, Audie. "Kurosawa." *Take One*, March 1979.

Henstell, Bruce. "Can George Lucas Give Us Another *American Graffiti*?" *Los Angeles* magazine, November 1978.

Rosenfield, Paul. "George Lucas: *Graffiti* Sequel." *Los Angeles Times*, March 1, 1978.

Internet Sources

Access Online. "Arthur Newman Reflects On The Loss Of Paul Newman: 'He Was My Role Model.'" October 1, 2008. https://www.accessonline.com/articles/arthur-newman-reflects-on-the-loss-of-paul-newman-he-was-my-role-model-65535.

American Film Institute (website), various. https://www.afi.com/.

Baker, Nena. "Columbia Chairman Praises Sony as New Buyer." UPI, September 28, 1989. https://www.upi.com/Archives/1989/09/28/Columbia-chairman-praises-Sony-as-new-buyer/8295622958400/

Ebert, Roger. "Billy Wilder on *The Front Page*." May 26, 1974. https://www.rogerebert.com/interviews/billy-wilder-on-the-front-page.

———. "Interview with Joshua Logan." April 30, 1967. https://www.rogerebert.com/interviews/interview-with-joshua-logan.

———. "Interview with Karen Black." June 16, 1975. https://www.rogerebert.com/interviews/interview-with-karen-black.

———. "Sam Peckinpah: 'Dying Is Not Fun and Games.'" June 29, 1969. https://www.rogerebert.com/interviews/sam-peckinpah-dying-is-not-fun-and-games.

Flint, Hanna. "Sandra Bullock says she's owed a *Demolition Man* pinball machine: 'All the men got one.'" Yahoo, June 14, 2018. https://www.yahoo.com/entertainment/sandra-bullock-says-shes-owed-demolition-man-pinball-machine-men-got-one-exclusive-142344062.html.

Folkart, Burt A. "Arthur Knight; Film Scholar, Teacher." *Los Angeles Times*, July 29, 1991. https://www.latimes.com/archives/la-xpm-1991-07-29-mn-99-story.html.

Foundas, Scott. "Coppola Rising." DGA, Spring 2007. https://www.dga.org/Craft/DGAQ/All-Articles/0701-Spring-2007/DGA-Interview-Francis-Coppola.aspx.

French, Mike, and Gilles Verschuere. "Deborah Nadoolman Interview." TheRaider, September 14, 2005. http://www.theraider.net/features/interviews/deborah_nadoolman.php.

Hindes, Andrew. "Distrib Tricor shouts Good Morning, Vietnam." Variety, April 21, 1999. https://variety.com/1999/film/news/distrib-tricor-shouts-good-morning-vietnam-1117493474/.

Joyner, C. Courtney. "Lights, Camera, Miracle?" True West Magazine, August 6, 2013. https://truewestmagazine.com/lights-camera-miracle/.

LA Times (website), various. https://www.latimes.com/.

Lawrence, Derek. "Mark Hamill gets Walk of Fame star with Harrison Ford, George Lucas in attendance." EW, March 8, 2018. https://ew.com/movies/2018/03/08/mark-hamill-walk-of-fame-star/.

McCormick, Lynde. "What's Happening to Hollywood?" Christian Science Monitor, December 12, 1980. https://www.csmonitor.com/1980/1212/121254.html.

Pizzello, Stephen. "Conrad Hall homage." American Society of Cinematographers, May 2003. https://theasc.com/news/in-memoriam-conrad-l-hall-asc-1926-2003.

Rabin, Nathan. "Austin Pendleton Interview." AV Club, July 29, 2009. https://film.avclub.com/austin-pendleton-1798217219.

Radish, Christina. "Mark Hamill on Pop Culture Quest and That 'One of Everything' Star Wars Toys Rumor." Collider, November 17, 2016. https://collider.com/mark-hamill-pop-culture-quest-star-wars-interview/.

Saravia, Jerry. "An Interview with Fred Sorenson: Raiders' Pilot Still Shows Backbone." Jerry Saravia on Cinema (blog), May 17, 2011. https://jerrysaravia.blogspot.com/2011/05/interview-with-fred-sorenson-raiders.html.

Simon, Alex. "Philip Kaufman: The Hollywood Interview." The Hollywood Interview (blog), December 12, 2012. http://thehollywoodinterview.blogspot.com/2008/03/philip-kaufman-hollywood-interview.html.

Spry, Jeff. "Mellow Greetings and Musings from Director Marco Brambilla on Demolition Man's 25th Birthday." Syfy Wire, October 8, 2018. https://www.syfy.com/syfywire/mellow-greetings-and-musings-from-director-marco-brambilla-on-demolition-mans-25th-birthday.

The Telegraph. "Fred Astaire used cannabis, claims Petula Clark." August 29, 2012. https://www.telegraph.co.uk/culture/culturenews/9505840/Fred-Astaire-used-cannabis-claims-Petula-Clark.html.

Turner Classic Movies (website). http://www.tcm.com/.

Wikipedia (website), various. https://www.wikipedia.org/.

Williams, Phillip. "The Road to Perfection." MovieMaker, February 3, 2007. https://www.moviemaker.com/the-road-to-perfection-2766/.

YouTube. "David Letterman Tom Selleck's Indiana Jones Audition." Uploaded by Paul Olson, September 2, 2016. https://www.youtube.com/watch?v=hbiKTuTT0Pg.

Other Media

ABC7. "Eye on L.A." Filmed news coverage of Return of the Jedi opening, 1983.

"Reel Conversations with Howard Kazanjian." Reel Conversations (podcast), 2017.

INDEX

351

OPPOSITE: *Kazanjian acts as host of a University of Southern California documentary that tells the story of its venerable Cinema Department. It was founded circa 1940 in horse stables originally built in 1923, but that building was demolished shortly after the documentary was completed in 1984. Since then, the cinema school has occupied newer, more modern facilities.*

OPPOSITE, FAR RIGHT: *A note from Kazanjian per his "Word of the Week" and two examples of the words in action. "Communication" is dated February 14, 1980.*

Acknowledgments

O n a project such as *Return of the Jedi, Raiders of the Lost Ark*, or any movie for any size screen, one doesn't work alone. It is a team effort of sweat, tears, and sometimes blood. I cannot let this book go to print without acknowledging so many people in my life.

My thank you to longtime friend George Lucas, of fifty-plus years—innovator, writer, director, super filmmaker, and one with the foresight to move our industry forward even at his own expense. You broke the mold and set in motion how movies would be written, directed, produced, and certainly edited in the future. You knew how to pick a team of illustrators, visual effects wizards, sound creators, and talent.

Thank you to Miki Herman who was there from the first *Star Wars*. Miki is a real *Star Wars* fan, one who knows all about the saga. She is dedicated and loves her work.

Louis Friedman was my right-hand man. I'd work with Louis anytime, anywhere. He often sensed what I was about to say and carried forward with silent commands. We have exchanged birthday greetings every year since, with Louis's thoughts and pictures much more exciting than mine could ever be.

Duwayne Dunham was also there at Parkway House. From running errands for the Lucases to becoming a fine editor and later a director. I had the pleasure of hiring Duwayne a few years later as a director on two episodes of *JAG*. We still keep in touch.

To Jane Bay, thank you for all the years we've worked together. From the time I first met you at your interview to the day you retired, you have truly been George's right-hand woman, handling all the challenges of daily life for him and his family. I know how much you have given to the Lucases.

Tom Smith of ILM—we still have lunch several times a year. Thank you, Tom, for the times I needed your assistance.

Ben Burtt, tremendous talented friend. Always there. Extremely hard worker and innovator. Multi-Oscar winner, longtime confidant to George. I wish I had more time to spend with Ben.

PROD. NO. U.S.C. R+D.

SCENE 7 TAKE 9 ROLL # 1

DIRECTOR HOWE

CAMERAMAN Morrill

DATE -84 EXT. INT.

MIURA

For years I have been asked to divulge some of my trade secrets in how to be the best production oriented person. I've now decided to share some of my classified and long protected secrets with you.

Each week I shall be sending out my "Word of the Week" to this very elite group.

Howard

2/14/80
Word #2

LUCASFILM Ltd

COMMUNICATION

is the word of the week

CC: Jim Bloom
Rita Bozyk
Debbie Fine
Louis Friedman
Mickey Herman
Laura Kenmore
Kathy Kennedy
Frank Marshall
Leah Schmidt
Patty Rum HOWARD KAZANJIAN

STAR WARS
REVENGE OF THE JEDI   HOWARD KAZANJIAN

ANTICIPATE

is the word of the week

And then there is Debbie Fine, who did marvelous research for our pictures, and was a friend from the day I hired her. Debbie is missed. And to my assistants, PAs, and all those early people at the Egg Company, Skywalker Ranch, ILM, Sprockets, etc.—cast, crew, staff, and administration, a warm thank you for your tireless work.

Thank you to Lucy Autrey Wilson who was the first person I met when I walked into Parkway and warmly greeted me. Lucy was always there for George and all of us when in need. Lucy was one of the first, if not the first, hired by George Lucas.

And to Brandon Alinger, a huge *Star Wars* and *Indiana Jones* fan who might even know more about the saga than me. He is a collector himself of *Star Wars* and *Raiders* original artifacts and has traveled to many of the original locations where the films were shot. Thank you, Brandon, also for the introduction to J. W. Rinzler, whose name appears on this book as the author. Jonathan is a fine writer with wonderful credits to his name. This book would not have happened if it were not for Jonathan.

Thank you all for making Lucasfilm what it was and for the wonderful films we made. It takes hundreds of people to make a movie, not just one. From the workers in the mills and the assistant directors to the auditors, directors, and producers, I thank you.

And thank you to my wife, Carol, who was there through it all and kept me going. The support I had was endless, even through childbirth of our three boys. And I must salute friend Marcia Lucas who stood by George during the good times and challenging ones. Marcia's brilliance as a storyteller can be felt through her editing skills. There are few in the world with her talent. I am pleased Carol and I can call her friend.

Again, to George Lucas, who made it all happen. Friend, innovator, out-of-the-box thinker. Well done, George. You will be forever remembered by countless millions and generations to come. I am so pleased we shared those moments together.

—Howard Kazanjian

CAMERON + COMPANY
149 Kentucky Street, Suite 7
Petaluma, CA 94952
www.cameronbooks.com

PUBLISHER *Chris Gruener*
CREATIVE DIRECTOR *Iain R. Morris*
DESIGNER *Rob Dolgaard*
MANAGING EDITOR *Jan Hughes*
EDITORIAL ASSISTANT *Mason Harper*

Library of Congress Cataloging-in-Publication Data available.

ISBN: 978-1-951836-18-4
10 9 8 7 6 5 4 3 2 1

Printed in China

CREDITS

INTERIORS: From the Howard Kazanjian Collection: 2, 4, 26–27, 31, 37, 42–44, 72, 100, 105, 159, 163, 188, 207 (bottom), 276 (top); Lucasfilm: 11, 204, 207 (top row), 223, 238–239, 244, 247, 269, 270–271, 276 (bottom), 277–279, 284, 285, 287, 357; Warner Bros.: 49, 52, 73, 85, 101, 106–107, 118, 305; Universal Pictures: 126, 134, 139, 150, 151, 158, 169, 177; RKO Pictures: 302; Paramount Television: 313

INSERT A: *American Cinematographer*, 1; From the Howard Kazanjian Collection: 2–3, 5–9, 11; Warner Bros.: 4, 10; Universal Pictures: 12–16

INSERT B: From the Howard Kazanjian Collection: 1, 2–3 (top), 7, 9 (middle and bottom), 12, 13 (bottom), 15, 16; Louis Friedman: 2–3 (bottom), 10 (bottom); Lucasfilm: 4–6, 8, 9 (top), 10 (top), 11, 13 (top), 14

INSERT C: Lucasfilm: 1, 5 (top), 6–10, 13, 15 (top); From the Howard Kazanjian Collection: 2, 3, 4, 5 (bottom), 11, 12, 15 (bottom), 16; Paramount Television: 14